This book is

a gift to:

_____

From:

_____

Date:

_____

FOUNTAINS

of

366 DEVOTIONS
TO HELP YOU
WALK WITH GOD

BLESSING

Solly Ozrovech

CHRISTIAN ART
PUBLISHERS

Originally published by Christian Publishing Company
under the title *By Fonteine van Seën*

© 1997

English edition © 1998
CHRISTIAN ART PUBLISHERS
PO Box 1599, Vereeniging, 1930

First edition 1997
Second edition 2002

Translated by Linda van Tonder
Cover designed by Christian Art Publishers

Scripture taken from the New King James Version Copyright
(1995) by Thomas Nelson, Inc. unless otherwise indicated

Set in 12 on 14 pt Southern by Christian Art Publishers

Printed and bound by Paarl Print, Oosterland Street
Paarl, South Africa

ISBN 1-86920-041-1

02   03   04   05   06   07   08   09   10   11   –   10   9   8   7   6   5   4   3   2   1

Dedication

This work is dedicated with much love and appreciation to:

- Herman and Dirkie Barnard of Brits for their friendship, love, hospitality and spiritual fellowship.
  "I thank my God every time I remember you" (Phil. 1:3).
- The extended Barnard family of Brits, who has also become our family in Christ.
  "Therefore my brothers, you whom I love and long for, my joy and crown, that is how you should stand firm in the Lord, dear friends" (Phil. 4:1).
- The ministers and congregation of the Dutch Reformed Church, Krokodilrivier, Brits, with whom I have a very special spiritual relationship.
  "May the Lord make your love increase and overflow for each other and for everyone else, just as ours does for you" (1 Thes. 3:12).

Table of Contents

reface

In all humility I offer you this book, praying that it will enrich you spiritually in all the facets mentioned, while you spend time with God in solitude. The title was derived from Isaiah 3:12 *"With joy you will draw water from the wells of salvation."*

May the Holy Spirit be your guide and your teacher while you read and may this book help to strengthen your union with Him while it also enriches your inner man. And may the words of Jesus in John 7:37-38 be true of your life, *"If anyone is thirsty, let him come and drink. Whoever believes in Me, as the Scripture has said, streams of living water will flow from within him."*

The Fountain is available in abundance; may you be blessed as you draw from Him and may you be refreshed as you drink.

Soli Deo Gloria!

– Solly Ozrovech –

THE FOUNTAIN OF GOD'S ACCOMPANIMENT

Jesus, You lead us. When we walk in Your steps we have the assurance that You take us by the hand and lead us to the fatherland. (Paraphrase of Hymn 189:1)

Heavenly Father,
Standing here at this point of departure into the new year,
I feel so very insignificant and inadequate.
You are omnipotent, omniscient and omnipresent and You have promised to be with me always.
At this moment it is such good news to me that I can hardly believe it, but my guarantee is Your Word as well as Your Spirit who is my guide.
I'm entering into this vast unknown, holding the hand of my loving Father whom I know and who has undertaken to accompany me along this road.
Therefore, I bow before You in awe and gratitude, and praise Your holy Name:
Emmanuel – God with me!

January

*M*oving on in faith

"Now faith is being sure of what we hope for and certain of what we do not see." (Heb. 11:1)

or most people the dawn of the new year involves feelings of anticipation, hesitation, contemplation and even excitement. You anticipate opportunities, but perhaps you are worried or anxious. At this moment you stand on the point of departure into the unknown year which lies ahead. It is important for you to decide now that you will accept the challenges you will have to deal with as this year unfolds before you.

There are those whose negative attitude and anxious countenance give clear evidence of how they feel, revealing their innermost fears and uncertainties. You will always encounter those who fear the worst, and who meet every new day with nervous concern. They expect – and prepare themselves for – the worst, and their lives are embittered by their negative attitude.

Yet, today, at the beginning of this new year, the living Christ invites you to put all your faith and trust in Him. He promised to be with you at all times. He invites you to let Him be your guide and accompany you through that which presently seems to be nothing but a pitch-dark and unknown wilderness.

Therefore, act in faith now: invite Christ to fill you with His Holy Spirit in order for Him to influence your thoughts and actions, your attitudes and decisions as He did in the past. The triune God will accompany you into the future.

In the final analysis faith is the only key to the universe. The eventual meaning of all human existence and the answer to all the questions which our happiness depends on, cannot be found in any other way. (Thomas Merton)

Lord, I invite You _____

_____

A new life for a new year

"Trust in the Lord with all your heart and lean not on your own understanding; in all your ways acknowledge Him, and He will make your paths straight." (Prov. 3:5, 6)

*Y*ou receive a new day and a new year from the hand of God. In addition, He also promises to accompany you along this unknown road. Today is once again the beginning of the rest of your life and decisions that you make today may have far-reaching effects for the rest of your life.

Therefore it will not be a waste of time to spend some time constructively in God's presence. Consider the past under the scrutinising and revealing eye of the Holy Spirit. Discover and confess those hidden sins and accepted weaknesses which, till now, you refused to acknowledge, or thought you could do nothing about. Start the year with a session of confession which will let you enter into a real experience of God's forgiveness. This is how you prepare yourself for God's guidance.

This new life is founded on total trust in the risen Christ. Surrender fully to Him. Nobody who has sincerely yielded to Him has ever failed. His indwelling Spirit will reveal new prospects of what life has in store for you. Your set of values changes and you start looking at life from a different point of view.

A positive faith in the Master causes you to discover that His Spirit is working through you you can live in total harmony with Him. Then your utmost desire will be to do His will only. Having the attitude of Christ is the summit of Christian experience. Therefore, be adamant to deepen your fellowship with Jesus Christ this year by sailing out into the deep waters of the Spirit.

> God is faithful and if we serve Him faithfully, He will provide every need. (Richard of Chichester)

Faithful Master, strengthen me _____

"Jesus, You lead the way"

"He restores my soul. He guides me in paths of righteousness for his name's sake." (Ps. 23:3)

Are you perhaps one of those people who today is afraid of the future? Perhaps a feeling of insecurity is shrouding your mind like a dark shadow. Perhaps you are afraid that you won't be able to fulfil all your responsibilities and that robs you of your confidence. Fear of what the future holds can sometimes totally paralyse your mind and your spirit.

If this is true in your life, it is true because you allow it to be. It is not at all the Lord's will for you to be robbed of all power and beauty because of the awful presence of fear. His desire is for you to be totally free from debilitating fear.

This is only possible if your trust in God exceeds your faith in fear. Accept the glorious fact that God is omniscient and that He presides over the past, the present and the future and that He desires only the very best for your life. This will bring such balance into your everyday life that no amount of fear will be able to upset you. Because God is also omnipresent, you need to realise that He is always with you. Allow your life to be controlled by His standard and norm.

Never forget that while you are moving into the future, God is already waiting there. He knows the future and He knows the right road to follow. You can put all your trust in Him. If you truly and totally trust Him, such profound peace will descend upon your life, that, even if storms of fear and insecurity rage around you, they will never be able to paralyse or destroy you.

> He who trusts in himself is lost. For the one who trusts in God, all things are possible. (Alphonsus Lignori)

Jesus, lead me _____

_____

ⴊhe right way

"Walk in all the way that the Lord your God has commanded you, so that you may live and prosper and prolong your days in the land that you will possess." (Deut. 5:33)

℘any people wonder if it is worthwhile trying to lead a good life. They maintain high standards of honesty, integrity and righteousness, yet they see others experiencing prosperity and success in spite of their dubious lives. When this happens, the danger exists that they will be tempted to compromise their high standards and follow those whose principles are doubtful.

If you should be tempted in this way, then remember that you can never hide your actions from God. He knows your life inside out and His scrutinising gaze will shine into every dark and hidden corner of your life, exposing your innermost spirit. In these circumstances your conscience will be quick to address the issue and torture you. You will feel ill at ease and unhappy because you know what you are doing is wrong in His sight.

To ensure a life of peace and liberty for yourself you must always try to follow the example of Jesus Christ. His whole life was a testimony of honesty, integrity, righteousness, compassion and love. In order to experience the abundant life which He offers, you need to live according to His prescriptions and follow His example. This is the only way in which you will taste the joy and fulfilment that are the portion of those who walk along the way established by the living Guide.

> God has placed good and evil within our ability and with that He has given us the freedom of choice. He never forcefully holds back those who are unwilling, but He surrounds the obedient with His love. (John Chrysostom)

Holy Spirit, Your way is _____

*H*andle the pressure with Jesus

"Those who pursue us are at our heels; we are weary and find no rest." (Lam. 5:5)

In spite of the fact that we live in a time of breathtaking progress, more and more people find it extremely difficult to deal with daily stress. The extensive pressure of modern life causes tremendous tension. Insecurity about the future creates a sense of danger. The amount of tension that is built up, robs many lives of their sparkle and purposefulness. Thus people break down under the pressure and unbearable load of their fears and problems.

Despite the fact that man regards himself as strong and self-sufficient in many areas, it is far from the truth. In due course man will discover the truth of Christ's words in John 15:5 *"... without Me, you can do nothing."* Our human efforts may prove to be successful for a limited time, but a day will come when our achievements will diminish and life will start losing its meaning and purpose.

In order for you to live confidently in these demanding times, it is imperative that your life and work must be dedicated to the living Christ, allowing Him to guide you. It is only through Him that all things become possible. It is through His guidance only that you will be able to live life to the full and be happy. Make the Lord your guide and companion on your pilgrimage, and fears and worries will not have a paralysing effect on your life. He overcame the world and He promises to be with His children always.

> When You are our strength, it is real strength, but when we are our own strength, it is only weakness. (Augustine of Hippo)

Loving Guide, with You by my side _____

_____

On the way with Jesus

"I have told you these things, so that in Me you may have peace. In this world you will have trouble. But take heart! I have overcome the world." (Jn. 16:33)

*Y*ou dare not enter the new year with your own insights or in your own strength. You need a companion and a mentor who will show you the way and guide you with wisdom. The prospect of a new year can be simultaneously exciting and upsetting: exciting because it is filled with unknown opportunities, yet upsetting because you anxiously stare into the unknown, wondering which disasters from the past will repeat themselves.

It is a common mistake to allow the past to cloud our view when we consider the future. Crises, financial setbacks, droughts, floods and personal disappointments tend to determine the pattern of your life. Thus you can find yourself at the gateway to the new year, but full of anxiety, worry and fear about the way ahead.

More than any other time of the year, you need to make a quality decision to put all your trust in the triune God. He loves you and cares about you. He wants to be your companion, but the choice is yours. Steadfastly believe Jesus' promise that He has already overcome the world. Enter into the new year, holding His loving hand. He will lead you through the maze because He knows what is best for you. Your duty is to obey Him; then your fear and anxiety will be replaced by an increasing assurance that the Lord loves you. And you will become a partaker of His peace.

> Show steadfast courage. God is mightier than Satan. We are on the winning side. (John Chapman)

Saviour, in this world _____

God's holy presence

"The hand of the Lord was upon me there, and He said to me, 'Get up and go out to the plain, and there I will speak to you.'" (Ezek. 3:22)

There are always those who are sceptical about people who say that the Almighty has spoken to them. They simply don't believe it or they regard those people as religious fanatics or freaks who need to be endured tongue-in-cheek. If only these sceptics could realise that this attitude is robbing them of one of life's greatest experiences.

There is no doubt whatsoever that God reveals Himself and His will to you in various ways. He may do so through circumstances or other people. You may have a sure inclination to go in a certain direction, or you may experience a sweet peace of mind descending upon your life. That is how God wants to indicate to you a specific direction which He wants you to follow.

In order to prepare yourself for such an experience, it is imperative that you spend time in solitude, prayer and meditation. In these quiet moments, dedicate yourself totally to the risen Christ. Open up your life and mind to the Holy Spirit in order to be in complete harmony with Him. Wholeheartedly obey that which the Holy Spirit whispers to you and you will be inspired to do that which you have to do, with the assurance that Christ will be with you all the way.

We only have to be obedient. There is guidance for each one of us and by listening humbly, we will hear the right word. (Ralph Waldo Emerson)

Thank You Father, that You make me sensitive to _____

Trust God totally

"You will only find yourself fighting against God." (Acts 5:39)

ome people are aggressive by nature. They mistrust others and have such an aggressive approach towards life that it isolates them from their fellowmen. They are convinced that everyone is against them and therefore they have very few friends.

If you have made yourself an enemy of life, the time has come for you to change your attitude and become its friend. Be on the look-out for mutual points of contact rather than stressing the differences. See the good in others and remember that we all have flaws – you too! Get rid of your self-centredness and find joy and fulfilment in helping others without considering payment. Always choose the edifying and constructive way, even though it might require a greater sacrifice. There are just as many ways to live constructively as there are to live destructively. Why then would you choose the way of a negative and painful lifestyle?

Perhaps you think it's impossible for you to change. Such a train of thought only serves to confirm the extent to which wrong thoughts are already controlling your mind. The essential truth is that wholehearted cooperation with God, where you allow the Holy Spirit to take total control of your life, will also bring you into a completely new relationship with other people.

This new life, which is the result of obedient cooperation with God, is a powerful and miracle-working experience. You become aware of His Godly guidance. Instead of your life remaining one hectic drama, it becomes the unfolding of His holy plan, bringing harmony and peace into your daily life.

> What can be more uplifting or inspiring than the obedient heart who is willing to risk everything on the Word of God? (John Henry Newman)

Lord, I thank You _____

_____

Examine yourself honestly

"Examine yourselves to see whether you are in faith; test yourselves. Do you not realise that Christ Jesus is in you – unless, of course, you fail the test?" (2 Cor. 13:5)

A large number of people have a very poor opinion of themselves and their abilities. When requested to do a simple little task, they refuse, using the excuse that they are not fit to do it. They don't accept invitations because they have no self-confidence. They live unhappy and frustrated lives, because what you believe about yourself, you portray to the world around you.

As a disciple of Jesus Christ, sooner or later, you have to evaluate yourself in the scrutinising light of the Holy Spirit. This can be destructive, yet it is also constructive. You will see yourself as you really are, with all the pettiness and hypocrisy. Of course this is uncomfortable and humiliating. Then, while you are asking God's forgiveness for what you have been, you also start to realise what you can become through His wisdom, power and guidance.

When your spirit is filled with hope and inspiration, which are gifts of the Holy Spirit, your self-confidence increases. It is not created by proud self-sufficiency, but by the realisation that you are a vessel into which God is pouring His love. As such you are very precious and special to Him. Because He loves you, and because He wants to use you in His service, the feeling of inferiority vanishes, because now you know for sure that you are God's child. With your mind enlightened like this, you cannot possibly think derogatory thoughts about yourself.

It is only when the Spirit of God takes control of and renews the "old man" that a person is made whole. It is only when this line is crossed that a personality assumes its full meaning and importance. (Emile Gailliet)

Jesus, through Your merit _____

_____

Holy and omniscient

"The Lord has established his throne in heaven, and his kingdom rules over all." (Ps. 103:19)

In adverse circumstances, people often experience a decline in their perception of God's power and majesty. When devastated by trouble or when they experience problems, when tragedy strikes or when they encounter hardships, their faith often wanes and the obstacles of life cause them to stumble. This kind of experience is not unusual and even some of God's most devout children fall prey to it. A study of Scripture will indicate exactly how many of the well-known Biblical characters fell prey to the affliction of despondency and depression.

When you find yourself in the midst of such circumstances, it is important that you should hold on to your faith and put all your trust in the victorious Christ. Meditate on Scripture and the history of the human race during times when it seemed as if evil had gained the upper hand – then pay attention to what happened when God stepped into the situation. In all the millennia since Creation, there is not one instance when the righteousness of God did not triumph over evil.

This same God wants to be your companion this year. Let your faith be powerful in all situations and believe fearlessly in the omnipotence of the living Christ and that He reigns supremely over everything and everyone. Let this be your strength and power in the new year with all its problems and demands.

> God is always with us, why should we not always be with God? (William Uttathorne)

Father, I find my strength and inspiration in knowing _____

*W*ho do you need to be?

"What a wretched man I am! Who will rescue me from this body of death? Thanks be to God – through Jesus Christ our Lord!" (Rom. 7:24, 25)

*U*nfortunately there are many disciples of our Lord who have become comfortable living a substandard Christianity. Perhaps they dedicated their lives to Jesus Christ many years ago and for a time they did experience the inspiration of a vibrant Christian life. Then this experience started to wane, until only a shadow remained and the power of their faith disappeared.

While their faith became ineffective, they nevertheless knew that it was not God's will for their lives at all. God only wanted the very best for them: fullness of life linked to an inspired purpose for living; a spiritual power to enable them to live triumphantly; an inner peace which secures peace of mind for daily living; an intellect which rejects the negative and builds on the positive. These, and many more gifts of grace, God is willing to bestow on those who dedicate themselves to Him totally.

God has never withdrawn Himself from you, and that deep longing in your heart to experience spiritual reality is actually a divinely inspired restlessness through which God is calling you back to Him. You know who you can be through the power of Christ, and you know who you are now because you allowed your faith to wane. God doesn't offer you an unattainable vision. He is calling you to dedicate yourself to Him afresh in order to regain the full stature of your faith. Then you will, once again, experience the glory and power of the living Christ and His Spirit in your mind, your spirit and your life.

> Remorse and confession are more than just being sorry about your sin: it involves a change of your total nature which will cause heaven to rejoice. (Lew Wallace)

Father, by a total commitment to Your Son _____

*S*et free by the Holy Spirit

"Where the Spirit of the Lord is, there is freedom." (2 Cor. 3:17)

*H*ave you ever felt that you are able to achieve more than you do presently and that you are not nearly reaching your full potential? You might be frustrated because of the monotonous routine of your life. You don't expect anything exciting to happen to you any more and life has lost all its beauty and sparkle. Your life is probably being shrouded by increasing triviality which seems to be suffocating all rightful ambition within you. Even though you may experience a stirring in your spirit every now and then, it is never strong enough to launch you into positive, creative action.

It can be a supreme tragedy if you carry on through life thwarted by a mediocre existence, while the liberty which the Holy Spirit offers, could be yours.

When you allow the Holy Spirit to come into your life and take control, you can expect some radical changes. Those inhibitions which prohibited you from living life to the full, will start to vanish. In practising this new-found freedom, you will become aware of the needs of others and you will start living a life of unselfish service. When the Spirit of God accompanies you, you will become aware of a certain pattern taking shape in your life. Suddenly there will be meaning and purpose in your life and you will be empowered by an indescribable feeling of real freedom. Your travelling companion, the Holy Spirit, is not only your guide, but also the One who protects and inspires you!

> Every time we confess: "I believe in the Holy Spirit" we mean that we believe there is a living God who has the ability and who is willing to penetrate the human personality and change it. (J.B. Phillips)

Father, through the wisdom and power of the Holy Spirit _____

God is always there

"My God, my God, why have You forsaken me? Why are You so far from helping me, and from the words of my groaning?" (Ps. 22:1)

Few things can be as destructive to the health of a person's soul than the feeling that you are totally on your own. Many people experience this because they separate themselves from others on purpose. Some really are without friends. It might be that they've been pushed aside into loneliness by other people. This loneliness is almost unbearable and could have devastating results.

Perhaps you are going through such an experience. The only way to set matters straight is for you to honestly assess yourself and your activities. Did you perhaps erect a barrier to exclude others on purpose? Have you been so possessed by your own affairs that you withdrew into your own small world, with no interest in others at all? Or did your attitude and actions push away those friendly people who are afraid to get hurt?

Yet God will never desert you. He promised to be with you always (Ref. Matthew 28:20). Turn to Him for guidance and wisdom to be able to handle your circumstances. Ask the living Christ to come in and take over your life making you an instrument of His peace and love. You can take the first step in bridging the gap between yourself and others by showing a loving interest in them as people. Your reward for doing this will be that Christ comes back into your life and His love will be your guide into the lives of others – and away from a life of seclusion.

People give love because they are afraid of themselves; afraid of the loneliness that lives inside of them and they need someone to lose themselves in as smoke gets lost in the blue sky. (W.F. Calverton)

Lord, help me through Your love in my heart, to _____

_____

"Your will be done!"

"'My food is to do the will of Him who sent Me, and to finish his work.'" (Jn. 4:34)

In order for you to experience abundance, joy and fulfillment in this new year you need to do that which you believe is God's will for your life. This might seem to you like a very typical religious approach which has no practical value at all. However, this is the highest form of wisdom according to which you can conduct your life. Anybody who diligently obeys the will of God, has powers at his disposal that the world will never be able to understand. He has an inner strength which becomes stronger as the adverse powers that work against him increase in violence. In moments of confusion he receives wisdom. In times of darkness he becomes aware of an inner light guiding him. God's will and His way are not so shrouded in mysticism that they have no earthly value for those who wish to hold His hand and follow His will. These people are not dreamers who constantly ignore the harsh realities of everyday life.

However, when your whole life is set on doing the will of God, then you come to a full understanding of the real meaning and purpose of life. You will never allow the following futile question to escape from your lips, "What is the meaning or purpose of life?" You will know that it is your highest goal and greatest joy to do the will of God. While you dedicate yourself to achieve this objective, the real purpose of your life will unfold before you. While you practise to do the will of God, you will discover that you have an inner strength which results from obeying His will. Like the living Christ you will also know by experience: My food is to do the will of Him who sent Me.

We are born as slaves, yet to obey God means absolute freedom. Those who do that will be free, safe and happy. (Seneca)

Father, my food is _____

_____

*P*ractical Christianity

"So, affectionately longing for you, we were well pleased to impart to you not only the gospel of God, but also our own lives, because you had become dear to us." (1 Thes. 2:8)

*W*hen we study the gospel there is always one issue which is clearly revealed time and again and that is Christ's practical approach to people and to life in general. In no way did this approach damage the spirituality of His Godly nature. On the contrary, it often enhanced it, adding depth and meaning to His nature.

The ministry of the Lord Jesus Christ to man came exactly at a time when the religious authorities and office bearers were so entangled in the structures of the law and all the rituals and formalities, that they practised a religion that was void of all love and mercy. The result was a false piousness, snobbishness and hypocrisy. This inevitably caused the needs of men to be ignored while the inflexibility of the law received preference over love. People only had a vague, erroneous image of a distant, terrifying God who dealt out punishment in a judgemental fashion.

When Jesus Christ came to earth, He introduced God's true grace and love to all people. He did not spare Himself in His care for others. In every facet of His ministry He revealed a loving compassion which was unknown before then. This reached its culmination when our Saviour laid down His life for us.

And this is the example which we have to follow this year along our Christian pilgrimage. Live the true meaning of the gospel: reveal love and compassion in your daily life.

> Love and compassion will heal more sins than condemnation would. (Henry Ward Beecher)

Lord, this is how I want to _____

_____

God is working through you

"For it is God who works in you both to work and to will for his good pleasure." (Phil. 2:13)

It is an overwhelming yet inspiring thought that God wants to work through us. The challenging fact is that whether you are cooperating with Him or whether you resist, God has a plan for your life and within the framework of that plan are those qualities which are needed to give full and perfect expression to the life God has given you.

You may be vaguely aware of your calling and destiny, yet the awareness might just not be strong enough to let you walk along the road which God has laid out for you. Therefore you live your life arbitrarily and not according to God's will. This self-chosen road always leads to dissatisfaction and frustration as you plod along the blind alleys which your evil heart follows. You do this in your own strength and you are more conscious of your failures than your victories. You find that every door has to be forced open and it seems as if few things ever work out well for you.

However, if you acknowledge with strong inner conviction that God is at work within you, and if you are adamant to obey Him in all things, God becomes your partner in the art of living. When this is so, incredible things start to happen in your life. Obstructions either vanish or you approach them with strength and wisdom not of your own doing. New prospects develop in your life, causing your vision to extend and all bitterness to disappear. You are filled with inspiration which unfolds more clearly as you move ahead, holding God's hand.

The Holy Spirit imparts love; then He inspires us with hope. Thereafter He gives freedom; and that is just about the last thing many of us have in our churches. (Dwight L. Moody)

God, in Your mercy, give me Your Holy Spirit that _____

*Y*our shield and your stronghold

"The Lord is my rock and my fortress and my deliverer; My God, my strength in whom I will trust; My shield and the horn of my salvation, my stronghold." (Ps. 18:2)

*R*egardless of who you are or what your circumstances may be, there comes a time in your life when you need someone you can fully trust. You might need advice, assistance or encouragement and you look for someone you can trust to assist you in your particular situation.

The problem is that people are often fickle and not to be trusted. Sometimes those you approach for help are so engrossed in their own problems that they have very little time to assist you, thus causing you to become disappointed and vulnerable.

The joy of Christianity is the fact that God is only a prayer away. Whatever your problem or need, whenever it may occur, the Lord is waiting for you to turn to Him. Submit your problems to Him as He accompanies you on the way He has laid out for your life. Because He is omniscient, omnipotent and all-seeing, you can rest assured that His way will eventually be to your benefit.

The absolute trustworthiness of the risen Christ, who is the same yesterday, today and forever more, is your guarantee that God's way is the best for you. This fact has been proven over and over again through the years. Therefore, when you are in need, turn to Him and allow Christ to enfold you with His love and to protect and encourage you.

> The more we trust God, the more trustworthy we find Him to be. (Cliff Richard)

Lord, with the psalmist I confess _____

*W*hy are you afraid?

"But the Lord is faithful, who will establish you and guard you from the evil one." (2 Thes. 3:3)

W hy are you afraid of what the future may hold? Does the idea of serious illness fill you with despair? Or is your heart disturbed by omens and fear? You might feel that the suffocating influence of evil wants to possess your life and that you have no power to resist it. At such times you may find yourself being strangled by the clutches of fear and your life becomes miserable and unbearable.

If this is your experience, perhaps, for a minute you have forgotten the fact, "God is faithful!" You may believe it in theory, but find it extremely difficult to apply in your daily life. If you really believe, you will not be afraid. Faith and fear cannot coexist in the same heart. It is important that your faith in God exceeds your fear of the unknown. God has given you the gracious gift of faith, but it is your responsibility to develop it through prayer, meditation and His eternal Word. You also have to apply your faith in the practical world. It makes no sense at all to talk about faith unless you give it full control over your life.

Faith and fear can never be sleeping partners. If you are being torn between faith and fear, then it is important that you learn to control your emotions through the power of the Holy Spirit. Build up your relationship with your heavenly Father and learn to trust Him unconditionally. Then your fear will vanish into thin air like mist in the bright morning sun.

> When the wise man encounters a storm, he doesn't pray to be set free from danger, but for deliverance from fear. It is the storm on the inside that is important and not the one on the outside. (Ralph Waldo Emerson)

Lord, inspire and accompany me _____

_____

Be encouraged in the Lord

"O Lord my God, You are very great: You are clothed with honor and majesty." (Ps. 104:1)

It is a natural tendency to restrict Jesus Christ to your religious world of thought and to allow Him entrance into your daily life only when you feel pious or are experiencing some deep emotional feeling. By limiting Jesus to a religious figure, thus separating Him from the activities of your daily routine, you are robbing yourself of the rich and rewarding experience of acknowledging Jesus in your everyday life and of sharing everything with Him.

Wherever you go, you can take Christ with you. Yet, if you should visit places or do things that your conscience warns you against, knowing that you cannot share them with Him, it would be wise to stop such activities immediately. To be involved in activities where you have to leave your Lord and Master outside, could be detrimental to your spiritual life and your testimony as a Christian. It is a sign of spiritual immaturity. You are also forfeiting abundant life in Christ because of your sinful tendencies (Ref. John 10:10).

When you allow the fullness of Christ to take possession of you, your intellectual and spiritual perceptions are enriched and you experience the Master working in the most unexpected places. You experience His activity in the lives of people you never regarded as religious and you develop an understanding of hidden motives which you never had before. This inner sensitivity, created by the indwelling Christ, elevates your faith and becomes a powerful dynamic, at work in every area of your life.

I have a great need of Christ; I have a great Christ for my needs. (Charles H. Spurgeon)

Saviour, please use me everywhere to _____

More than conquerors

"Yet in all these things we are more than conquerors through Him who loved us." (Rom. 8:37)

Things could seem worse to you right now than they have done for many years. You might have many reasons to be discouraged. You may very well be asking yourself, "Is it worth the trouble to slave like this, without attaining anything? I might as well give up."

Remember, you are never defeated until you admit defeat. Unfortunately life is teeming with people who have accepted defeat as a fact and whose pessimism has influenced others very negatively. It is so easy to become one of this great throng and become a loser through self-pity.

There are many inspirational stories about people who, when faced with defeat, eventually managed to gain victory in spite of tremendous odds against them. People who are dispirited by looming defeat would be wise to read these inspirational stories.

Before you give up in total despair, first ask yourself the following questions: Whom do I submit myself to in my despair? Will life be easier once I have admitted defeat? Will I be able to escape from moral responsibilities and obligations because I feel that I cannot cope any longer?

To answer the first question: You submit to your fear and unless you resist and overcome fear through the power of the triumphant Christ, you will certainly go under. It is through faith in Jesus Christ that you obtain victory.

If Christ is with us, who can be against us? If you are sure of the victory, you can go into battle with great courage. With Christ and for Christ victory is certain. (Bernard of Clairvaux)

Christ, I praise You, because I triumphantly _____

_____

God's wise counsel

"For the Lord gives wisdom; From his mouth come knowledge and understanding." (Prov. 2:6)

In every area of life there are people who seek advice and people who give advice. People need help in their personal lives as well as in their businesses. They look for wise counsellors in both their spiritual and secular lives. Sometimes they will ask advice from a professional person. At other times they will go to a trusted and respected friend or acquaintance. Regardless of the situation, the one who has a problem needs help to find a solution.

You may be in such a situation. You will benefit if, before going to anybody for assistance or advice, you first pray. Ask the omniscient God to guide you in finding the person of His choice, thus you will know that you are approaching the right person. Ask Him to make you sensitive and receptive to the prompting of the Holy Spirit so that you can draw from the Spirit's gifts of wisdom and discernment.

Above all, pray for the person you will be approaching for counsel. Ask God to bless this person with the ability to understand and to give effective counsel. When you have done this you can wait on the Lord to guide you. Put your trust in God and not so much in people. Accept the advice that you receive as if it comes from your heavenly Father. You will have peace and tranquillity of mind knowing that you've acted within God's perfect will.

> To benefit from wise counsel, requires more wisdom than to advise others. (John Churton Collins)

Holy Father, it is only with You that _____

_____

Your communication with God

"I waited patiently for the Lord; And He inclined to me, and heard my cry." (Ps. 40:1)

In this new year, your communication with God is your lifeline. If you should experience a time where God seems to be far from you and unreal, then this dry desert patch is your handiwork and not His. Of course, it is difficult to admit to this because then you confess that somewhere along your spiritual pilgrimage you allowed pride and self-assertiveness to lead you in trying to plan your own way, and disobedience crept into your life, destroying your communication with the living Christ. Whenever there is a case of broken fellowship between God and man, you will find some obstinate disobedience from man's side. If you wish to experience the reality of Christ in your life and mind, you need to be absolutely obedient – even if you have to deny yourself.

If you feel that you are far from God and, after investigating your life, still cannot manage to detect the cause of this, it means that you did your spiritual evaluation in the strength of your own restricted wisdom and not in the revealing light and power of the Holy Spirit. In order for you to discern spiritual powers or weaknesses within you, you need to open up your life to the Holy Spirit. He will reveal to you who you really are.

Inviting the Holy Spirit to work in your life could very well create a spiritual storm. That which you regard as good, might be revealed to be second best; the good deeds that you perform might prove to be a form of escape from greater spiritual challenges. If you have the courage to accept the challenge of the Holy Spirit, you will have an exceptional experience of His power and inspiration along your pilgrimage.

> That which lies behind or ahead of us is insignificant when compared to what lies within us. (Ralph Waldo Emerson)

Holy Spirit, give me a revelation of myself so that _____

_____

*W*ake up my soul!

"'Our friend Lazarus sleeps, but I go that I may wake him up.'" (Jn. 11:11)

*H*ow appropriate are these words that Jesus uttered in the past, for today! He was on His way to Lazarus' grave to perform the great miracle of raising someone from the dead. They are appropriate today because there are so many people who need to be raised from their indifference, their general attitude of throwing in the towel, their hopelessness and helplessness. They willingly submit themselves to the worries and anxieties which torture them daily. Yet, in the midst of all the problems encountered in the world today, it is not only important, but imperative, that your whole life and total existence be founded on your faith in the living Christ. This is your guarantee of a new life of powerful faith.

In an era where standards continually decline, it is easy to give in to the temptation of taking the easy road of compromise and disinterest; or just to give up the fight and drift along with the current rather than living the life God expects you to. If you are trusting in your own resources and ingenuity, there is little doubt that you will go under.

Nevertheless, just as Christ raised Lazarus from the dead, He will raise you from your spiritual sleep of death and inspire you to live a life of victory and achievement in His service. The only thing that the life-giving Saviour asks of you is that you accept Him as the Lord of your life. Can you afford to refuse an offer so rich in mercy?

Fellowship with Christ means participation in the Godly life which finds its highest expression in victory over death. Life is a more powerful word than resurrection, but resurrection is, so to speak, the essential quality of life. (William Temple)

Lord Jesus, I worship You as the _____

_____

We believe without seeing

"So we are always confident ... For we walk by faith, not by sight." (2 Cor. 5:6,7)

Meditate on your faith for a while. When you are battling with problems, difficulties or disappointments, or when you have to make extremely important decisions, do you trust God sufficiently to place yourself and your future unconditionally in His hand; and are you sure then that, regardless of what He brings across your path, it will always work together for your good? Or do you try to struggle through the problems in your own strength until defeat overtakes you?

Jesus came to confirm that God loves you unconditionally. His care, help and compassion are unquestionable. You are precious in His sight. Read John 3:16 again and remember that He died on Golgotha for your sake and in your place. And if that is certain, then it is equally true that Christ will not allow anything that will cause you irreparable loss. On the contrary, He wants what is best for you. With this assurance, you cannot do otherwise than trust God unconditionally in everything you undertake. Then you will walk along His way, doing His will.

To ensure peace and tranquillity of mind, place yourself, your plans and your problems in the hands of your Saviour. Discuss your problems and secret fears, or those important decisions that you have to make with Him in prayer. Remember you are talking to someone who, by grace, calls you His friend.

In this way you will experience the living presence of Christ in every situation of life. He will guide you through His Spirit and accompany you to the place where you experience peace and tranquillity of mind. Even though you cannot see the complete road ahead, faith will carry you through.

Faith is the inner eye of man's soul. (Alexander Maclaren)

Lord, accompany me to _____

*𝒫*urposefully into the future

"In all your ways acknowledge Him, and He shall direct your paths."
(Prov. 3:6)

*𝒜*n experience with the living Christ gives purpose and meaning to your life. People who exist without any purpose will never experience the joy of achievement and life-fulfilment. To plod along from day to day hoping only for better days to come, without doing anything to bring them about creates a don't-care attitude. Purposelessness is the result of a lack of drive and motivation.

Ambitious people know what they want and are willing to work hard to achieve that. Often they are willing to sacrifice their time, health, family life, social contacts and money in order to reach their goal. Because they invest all their energy in realising their ideals, they usually achieve success. The tragedy, however, occurs when, after they have achieved everything they set out to achieve, they still have the gnawing feeling that, in spite of all their efforts, sacrifice and hard work, they have missed out on something important.

If you have disregarded the spiritual aspect of life, you probably missed the most important truth. It is impossible to experience fulfilment in life if you are careless about the reality of your spiritual life. You are a spiritual being, created in the image of God. If you wish to follow in the steps of the Master, you should be aware of your spiritual nature, regardless of what your daily task might be. Whether you are a clerk, a housewife or factory worker or whether you practise a profession, your primary objective as a Christian disciple is to do the will of God. God has bestowed upon you the gracious gift of life in order for you to serve Him.

> Hard work is a joy and an excitement if you are in God's will with it.
> (Robert Cook)

Lord, please hold my hand _____

Power from on high

"But you shall receive power when the Holy Spirit has come upon you" (Acts 1:8)

Many well-meaning Christians never succeed in developing their full potential while on their spiritual pilgrimage because they don't understand the person and work of the Holy Spirit. Sometimes it is sheer ignorance, sometimes it is due to wrong or incomplete teaching. Whatever the case may be, it has a negative influence on their discipleship, resulting in their not having the ability to serve Christ as effectively as they should.

If you are depending on your own strength only in your service to the Master, you are sure to fail. This kind of service can never be effective. Jesus Himself said, *" ... without Me you can do nothing"* (John 15:5).

It is not something which you can earn or bring about. It is a serious matter. The anointing is your gift of grace when you submit yourself to the authority of the living Christ and when you pray seriously to willingly receive the blessing and the privilege and the responsibility of this gift. Do not expect your experience to be the same as someone else's and accept the fact that the gifts of the Spirit can manifest themselves differently in your life.

Accept God's gift with gratitude and joy, and allow the Spirit to lead you along the ways of service that He has chosen for you. Then serve Him with a new-found spirit of trust, authority and peace.

Every time we say "I believe in the Holy Spirit" we mean that we believe there is a living God who is able and willing to penetrate the human personality and change it. (J.B. Phillips)

Spirit, re-create me in order for Your kingdom _____

Don't miss opportunities

"Do not despise the day of small things." (Zech. 4:10)

There are always people who are so busy battling with life's problems that they miss its opportunities. They don't realise that opportunities often come to us disguised as problems. If they realised that, they would discover the secret of how to transform possible defeat into glorious victory.

Many people complain that they never had any opportunities. Probably the truth is rather that they waited for something big and sensational to happen in their lives and therefore allowed many opportunities to slip by unnoticed and unused. The tragedy of many lives is not a lack of opportunities, but the inability to recognise them when they knock.

It often happens that opportunities come unobserved into a person's life, and one requires insight to be able to see their full potential. Therefore a wise person will never regard small things as unimportant. He always remembers that the massive oak tree was once an insignificant acorn. The ability to appreciate that which seems small and unimportant is one of the beautiful by-products of a Christian's life. And this often opens doors of great opportunity which remain locked for those who don't appreciate the value of small things.

The same God who created the universe, also created the mustard seed. No part of God's creation is unimportant to Him. Appreciate the small things in life and the big opportunities of life will be revealed to you.

The secret of success in life is to be ready when opportunity knocks. (Benjamin Disraeli)

God of grace, the small things and the big opportunities _____

God's accompaniment is practical

"I will instruct you and teach you in the way you should go. I will guide you with my eye." (Ps. 32:8)

Many people think that God's guidance is obscured by a cloud of mysticism. When they encounter problems or insecurities they pray fervently for God to guide them, but when things are back to normal, they feel confident to make their own decisions and walk along the paths of their own choice again.

To seek God's guidance for special occasions only causes people to overlook the value it has in the smaller and routine matters of life. The result is that these people never cultivate a relationship with their heavenly Father, because this is only attained through sustained obedience to His all-wise guidance.

God gives guidance in every area of life. It is given through ordinary common sense, which is such a common occurrence that it is often not recognised as His guidance. To wait for guidance while common sense already prescribes what needs to be done, is like waiting for a present which you have already received.

Your common sense needs to be motivated and inspired through an active prayer life. Such a prayer life causes your mind to be in harmony with God. Then, as time goes by, your thoughts are inspired and your whole life comes under God's control. Godly guidance should not be sought in times of crisis only. If you seek His guidance in the small issues of life, it will be much easier to recognise His will when important decisions have to be made.

> God expects each one of us to work as diligently as he possibly can, not withholding anything and exerting himself to the utmost. When there is nothing more that we can do, He stretches forth His holy arm and then He takes control. (Dom Orione)

Jesus, Your example has taught me _____

_____

He is the God of this moment

"But as for me, I trust in You O Lord. I say, 'You are my God.' My times are in your hand." (Ps. 31:14, 15)

*I*t is an irrefutable fact that one can only think one thought at a time. Even though they may succeed one another at breathtaking speed, the thought that is in your mind at this very moment is the one that crowds out all others. Your thoughts of the moment are very important because they could prevent you from thinking more serious, nobler thoughts.

Many people waste the preciousness of the present moment by allowing themselves to be absorbed by the failures of the past and to recall those incidents that rob the present of its joy and beauty. Yet others forget the past, disregard the present and indulge in idle dreams about the future, without taking any constructive measures to realise those dreams. Your past has reached its summit in the present and your future starts now.

As the present is of essential value for the future, you need God's guidance to make wise decisions. God loves you and He cares for you. If your thought life is dedicated to God, He will guide you even when your thoughts are confused. God is omniscient and though you may not be aware of His living presence, He is with you. He will keep you, even if your duties require your thoughts to concentrate elsewhere.

Trust this unique God who promised to guide and keep you and never to let go of you. He is your guarantee of a blessed future.

> Often God gives to us in one fleeting moment that which He has denied us for a long time. (Thomas á Kempis)

My Guide, I bow before You in humble gratitude _____

_____

Reach your goal

"And keep the charge of the Lord your God: to walk in his ways, to keep his statutes, his commandments, his judgements and his testimonies as it is written in the law of Moses, that you may prosper in all that you do and wherever you turn." (1 Kgs. 2:3)

The objective and desire of every person is to successfully achieve his ambitions and ideals. There are few people, if any, who can honestly say that success doesn't mean anything to them; that they will be satisfied, regardless of what happens to them in life. On the contrary, life would be empty and meaningless for the person who has no goal or ambition.

On the other hand, for those who have a heart-felt desire to succeed, failure could be a bitter pill to swallow. It can deal a serious blow to their confidence. Many people give up their future because they despair of ever obtaining success. Every disappointment or failure is a destructive blow to their ambition.

Along your pilgrimage on earth it is important that you should discover and accept the fact that it is impossible to be successful through your own abilities only. One needs Jesus Christ's guidance and support to ensure that you make the right decision and choose the right direction. If the living Christ is your travelling companion and partner, then you can rest assured that you will experience an honest and pure fulfilment in everything you take on. Will you dare to attempt the pilgrimage without His guidance and accompaniment? That would be nothing but a recipe for disaster!

> The pilgrim who wastes all his time to count his steps, will make very little progress. (Jean Pierre Camus)

Holy Spirit, please help me to stay on course _____

_____

Where are you going?

"Now thanks be to God who always leads us in triumph in Christ" (2 Cor. 2:14)

Some people seem to achieve success with seeming ease, while others are plagued by defeat. To ascribe this to co-incidence would be unrealistic and contrary to the law of cause and effect. Nothing happens by chance – at least not in the lives of God's children. Nobody is successful by accident, nor is anybody a failure by choice.

Every person makes his own choice as to what he wants to be and where he wants to go and this choice involves much more than wishful thinking. It is not always easy to choose which road you should follow. And this is where the acceptance of Christ as Lord of your life puts divine powers into action. It has a positive and constructive influence on your life – your values take on the right perspective and you can choose those which will supply you with an inspired yet practical goal.

Choosing your goal with Christ's guidance is the highest form of common sense. It implies cooperation with God which can only result in tremendous blessing in your life.

Choosing your objectives with Christ's help causes you to put your feet on a road which you can follow with a clear conscience. It will bring joy, confidence and enthusiasm into your life. A by-product of such a way of living is that the relationship between you and the triune God becomes more intimate on a daily basis. Striving to reach the goal then becomes just as joyful as its attainment. If you walk your path of life in the light of God, the whole journey becomes a joyous experience.

Ideals are like stars – we don't really reach them, but like seafarers we use them to determine our direction. (Carl Schultz)

Dear Guide, thank You that I am part _____

_____

THE FOUNTAIN OF
GOD'S ENCOURAGEMENT

Faith is to see the light with your heart when your eyes can only see the darkness. (Alexander Maclaren)

Lord, my God, thank You for all the encouragement which Your Holy Spirit and Your Word offer me. I want to walk along life's road with courage and faith, but I know I can only do it when I hold on to Your almighty hand.

Please hold me, Lord, so that I will not take the wrong paths; that I won't follow my own foolish heart; and that I won't despair because at times the path seems to be too steep.

Strengthen my faith in order for my spiritual eyes to see clearly; grant me wisdom in order for me to choose Your path only; grant me strength not to give in to self-pity.

Thank You for Your encouragement every step of the way.

*T*ake courage

"Be strong and of good courage; do not be afraid, nor be dismayed, for the Lord your God is with you wherever you go." (Josh. 1:9)

*Y*ou still need to grow beyond that point in your spiritual life where you believe that God is a super-examiner who finds great satisfaction in penalising you for every mistake you make. To have such a concept of your heavenly Father in your heart, is to do Him great injustice. It also creates a serious barrier, preventing His loving encouragement from flowing into your life.

It is God's desire for you to live in intimate fellowship with Him; that you will experience His creative abilities; that you will express His wisdom in your relationship with others; that you will draw from Him strength when you are weak, courage when you are discouraged and inspiration when you are despondent. Your heavenly Father does not take pleasure in your failures, but He waits for you to ask Him to meet you at the point of your need and to enable you to become that which He expects you to be.

If you make God your partner and the consciousness of His living presence becomes a reality in your life, then your perception of God will change radically. Then you won't regard Him as One who takes pleasure in condemnation, but as the main source of encouragement and inspiration. Then He becomes your shining light of encouragement when you are downcast, or when you experience bitterness, failure and disappointment. Then He will be there to whisper to you, "Do not be afraid, nor be dismayed."

Encouragement is the oxygen of man's soul. (George M. Adams)

Father, Your constant encouragement and inspiration _____

_____

ᴄᴀ God who encourages

"Now may the God of patience and comfort grant you to be like-minded toward one another, according to Christ Jesus" (Rom. 15:5)

Every one of us experiences times in our lives when we are threatened by heaviness and depression. For no apparent reason it feels as if you cannot handle the demands of life any more and you give in to every passing mood of despair. Everything you try your hand at seems to fail, you become discouraged and believe you are no longer able to cope with life's struggles.

When you've come to the end of your own abilities, it is good to become silent before God for a while and there receive the encouragement that only He can give. It requires an absolute stillness and submission of yourself and your mind in order to receive His encouragement. Otherwise, all the old familiar attitudes of despair will take hold of you again.

In the silence of being conscious of God's divine presence, you can recall all His glorious promises of encouragement. That will revive a positive and encouraging attitude in your mind and emotions. Reassure yourself afresh that both in the storm and the hush, God, in Christ Jesus, is with you. Remember that He promised to make all things new. He will give to you the singleness of purpose as well as the strength to complete the task which He has given you to do.

It is not God's will for you to permanently remain in the dark valley of despondency. He will give you the encouragement which will make your life meaningful and beautiful again.

God's power to guide me; God's omnipotence to protect me; God's wisdom to teach me; God's eye to keep watch over me; God's ear to hear me and God's Word to purify me. (Patrick the Pious)

Holy God, when life is too much for me _____

Find your strength in Him

"Strengthen the weak hands, and make firm the feeble knees. Say to those who are fearful-hearted, 'Be strong, do not fear, your God will come.'" (Is. 35:3, 4)

It is a lamentable fact that there are many people who don't realise what their full potential is, because they live in fear and underestimate themselves. They do have the ability, but when the time of testing comes, their bashfulness or aloofness causes them to withdraw. Numerous people who can account for themselves in a specific area, fail because of this flaw in their personality. As a result they experience a feeling of inability which only serves to increase their feeling of inferiority.

A Christian should never suffer loss like this. As a child of God you have the promise of His Son, Jesus Christ, that He will take your burdens upon Himself and will bear your guilt. He wants to be your inseparable companion through life. He invites you to come to Him with all your fears, anxieties and insecurities. You have His Word of promise that He will never leave you nor forsake you (Ref. Hebrews 14:5).

With the promise of His divine support and the steadfast assurance that the Son of God is with you in every situation, you can move forward in confidence: secure in His Name and unafraid of what may lie ahead. Just as He was in the past, God is in the future as well. Does one need greater encouragement than that?

Our trust in Christ doesn't cause us to be lazy, irresponsible or reckless; on the contrary, it awakens and ignites us, activating us to do good and live righteously. No self-confidence can be compared to this. (Ulrich Zwingli)

Living Lord Jesus, with You at my side _____

Life is an open door

"See, I have set before you an open door and no one can shut it." (Rev. 3:8)

There are people who complain that life is empty and meaningless. For them life is one dreary hour after the next, one uninteresting day after the next and time drags by while they lead a useless existence. It doesn't take them long to wilt intellectually and to develop a negative, narrow-minded attitude towards life.

It is totally unnecessary for such a situation to develop in your life, because Jesus Christ has given to you, and to all others, the promise of an abundant life – and the opportunity to experience it to the full (Ref. John 10:10). Scripture, history and your personal experience offer ample testimony to this fact. It testifies that an ordinary, dull life is transformed by the power of the living Christ and through His Holy Spirit.

Through the wonder of God's grace sadness is transformed into joy, defeat into victory; fear disappears; hate changes into love and despair into hope – even death becomes life. The moment you accept Christ into your life as Redeemer and Saviour, everything in life gets new meaning and purpose. You enter through the door of redemption into a new world. Paul says, *"Therefore, if anyone is in Christ, he is a new creation; old things have passed away; behold, all things have become new"* (2 Corinthians 5:17).

This new life of abundance which Christ offers you, is yours for the taking. If you only exist, without really living, turn to Christ and He will open the door for you to a new, meaningful life.

> Conversion must find concrete expression in small and big deeds of faith. (Robert H. Benson)

Lord Jesus, the open door of Your grace leads me _____

_____

Encouragement for lonely days

"I alone am left." (1 Kgs. 19:10)

Sometimes one finds oneself dismally lonely in the midst of a crowd of people. Suddenly everything looks strange to you. Perhaps you were used to the privacy of your own room, and suddenly you have to share a ward with others. It could be that their company is not the type that you are used to, and you feel very uncomfortable in their presence. You find that even though you are among people, you are still isolated.

This kind of loneliness is experienced by everyone who is dissociated from a familiar environment and it is accentuated when the new surroundings are unsympathetic. A child leaving his parental home to move into a university residence; an elderly person taken from his familiar environment into a home for the aged. Remember then that in the circle where you find yourself now, there are others who feel just as lonely as you do. Often the ones who are the loudest are the loneliest. Therefore, don't be fooled by their pretence.

The secret of overcoming loneliness in every form lies in knowing that the living Christ is with you at all times. In order for you to experience this, it is important that you constantly confirm His presence in your mind and your spirit. You must know and trust that He is with you in the taxing times of life. There are many dedicated children of God in all areas of life who are waiting to share their Christian experiences with you. Yet, the most important of all is this, your heavenly Friend is always there for you.

People are lonely because they build walls instead of bridges. (Josef F. Newton)

Lord Jesus, Your unceasing presence _____

Varying spiritual experiences

"Nevertheless, God Who comforts the downcast, comforted us by the coming of Titus." (2 Cor. 7:6)

Many of Jesus Christ's disciples live from one elevating spiritual experience to the next. When their lives take a normal course, they think something is wrong with their Christianity.

The mountaintop experiences of a Christian's life are filled with inspiration and the consciousness of the presence of the living Christ. Just as the disciples shared those glorious moments with their Master on the Mount of Transfiguration, so the present-day disciple cherishes those intimate moments when Christ becomes a living reality to him. These moments serve to light up the commonness of life.

However, many disciples refuse to accept the commonness of life as a reality and they expect to live continually on spiritual summits. Then, when they encounter problems, they find themselves in a dark valley. They are convinced that their Master has forsaken them, or that their faith is not what it should be.

Even our Lord experienced times when He was sad and distressed. We read in Scripture that in Gethsemane He *"began to be sorrowful and deeply distressed"* (Ref. Matthew 26:37). That was anything but a mountaintop experience; on the contrary, those were moments of deep affliction. If you are disappointed because your faith isn't always at the highest level, then remember that your Saviour understands and that He will guide you to steadfastness and victory. Allow this guarantee to be your encouragement for today.

> Conviction is truth which is settled in your mind; faith is the fire that burns in your heart. (Joseph Newton)

I praise You, great God _____

_____

$\mathcal{A}$ttempt great things

"He is your praise, and He is your God, who has done for you these great and awesome things which your eyes have seen." (Deut. 10:21)

$\mathcal{T}$he great majority of people adapt their lives according to what others think of them. Because society expects nothing from them, they expect nothing from themselves. They merge into oblivion among the masses and become quite happy to lose their identity in this mass. At times they become aware of deep, strange stirrings in their spirit. This is because, even though they are a minute particle of human society, they have the basic elements of eternity in them. One of an innumerable multitude and yet partakers of God's life-giving breath.

Everyone who is aware of this, starts searching for vaster horizons of spiritual and mental experiences. They become dissatisfied with their present situation and yearn for the ability to expand their future. At this point however, they experience the impact of the ordinary, unfulfilling life they lead. While they long to move ahead with new insights, there are influences and powers which hold them back. Many fear that they will never be able to escape from the past and regress into their old life, with crumbled hopes and shattered dreams of what could have happened.

If God has given you a vision or a mission, then you can be sure it will require effort and hard work. God guides individuals by entrusting them with tasks which seem to be above their ability. Only if you accept the challenge and trust God, will you be able to find out what you are really able to do.

> God is the God of promise. He keeps His Word even when it seems impossible; even when circumstances indicate the opposite. (Colin Urquhart)

My Lord, I pray _____

_____

Discover God's will for your life

"But the manifestation of the Spirit is given to each one for the profit of all." (1 Cor. 12:7)

Have you ever felt as though you are drifting aimlessly through life and that it would make no difference whether you were here or not? Day upon dreary day comes and goes without your achieving anything worthwhile and your spiritual life has lost its sparkle.

Such a sad state of affairs is not God's fault at all. First of all you need to rediscover the reality of your spiritual experience. Then you have to search for God's will for your life in order to have a positive goal. With Christ in control of your life, you will stop drifting around aimlessly and become an inspired and positive Christian.

The renewal of your spiritual experience starts when you invite Christ into your life and open yourself up to the working of the Holy Spirit allowing Him to take control of your thoughts and actions. Then you discover that as you are living in harmony with Him, new areas of service are revealed to you. You realise that you are being led by the Holy Spirit into spheres of life which you had not even considered before.

When you have a feeling that God is guiding you, you need to confirm it in prayer. Be courageous, act confidently and trust steadfastly in God. To discover God's will for your life not only requires faith, but positive action as well.

God's encouragement is to be found in the fact that He is with you always; that He loves you and cares for you. What more does one need?

> Do not carry one single burden, because one is too much for you. The work is Mine and Mine only: your job is to rest in Me! (Isaac T. Hecher)

Loving Master, with renewed courage I'm going to _____

_____

God is omnipresent

"The steps of a good man are ordered of the Lord, and He delights in his way. Though he fall, he shall not be utterly cast down, for the Lord upholds him with his hand." (Ps. 37:23, 24)

Christians are not exempt from deep emotional experiences. Sometimes they find themselves on cloud nine with spiritual joy, while at other times they are cast into the depths of spiritual despair. It is important to maintain a healthy balance between these two extremes and to keep your grip on your faith.

Don't convince yourself that you've disappointed or denied the Master. He knows what it means to be upset and He understands your moods. He also understands your moments of spiritual ecstasy when your spirit reaches out to God. He is the Lord of every frame of mind, because He became a man.

You must take care that your despondency is not caused by physical weakness, because it can create apathy in spiritual matters. The most common cause of despondency and depression however, is disobedience to the law of God and His plan for your life. When a Christian disciple refuses to do the will of God, he experiences an inner turmoil which results in frustration and despair.

The remedy for this state of mind is a more intimate walk with God. This means more time in prayer and meditation; a disciplined quiet time and a consciousness of the presence of the living Christ. Your encouragement is that when you search for Him, He is already there to receive you.

God is everywhere and in all things; not as a part of their being and also not by accident, but like an agent is present in the medium which it has an influence on. (Thomas Aquinas)

Thank You, Father, for _____

_____

Inspiration has many faces

"But there is a spirit in man and the breath of the Almighty gives him understanding." (Job 32:8)

If you really want to enjoy life, you need to discover the fact that, along your path, there are hidden sources of inspiration waiting to refresh you and spur you on to greater effort. To deny the existence of these sources, is to rob yourself of something which has immeasurable value and for which there is no substitute.

The sad truth is that most people rush through their daily activities without any desire to be inspired through truths which they discovered themselves. When something great or lofty comes to them, they are elevated for a moment, only to sink back into their old sluggishness very soon. They don't succeed in seeing the small inspirations of life and isolate themselves from any form of inspiration which could bring beauty and strength into their lives.

The joy of these small inspirations is that you have to discover them yourself. They will not force themselves upon you, but, like beautiful flowers, they need to be picked from the common experiences of everyday life: a friendly word, a pleasant attitude, a word of comfort to someone in deep sorrow. Has the rising or setting of the sun filled you with enchantment lately or has it become so commonplace that you never notice it any more? Are you still made glad when someone puts trust in you? There are numerous blessings which are waiting to be used by you for inspiration. To make the most of your life, make sure that you don't miss them.

> Have a good look at your innermost being; there is always a source of inspiration if you would only notice it and use it. (Marcus Antonius)

Holy Teacher, please teach me the art of living _____

God wants to be your friend

"So the Lord spoke to Moses face to face, as a man speaks to his friend."
(Ex. 33:11)

In their search for God many people experience only silence in His presence. They feel as if they are in a spiritual void. They try to empty their minds of all thoughts in order to be filled with a consciousness of the living God, only to find that their minds are being filled with petty and confusing thoughts.

One method of getting to know God, is to accept Him as a tried and trusted friend. Share your deepest thoughts and feelings with Him. Include Him in your everyday thoughts, thus making Him an integral part of your life. The development of such familiarity will in no way decrease the respect that you have for Him. On the contrary, the development of such an intimacy enables you to enter the silence of God, thus strengthening your inner life and refreshing your spirit.

Many well-meaning disciples exert themselves to the utmost in an effort to enter the quietude which is found in God. This can never be achieved by force, but only through the sanctified friendship which the Master offers to His committed and dedicated disciples.

God wants to be your friend. Make Him your friend. Share with Him your deepest thoughts. Enjoy fellowship with Him constantly in the quietness of your spirit. Then you will discover those beautiful moments that are filled with His presence. The thoughts that you share with Him fill that void and make you receptive to His encouraging closeness.

> The reality of our fellowship with Christ, and through Him with one another, is the increase of love in our hearts. (William Temple)

Lord, I praise Your great Name because _____

_____

Be strong

"Wait on the Lord; Be of good courage, and He shall strengthen your heart. Wait, I say, on the Lord!" (Ps. 27:14)

Sometimes things just get too much for us. You feel as if you cannot go one step forward. Sickness, affliction, worries, death, disappointment, old age, hardships, you name them ... they all make your path steep, your life dark and your future insecure.

If this is how you are feeling at this moment, the Lord wants to encourage you through His words, *"Be of good courage, and He shall strengthen your heart."* In the dark hours of his life David made the following discovery, *"The Lord is the strength of my life ... "* Even though the sun sometimes sets over your life, you never need to dwell in darkness. Where the Lord is, there is always light and the night disappears. *"For You will light my lamp; the Lord my God will enlighten my darkness"* (Psalm 18:28).

The Lord is also your Saviour. Even though you feel hopelessly ensnared in your crises and afflicting situations, the Lord will save you from all your distress and anxiety, even though you don't know when and how. *"He shall deliver you in six troubles, yes, in seven no evil shall touch you"* (Job 5:19).

The Lord is your refuge. A refuge is a place where you can flee to in a time of danger and where you will find protection, safety and rest. Are you looking for a place of rest, and refuge? *"The Lord is my refuge ... "* (Ps 27:1) (NIV). *"I will say of the Lord. 'He is my refuge and my fortress, my God in Him I will trust'"* (Psalm 91:2). May the Lord carry you in love with this encouragement.

Regardless of what happens to you, God is your Father and He is interested in you. This is His attitude towards you. (Martyn Lloyd-Jones)

Omnipotent Father, because You are my strength, my Saviour and my refuge, I will not _____

_____

God grants self-confidence

"It is better to trust in the Lord, than to put confidence in princes."
(Ps. 118:9)

Many of God's children lack self-confidence. Though they believe in God and in His goodness and grace, they enter every day with fear and trepidation. They avoid strangers and meet new people only when it's an absolute must. They are deeply disturbed and unhappy because they feel so inferior. They are convinced that others are better and work better than they do and assure themselves that others don't think much of them. They try to walk along life's path as unobtrusively as possible and prefer to be left on their own.

If you've had a real and living encounter with Christ, you will not suffer from an inferiority complex, because then you will forget about yourself. If you accept Him as the Lord of your life and you have made up your mind to serve Him and obey Him in everything you do, you will stop thinking about how you react to the opinion and actions of others. You will judge situations and things that happen through the Spirit of Christ who lives in you.

You have the Christlike view of life when you've accepted his invitation to *"Abide in Him"* (See John 15:1-8). Then He lives in you too. What others think or say then is of no concern to you. Christ has given you a new approach and you face each day with confidence. Your only desire is to please Christ and not men. Forget about yourself, live for Christ and your inferiority will be something of the past.

> The greater and more steadfast your trust in God, the more abundantly He will grant you self-confidence. (John Dewey)

Christ, I want to live for You so that I _____

_____

Godly assistance

"I can do all things through Christ who strengthens me." (Phil. 4:13)

How often have you side-stepped a task because you thought that you were unable to do it? In this you are not unique, because there are many people who find the responsibilities of a certain task too taxing and therefore they refuse to accept the challenge. The result is that they probably miss out on wonderful opportunities in life.

As long as you trust in your own abilities, there will always be times when you shy away from a challenge or responsibility. The result is a feeling of failure or inadequacy. This usually has a negative effect on your self-confidence and your ability to handle a crisis.

You must remember – and continually remind yourself – that when God calls you to do something, He chose you because He knows that you are the one to fulfil this specific calling. God does not necessarily call the ones who are able: He enables those whom He calls. In Christ your Lord, God will grant you the ability to fulfil your calling.

Regardless what task you are called to do, pray about it and dedicate your task to Christ. Seek the Holy Spirit's help and assistance and follow obediently and willingly wherever He leads you. You will not fail, because God Himself will be with you.

God only requires you to do your best and to trust Him. (Robert H. Benson)

Holy Master, I trust You to _____ me _____

*C*ssured of His presence

"By this we know that we abide in Him, and He in us, because He has given us his Spirit." (1 Jn. 4:13)

*I*n spite of the fact that the first disciples lived in such intimate fellowship with Jesus, they were still fallible. They saw His love towards all people; they were amazed at His miracles and healings; they rejoiced in His teachings which He conveyed to them with such clarity of logic; and they were overjoyed because they were His friends.

In spite of this beautiful intimacy and the wonderful privilege of sharing His life, they nevertheless revealed very real human characteristics. They contended with one another; they were jealous, proud and selfish. In general they had normal human weaknesses. And this carried on till the time of His death, when they betrayed and denied Him and fled from Him like cowards.

The wonderful truth is that the most glorious time in the disciples' lives occurred after the Master had gone from them. He promised that He would be with them at all times by giving them His Spirit. He undertook to dwell in their spirit in order that His wisdom and strength would enable them to live to His glory.

And the promise of the Master's indwelling Spirit has never yet been recalled. In these modern times His disciples can still be partakers of His Spirit and experience the assurance of His presence. To own this precious treasure, you have to believe that it's yours: you have to accept it in faith and nurture it through prayer, Bible study and meditation.

God is He without whom one cannot live. (Leo Tolstoy)

Living Saviour, come _____

_____

On his Majesty's service

"Therefore I have reason to glory in Christ Jesus in the things which pertain to God." (Rom. 15:17)

For many years a general complaint in the life of the average congregation has been that there are very few people who are willing to work. The excuses for this lack of involvement are legion: lack of time, inefficiency and lack of qualifications. The result is that there is so much to be done in the church of Christ, but there are very few willing to undertake the work.

Two things are essentially important and must be borne in mind when service to a church is considered. The first fact is that you are serving the living God and not people. You are doing it to His glory and honour. The second fact is that God will never call you to His service, without equipping you with the ability to do that specific task.

It is indeed an indescribable privilege, but also your Christian duty to offer your service to serve Jesus amongst His people. Thus, by grace you have the undeserved honour to reflect the love of God. That is why every task needs to be done with loving zeal. If there is any doubt with regard to your ability, then seek the help of the Holy Spirit. If you remain open to His guidance, He will inspire you with the power of the living Christ which will enable you to fulfil that task which He has chosen for you with gratitude and faithfulness.

Offer yourself and your talents to Him and experience the joy of fulfilment.

> Nobody offers himself freely and totally in God's service, unless he has tasted His Fatherly love and serve and worship Him in gratitude.

Take my life Lord, let it be _____

_____

I am with you!

"When you pass through the waters, I will be with you; And through the rivers, they shall not overflow you." (Is. 43:2)

I t requires great faith and a strong character to be able to work through adversity and disappointment. Many seemingly strong people eventually double up under their burdens and break down. When things turned against them they were not able to withstand the pressure. Of course the results can have a destructive effect on their lives – and also on the lives of others close to them.

The Lord never promised you will never experience a crisis because you have accepted Him. However, He did undertake to be there for you at all times to assist you and to help you over life's hurdles. This assurance in itself brings great comfort: knowing that you don't have to tackle the afflictions in life on your own.

To ensure your peace of mind, it is important that you should realise and hold on to the fact that Jesus is the living Christ. Through the Holy Spirit, He is just as much a part of you as you are of yourself. Because He was able to overcome the worst people had done to Him, He is now at your side every step of the way and every moment of the day.

When problems mar your view and put you under pressure, turn to Christ. He is your heavenly companion. Overcome your problems in the peace of His presence.

> There are three things which only God knows: the beginning of things, the cause of things and the end of things. (Welsh proverb)

Thank You, omnipotent Father, that I can say _____

_____

Your anchor in life

"No one is holy like the Lord, for there is none besides You, nor is there any rock like our God." (1 Sam. 2:2)

There comes a time in the life of every person when reassurance and support are needed. Even those who regard themselves as totally self-sufficient come to a point where their own resources are insufficient to meet the needs of the situation they find themselves in. Then they need something or someone to enable them to handle the situation.

Some people turn to professional counsellors; others go for medical assistance; yet others trust in the support of their friends. There are even those who try to fight their way through the dilemma in their own strength. While all these methods can partially help to solve their problems, they can never be totally sure of that. They also won't have the assurance that the problem won't occur again, or that they will be able to handle it if it does occur.

The only sure and lasting solution comes from God. Whether you seek for help elsewhere or not, never make the mistake of counting God out. He cares for you in every situation. Because Christ is the same yesterday, today and forever, you can be assured of His incessant and constant presence through all circumstances of life. While there are other things that can help you survive, only God can give you abiding peace and ease of mind. And without that, life can easily become a nightmare.

When you feel overly confident, remember your own weakness; when you feel weak, remember God's omnipotence. (Sir Thomas More)

Saviour, by putting my life in Your hands _____

_____

Be encouraged in the Lord

"O Lord my God, You are very great: You are clothed with honour and majesty." (Ps. 104:1)

In general, people are easily inclined to give in to feelings of pessimism. When they experience adversity or misfortune, when they go through worrying times, a heavy atmosphere of doom and gloom descends upon them and the burden of anxious care becomes too much for them.

When you experience feelings like these, it would be wise to consider the wonder of God's omnipotence. Through the ages there is ample testimony of the revelation of His omnipotence. Civilisations and even the world as a whole, have often been threatened, but the Lord stepped in every time and averted disaster. Evil tried to conquer good, but God's powerful hand conquered the evil one and rendered him powerless time and time again.

What seemed to be the biggest disaster, when the Son of God was nailed to a cross and died, dissipated when Christ rose triumphantly from death and became the victor over sin, evil and death for ever.

In your dark moments consider the wonder of God's royal majesty and thank Him for His encompassing love for humanity and the world. Be encouraged by the fact that the omnipotent Lord God reigns over everything, and approach life with faith and courage.

The very same omnipotent power which brought Christ from the dead, is at work in those who belong to Christ. The resurrection is an ongoing event. (Leon Morris)

Great God, to You be all honour _____

Encouragement in service

"Well done, good and faithful servant; you were faithful over a few things. I will make you ruler over many things. Enter into the joy of your Lord." (Mt. 25:21)

In this life few experiences give as much satisfaction as a task done to the best of your ability for the sake of your heavenly Father. To undertake a task which you believe was the will of God; to struggle and grapple and then experience the satisfaction of completion; to eventually lay everything before your Lord, knowing that you are laying before Him the best you could do – that gives deep and lasting satisfaction.

In conjunction with this satisfaction comes a feeling of achievement which elevates your spirit and brings about great happiness. Now you may sit back and think there is nothing more that you need to do for God. If you were faithful in performing one task, God will probably have some more which He will entrust to you. When you have proven your value in one instance, you should humbly ask God where He wants to use you next.

A true servant lives very close to the source of His inspiration and spiritual refreshment. That is why he never gets tired spiritually. When the body is tired and exhausted, it is refreshed through sleep. The spirit of man flourishes on a job completed well and the knowledge that he did his best in everything that was done for God. Thus he receives God's blessing on all his labour. May this also cause you to be encouraged in your service to the Master.

Service is God's way to liberate an individual, while slavery is man's way to destroy him. (Michael Harpur)

Lord Jesus, I offer my service to You _____

_____

*O*bedience creates trust

"Now He who has prepared us for this very thing is God, who also has given us the Spirit as guarantee. So we are always confident." (2 Cor. 5:5, 6)

*T*he person who is disobedient continually lives in fear that his disobedience will be revealed some day. Those who live a double life develop a feeling of insecurity which leads to secrecy. The result is a lack of confidence which is so necessary for a purposeful and joyous life.

If you desire to have faith and trust in God, it is important that you obey Him. Such obedience is not a reluctant acceptance of something which cannot be avoided, but a cheerful acceptance of whatever His all-wise will might be for your life.

God gives you His Holy Spirit and if you accept this divine gift, it will be your greatest desire to do God's will where ever He has placed you. Initially this seems to be very difficult, but because of the Spirit in you, you will receive power which enables you to live a life that is pleasing to God.

One of the richest rewards of living as God expects you to live, is that your trust in Him grows continually. Then you live without fear or a feeling of inferiority. While you go on in total obedience to the Spirit who dwells in you, you develop a relationship of trust with God, your fellowmen and a much greater appreciation of yourself.

It is impossible to live in complete obedience to the will of God and at the same time have no trust in the future at all.

Obedience to God is the infallible proof of true and total love for Him. (Nathaniël Emmons)

Master, I praise Your Name for _____

_____

*W*hen life becomes a problem

"We are hard-pressed on every side, yet not crushed; we are perplexed, but not in despair." (2 Cor. 4:8)

Regardless of what your problem might be, you dare not allow it to control your thoughts to the extent that God is excluded. If you allow your problems to soak your mind, resulting in a confused lifestyle, you are not allowing your heavenly Father to work out His will in your life. You are more aware of the problem than of God and that is a detrimental situation.

Make sure that you always approach your problem in a constructive manner. First make very sure what it really is. If it is vague and confused, it is alarming. When you've put it in writing and considered it honestly and handled it purposefully, you have already made it manageable. Set your problem out in the clearest and simplest words that you possibly can.

Once you've done that you can present it to God in a spirit of anticipation. Be assured that God is bigger than any problem which could ever arise. Share your problem with your Father and declare yourself willing to obey His will. Then be sensitive to His guidance. And then the words of Proverbs 3:6 will become true for you, *"In all your ways acknowledge Him, and He shall direct your path."*

Be watchful against panic and self-pity. Put your trust totally in the Lord. Allow His Holy Spirit to work freely in your life. This can be a liberating and victorious experience.

God's promises are like the stars: the darker the night, the brighter they shine. (David Nicholas)

Loving Father, thank You that You _____

_____

Overcome your fear

"Fear not, for I have redeemed you; I have called you by name, you are Mine." (Is. 43:1)

Most people will agree that we live in very uncertain times. Nations experience economic crises; violence and political instability are all around. Individuals feel disrupted and insecure in the midst of all these changes. Others feel unsafe and insecure when they look at the future. Such circumstances are not really conducive to peace of mind or a stable lifestyle. The result is that people are afraid.

Right from the beginning of man's existence on earth, fear has been a decaying factor. After the fall Adam confessed to God, *"I heard your voice in the garden, and I was afraid ... "* (Genesis 3:10). Fear can have very far-reaching results for your mental, spiritual, physical and emotional well-being. In some instances fear can be the cause of a total break-down and you are in danger of losing your hold on life.

History bears testimony to the fact that when individuals or nations turned to the Lord in times of severe crisis, He always equipped them to handle the situation. Biblical history reflects the wonderful way in which the love of God has overcome fear in the lives of people who put their trust completely in Him.

When you feel the icy grip of fear on your life, seek the comforting and encouraging presence of the living Christ. Seek Him in prayer and hold on to His love. Commit yourself totally to Him and hand over all your problems to Him. Then you will experience how the peace of God dispels all fear from your life.

Courage is not the absence of fear; courage is the conquering of fear. (R.L. Stevenson)

Jesus, my Guide, thank You that You are holding my hand _____

Christ will protect you

"But the Lord is faithful, who will establish you and guard you from the evil one." (2 Thes. 3:3)

There comes a time in every person's life – and especially in a Christian's life – when one falls into temptation. This doesn't necessarily mean that you are seduced into committing terrible crimes. Temptation has many faces but they all result in undermining your faith one way or the other.

When facing temptation the average person will always conclude that it is impossible to resist it. In general this is true, because there is very little you can do in your own strength to overcome it. It has been proven time and time again that people are weak and frail and easily influenced by the circumstances of the moment.

The living Christ has come to say to us that without God we can do nothing, but that with God all things are possible. This is where the tremendous message of hope and encouragement is to be found for all Christians: when all else has failed, God is still there and He is in control.

In order for you to be strengthened in your intention to tackle life with courage, it is important that you should be able to handle your problems. You will have to overcome all those temptations that descend upon your life like a plague. That is why it is important that you should allow the Spirit of the living God to enter into your life and control it. Thus you will receive the assurance and trust that Jesus Christ is with you in every temptation and every difficult situation.

> The one sure antidote for temptation is to experience the presence of God. (Francois Fenelon)

Lord, with You in control of my life _____

Excessive concern

"Therefore do not worry about tomorrow, for tomorrow will worry about its own things. Sufficient for the day is its own trouble." (Mt. 6:34)

There are many people who sit and count and cuddle their "worry-beads" all day long, thus losing their hold on life. It could be that life makes very high demands; that your responsibilities are many and massive; that it feels as if you have lost your sense of priority; as if all hope is dying. And it is in this chaotic breeding-ground that worry takes root and flourishes, because worry is the fruit of a confused mind and insufficient faith.

The first step to overcome worry is to clearly define that which creates the worry. For many people, worry is something vague and poorly outlined. However, it continually weighs down your spirit and mind, creating disastrous results. Outline your worries by writing them down – clearly and simply – on a piece of paper. Then look at them calmly, pray about them and scale them down to their real size. Confirm prayerfully that you are in control of the situation that has developed and that worry will no longer affect your tranquillity and peace of mind.

If you would only involve yourself in this creative action today, you will discover that you are prohibiting worry and concern from flooding your future. The secret is "prayerful confirmation". And that means to be conscious of Christ's presence so that He is a greater reality than your worries. Christ is all-sufficient for all our needs of today, tomorrow and every other day in the future.

Worry does not empty tomorrow of its sadness; it robs today of its power. (Corrie ten Boom)

Saviour, I praise and thank You that You _____ me ___

*W*hen everything seems lost

"Do not sorrow, for the joy of the Lord is your strength." (Neh. 8:11)

*T*here are many instances in life when the sky above us is overcast with ominous thunder clouds. The loss of a loved-one, a friend or even a pet can cause sorrow. To be separated from someone who has meant a lot to you and who has been an intimate part of your life, can be traumatic.

When this happens, many people have difficulty in filling the void again and thus they fall into a state of despair. This can cause untold damage to their mind, their emotions and their spiritual life.

It would be utterly foolish to expect you not to experience sadness when separated from someone you love, yet it is important to remember that with the help of Christ Jesus you can handle your sorrow with dignity. It is unthinkable that God's great heart of love was not grieved when His Son was sacrificed on the cross, or that Jesus was not grieved when He had to part with His disciples. But the love, joy and peace of God were the supporting graces. And even today, this is still the grace through which you can overcome sorrow.

In times when you experience tension, sorrow and pressure, surrender yourself to the risen Christ. Allow His power to support and encourage you.

> Sorrow is a fruit. God never allows it to grow on branches that cannot bear it. (Victor Hugo)

Lord, I thank You that You are my strength _____

Find encouragement in God

"Open my eyes that I may see wondrous things from your law." (Ps. 119:18)

Despondency and discouragement are common pheno-mena in the world today. People's emotions are like the rising and falling of mercury in a barometer, creating an unstable and insecure existence. The result is that many people are unhappy and not very sure of themselves. There is thus a tendency amongst the majority of people to be pessimistically inclined towards life. This influences their actions, plans and decisions negatively.

If you want to "live" in contrast to only "existing" it is important that you should be positive. If things are going well now, you must enjoy life and try to keep it up. Also thank God for it. If things are not going well, then you have to analyse the situation, identify the problem and then deal with it.

To achieve that, you will need to have a faith which is strong to enable you to bear the afflictions, handle the problems, overcome the obstacles and eventually live triumphantly. Such a faith is developed through prayer, during which you seek the assistance of the living Christ. And to prevent you from being tempted to give in to discouragement, something more is required. Constantly search the Scripture for examples of God's wondrous deeds. You will find one example after another where ordinary people were enabled to overcome superior numbers in the strength of the Master. Find your encouragement in Jesus Christ and in His Word and you will triumph over depression.

Like in paradise, God walks through the Scriptures, searching for people in need. (St. Ambrose)

Word that became flesh, I thank You for the future hope _____

_Light up your life

"'I am the light of the world. He who follows Me shall not walk in darkness, but have the light of life.'" (Jn. 8:12)

The effect that darkness has on the lives and emotions of people is multiple and varied. It could cause fear, depression, loneliness and sorrow. For most of us, when light comes, whether it's natural or artificial, it causes relief and is accompanied by a feeling of safety.

The darkness of the soul also has a negative effect on people. Because their spiritual lives suffer, they lose hope. Sickness, death, disappointment and sorrow are some of the causes that drive human emotions to the darkest depths of despair. The light of tranquillity and peace of mind seems to burn all the more dimly because of such experiences. It causes people to experience the commonly known feelings of despondency, depression and despair.

The only way in which you will manage to fight against, and overcome, these dark shadows, is through strong faith in God. Turn to Christ in every situation in life. Trust Him and believe that He will be able to guide you through the particular problem which you are experiencing right now. Don't just continue cursing the darkness. Light a small candle of faith and help to light up the darkness.

Walk in His light and soon you will acknowledge that the darkness has gone. Because His light is in your heart, and is lighting your path, the day becomes radiant for you.

While in the dark, we have no choice. It is the light which enables us to see the difference between things; and it is Christ who supplies the light. (C.T. Whitmell)

Loving Guide, while You hold my hand I am _____

God has a plan for you

"But now, do not therefore be grieved or angry with yourselves because you sold me here; for God sent me before you to preserve life." (Gen. 45:5)

It is often difficult to understand or to accept that God is busy fulfilling His plan in your life, especially when you are going through difficult or taxing times. When Joseph was sold into slavery, when an unscrupulous woman robbed him of his freedom and when his friends forgot about him, it seemed unlikely that he would discern the hand of God in all those happenings. Nevertheless, when after many years he looked back upon the road he had travelled, he did see the hand of God in his life.

If you are in deep waters of affliction right now, if you are experiencing problems and sorrow – remember that it might be part of God's tapestry. He determines the pattern of your life. In your darkest hour, hold on steadfastly to the belief that, in spite of the appearance of things, God is still in control because you have committed your life to Him.

Don't ever, in your imperfect and negative mind, confuse that which seems like an inevitable disaster to you, with the divine will of God. Rather discover that God can give purpose and meaning to Joseph's slavery, Moses' depression, Jeremiah's lamentations – and yes, even to Jesus' death on the cross. Life's darkest moments can be a testimony of God's perfect purpose for your life.

In your present circumstances, difficult and heart-rending as they might be, you have to hold on to the assurance that God is busy working out His perfect plan for your life.

> There is nothing which God cannot complete. (Cicero)

Faithful Guide, I will trust You _____

_____

ᴛHE FOUNTAIN
OF GOD'S PROTECTION

Faith is the beginning and the end of love, and God is the two of them blended in unity. (Ignatius of Antioch)

Almighty and omnipotent God, in Jesus Christ You are a refuge for us from generation to generation and every day You grant us Your love in abundance.

Thank You that those who seek shelter in You will never be put to shame.

It is such a comforting thought that You protect not only our bodies, but also our souls.

As individuals, as families, as a community and as a nation we need Your protection so much.

Please keep us from thinking that we don't need You.

Like little children we want to be protected by Your love and grace at all times.

Thank You for Your protection along our pilgrimage.

*O*mnipotent Protector

*"The Lord is my rock and my fortress and my deliverer; the God of
my strength in whom I will trust; my shield and the horn of my salvation; my stronghold and my refuge; my Saviour." (2 Sam. 22:2, 3)*

*I*n our times of affliction and need, the love and omnipotence
of God are our protection. We can overcome any challenge,
adversity or problem if we only steadfastly trust in His loving care
and grace.

He will command His angels to watch over us and protect us
from any danger. We will not be overwhelmed by Evil and rendered powerless.

Our inherent ability to choose, in His light, between that which
is good and right, or that which is wrong and unprofitable, will
enable us to act wisely. Thus we are protected against accidents,
loss or any terrifying experience.

Our ability to think and react quickly and then to act wisely, is
our protection against unexpected attacks and temptations from
Satan.

Our ability to adapt to our circumstances, to always be singing
in our inner being and be joyful, regardless of the situation and regardless of who we are with, protects us against times of loneliness
and depression.

Through the love that's in our hearts we give and receive love;
then peace and joy fill our minds and hearts, and we know that we
have an omnipotent Protector.

> The only true protection is to be found in the secret place of the Most
> High. (Dwight L. Moody)

Father, I bow before You in grateful humility _____

Under God's protection

"Blessed is the man who trusts in the Lord, and whose hope is in the Lord." (Jer. 17:7)

The whole world is experiencing ominous times. From every corner of the earth comes the news of famines, droughts, financial crises, violence, earthquakes, hurricanes, floods and many more destructive happenings which are caused by forces of nature. The result is that people are restless, insecure and afraid. And in the midst of these situations they are confused and don't know who to turn to or what to do for protection.

In order for you to maintain peace of mind, it is imperative that you place your faith and trust totally in God. He Who has promised to be with you till the end of time is there with you in every situation. He will protect you and will safely lead you from the darkness into His marvellous light. If your life is Christ-centered and if you acknowledge Him in everything that you do, He will protect you and lead you safely.

Regardless of how hopeless things might seem, never lose your faith in Christ's ability. He knows you and will protect you against the storms of life. Make Him your constant, inseparable companion. While you walk with Him, He will give you the strength to handle any imaginable situation; and also to overcome every disappointment and stroke of bad luck. Without His protection you are exposed to every possible danger and attacks from the evil one. You need not continue living like that while the glorious alternative is available to you: to live under the protection of the Most High.

The basis of peace is God and the secret of peace is steadfast trust. (J.B. Figgis)

With trust in You, O Lord, I experience _____

Protect the oasis of your life

"He makes me to lie down in green pastures; He leads me beside still waters." (Ps. 23:2)

For many people life is nothing but drudgery. Their daily routine has become so monotonous that all their initiative has died. The joy they once derived from the small, interesting things in life is now dead. They exist from morning till night without any purpose or expectation.

When you take a close look at these people who have lost their vision, you will find that they have neglected the oasis of their lives. They have plodded along without realising how important it is for them to come to a standstill, refresh their spirit and determine the course they are following. Their lives have turned into a desert. If you carry on without making time for spiritual refreshment and for adapting your course, life itself later loses all meaning and purpose. Then the monotony suffocates your spirit and you will not be able to appreciate the loftier things in life any more.

Cultivating an effective life is not a luxury, but a practical necessity. Life today is being lived at such a hectic pace that it is imperative for you to make time to withdraw for a while and spend time alone with God. Neglect this spiritual exercise and you can be sure that the tensions of life will overwhelm you.

You need to protect the oasis of your life with diligence and spend a quiet time with God in order for you to lead a meaningful life and to ensure that you are still within His sphere of protection.

> All of life's problems overcome us because we rebelliously refuse to go to our rooms daily and become quiet before God. (Blaise Pascal)

Holy Spirit of God, with Your help _____

_____

God protects His labourers

"Being confident of this very thing, that He who has begun a good work in you will complete it until the day of Jesus Christ." (Phil. 1:6)

From every generation Jesus Christ has His followers who preach His gospel and do His will. Some of them reach high positions in society; others perform the task He has assigned to them to the best of their ability. Regardless of their status they zealously love the Lord, to the extent that it challenges and motivates their fellow believers.

The spiritual giants of the Christian faith always have a vivid and unique experience with their Saviour. Paul never forgot his experience on the road to Damascus; Brother Lawrence loved being in his kitchen with Christ; John Wesley felt his "heart to be strangely warmed" in a room in Aldersgate Street in London. There are also many other disciples who experience the reality of the living Christ in various ways.

One thing that the followers of Christ should understand is that the Master comes to them in their own, unique circumstances, meeting everyone at his own level and place. The ordinary disciple does not necessarily have a Damascus Road experience.

As your relationship with Jesus Christ deepens, you will be guided into constructive service. You become aware of a divine plan unfolding for your life. Such a plan might perhaps not be dramatic, but it is God's plan for you, and in executing it you will find joy and a deep satisfaction – as well as His protection.

There is no nobler religion than service to mankind. To work amongst people for the sake of God, is the greatest confession of faith anyone can make. (Albert Schweitzer)

Master, make my experience _____

*W*alk with God

"Good and upright is the Lord; therefore He teaches sinners the way. The humble He guides in justice, and the humble He teaches his way. All the paths of the Lord are mercy and truth, to such as keep his covenant and his testimonies." (Ps. 25:8-10)

It is undoubtedly true that the best way to live is God's way. He is the source of all life, but He has given man the ability to choose his own path. This ability is crucial, because it either leads to constructive achievement or destructive failure. God has given you the gift of life, but what you do with it is your own responsibility.

In order to live successfully, you need a value system that is more trustworthy than your natural inclinations, and also a noble goal that you strive to achieve. God has supplied you with such a value system in the teachings of Jesus Christ. And the goal of every disciple should be to become Christlike and to do the will of the Father.

When you accept the Christian value system, and acknowledge it to be every Christian's duty to do God's will, then you have entered into a meaningful relationship with God. The consciousness of His divine presence then becomes a practical reality. You become aware of the hand that is guiding you. And God will surely guide you if you strive to walk in His way. Under His guidance you will once again discover the beauty of life. And with excitement you also discover what you can become through His omnipotence and Christ's guidance. Walk with God and you will discover the deepest meaning of life.

> Life becomes filled with meaning and purpose the minute Jesus Christ becomes part of it. (Stephen Neill)

In Jesus Christ _____

_____

C# quality life

"One's life does not consist in the abundance of the things he possesses."
(Lk. 12:15)

For many people riches and possessions are of crucial importance in their lives. Thus, most of their time is spent on these things. They hoard things and compete with others trying to outdo their colleagues or opponents.

This lifestyle will probably lead to tension, stress and unhappiness. It will definitely not lead to tranquillity, peace of mind or fulfilment, because, in the obsession to hoard earthly treasures, such a person is playing with the dangers of physical and mental illness.

True happiness, which will lead to a life of abundant fulfilment, is only found through a real and meaningful experience with the living Christ (See John 10:10). It is when you live in and through Him that you become a partaker of a life of true and constant abundance.

Through the centuries people have tried many substitutes for this abundant life in Jesus Christ, but it is only when you commit yourself to the Master's service and decide to live according to His precepts, that you realise true riches are to be found in the peace of mind and tranquillity that is not of this world. It becomes your rich inheritance, however, through your surrender to the Prince of Peace.

In His unfathomable love God wants to protect you from a life without quality. Addiction to earthly riches and possessions degrades the quality of your life. Through Jesus Christ, God offers you a quality life – and it is free.

Riches are like salt water: the more you drink, the thirstier you get. (Francis Bacon)

Divine Master, thank You _____

*P*lan with God

"That your faith should not be in the wisdom of men, but in the power of God." (1 Cor. 2:5)

*H*ow often have you, or others that you know and love, experienced the disappointment of unfulfilled dreams, watched carefully planned dreams disintegrate and hope collapse like a house of cards? It leaves you with a feeling of complete dejection. Many people who experience such a stroke of ill fate, never recover. They are therefore not willing to take upon themselves the risk of another disaster, and thus a tremendous amount of talent lies wasted and unused.

There are those who will mock the idea that you need to call in God's help to realise your plans. These people promote the idea of self-sufficiency in everything they undertake and they trust completely in their own ability. That is why, when success has been achieved, they also take all the praise for themselves. It is all very well as long as their plans are successful, but in the meantime they are submitted to the tension and pressure of insecurity. Then, if they fail, they experience the destructive results of failure.

When you trust completely in God for everything you do, if you want to follow His will and obey Him, you might feel that things are moving too slowly for you. However, be patient and steadfastly put your trust in God. Then you will have peace of mind, knowing that God is in control and that the fulfilment of your plans will be to your lasting benefit. Trust God's protective love when planning your life and your work.

> Realise how quickly people change and how little you can trust them. Therefore hold on steadfastly to God because He never changes. (Teresa of Avila)

Lord, I know _____

_____

The power belongs to God

"... that the excellence of the power may be of God and not of us."
(2 Cor. 4:7)

When God calls you for a task as a parent within a family, as leader of a group of students, as manager of a company, as an educator, as a sportsman or as an office-bearer in His church, He proves that He has confidence in you – even though you may doubt your own ability to do what He expects you to, and even though you offer various excuses as to exactly why He should not have called you.

God knows the potential of your character and personality, even while you are trying to convince Him that the task He has called you to do is far above your abilities.

If God has opened a door for you to a bigger area of service, you can do one of two things. You can be so completely overwhelmed by a feeling of insecurity that you can tell God He has made a mistake to call you. Many Biblical characters chose this option. On the other hand you can weigh up the task against God's greatness and be assured by His divine promise that, because He has called you, He will also equip you.

The most important element in God's service is not intellectual brilliance or experience – though both could play an important role – but obedience and faithfulness which compels you to become an instrument in His hands. The assurance that God will work through you and that He will bind you more securely to Him, is to be found in the knowledge that the power to fulfil your calling does not belong to you, but to God.

> What is impossible for God? Not that which is difficult for His omnipotence, but that which is against His nature. (St. Ambrosius)

Omnipotent Lord, I beg _____

A meaningful life

"A man's steps are of the Lord: How then can a man understand his own way?" (Prov. 20:24)

When God controls a person's life, there is no time for trivialities. This doesn't mean that you should regard small things as insignificant, but it implies that you must abide by the guidelines of love, virtue, forgiveness, goodness, faithfulness, compassion and self control. These are the God-given and God-inspired virtues. Then you will approach everything that happens in your life from this broader context.

In the truly spiritual life there is no room for pettiness or narrow-mindedness. To nurse a grievance against someone; to refuse to forgive; to be thrilled when someone else falls or fails; these are only a few symptoms of an immature spirit. And it is revealed in a sickly, mean and shallow attitude which could never be part of God's plan for your life.

If you sincerely strive to live according to God's will, something of the magnitude of your heavenly Father will be revealed in your spirit as well as in your attitude and actions. You will have the ability to distinguish between that which is important and unimportant. You will develop a perception which will enable you to appreciate the small things in life, without allowing them to divert your attention from that which is big and crucial. You will live to the glory of God and will be guided by His Holy Spirit. Thus, under His protective hand, your life will become meaningful.

> Happy are those who know that discipleship simply means a life which originated through grace, and that grace simply means discipleship. (Dietrich Bonhoeffer)

Lord Jesus, grant me a deeper understanding _____
_____

The secret of success

"He sought God in the days of Zechariah who had understanding in the visions of God; and as long as he sought the Lord, God made him prosper." (2 Chr. 26:5)

The majority of people plan their lives to please themselves. That is quite understandable, but what is not usually understood is the importance of having the right and pure motivation for achieving success.

To think of success in terms of money and prestige, is to ignore the deeper meaning of life. Success has spiritual qualities and it is only when we recognise them that our life can become that which God desires it to be. Experience has shown that a materialistic attitude towards life never guarantees joy and satisfaction. This is because God is being ignored, and our standards are lowered. Instead of loving God above all else, and allowing Him to control your life, money and possessions become the controlling power. This creates a hard, steel-like unyielding personality.

If God is not acknowledged it is impossible to be conscious of His Fatherhood. This means that the unique relationship which must exist between the Father and His child, has to be inspired by God.

If you seek God's guidance in your life and obey Him, you become God's co-labourer. Then you will experience success and prosperity that are founded on your spiritual values. Your life will be filled with meaning and purpose and you will be living under God's protection.

In Jesus Christ people find a reflection of their own ideals. (Granville Hicks)

Grant me, O Lord, success _____

The art of living

"As a shepherd seeks out his flock on the day he is among his scattered sheep, so will I seek out my sheep and deliver them from all the places where they were scattered on a cloudy and dark day." (Ezek. 34:12)

When watching the behaviour pattern of people, you will find many instances where, in some way, they act like sheep. In the same way that sheep sometimes follow one another, so are people inclined to follow the masses or public opinion. Just as sheep huddle together, so do people look for comfort and safety from each other in a time of crisis. In the same way that a sudden shock causes sheep to scatter, so are people driven apart in circumstances of shock and confusion. This kind of behaviour does not contribute to a stable lifestyle. The uncertainty leads to feelings of insecurity and nervous fear.

Many people will conclude that that is the way they were created and there is nothing they can do about it. That is not true. You don't have to maintain an unstable way of life. This certainly is not the life that Jesus Christ is offering you. This is also not why He came to dwell with us.

He is with you in every situation of life through the spirit of the living Christ to protect you. He is omniscient, omnipotent and all-knowing – a Father who watches over His children. He is always there, waiting for you to open the door of your life for Him, so that He can take over and lead you along His perfect way (See Revelation 3:20). At all times keep contact with the Master and you will be guaranteed a life of tranquillity and peace of mind.

During a storm a wise man doesn't pray for protection from danger, but for deliverance from fear. He knows it's the storm on the inside that is a threat, not the one on the outside. (Ralph Waldo Emerson)

Lord, with You I shelter, because _____

_____

The angel that goes before you

"For He shall give his angels charge over you to keep you in all your ways." (Ps. 91:11)

In the mind of modern man angels are associated with the Middle Ages or stained glass windows. If people think of them at all, it is to visualise them as shadow-beings with wings, dressed in long white robes. But the Scriptural portrayal of these beings as messengers and servants of God brings these spirit-beings into close contact with the human race. Most Scriptural references about angels are to be found in the New Testament.

Angels were present at the birth of Jesus Christ. After His exhausting experience in the wilderness where He was tempted by Satan, angels came to minister to Him. During His suffering in Gethsemane He was strengthened by an angel. Without doubt, angels were a reality to the living Christ.

These celestial beings were acknowledged and accepted by Peter, Paul and the early disciples. The writer of the epistle to the Hebrews call them *"ministering spirits of God"* (see Hebrews 1:14) and he urges believers to be hospitable because people could *"unwittingly have entertained angels"* (see Hebrews 13:2).

The Scriptural credibility of angels causes our belief in their existence to be above reproach. The object of their existence, as revealed in Scripture, is to be servants of the Most High. If they are true to their mission, they receive divine authority and, while serving people, they spread a consciousness of His protective presence. Thus we receive guidance, love, protection and a more intimate awareness of God's presence.

> An angel is a spirit-being without a body, created by God, in the service of Christianity and the church. (Martin Luther)

I praise and thank You, eternal God _____

_____

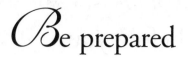

$\mathcal{B}$e prepared

"Do not be afraid of sudden terror, nor of trouble from the wicked if it comes; For the Lord will be your confidence, and will keep your foot from being caught." (Prov. 3:25, 26)

$\mathcal{T}$he motto of the Scouts and Guides movement is: "Be Prepared." How prepared are you to handle all the demands of life? The lives of many people are shaken right to their foundation by a sudden or unexpected disaster. A loved-one is taken away by death; circumstances force you to drastically change your lifestyle; financial need is felt to the core of your being; a wrong decision leads to failure or shame. These are but a few things which can destroy the root of your stability, leading to spiritual or psychological trauma. While some of the setbacks could be ascribed to a person's own actions or lifestyle, it often happens that these destructive events come upon you very unexpectedly – without any warning. And it is important that you should know how to prepare yourself to handle them when they occur.

Christ invites you to turn to God and to free yourself from the addiction to materialism which is so common to this world. He stresses the fact that the things of this world are subject to decay, while nothing could ever destroy your Christian heritage.

If you long to live victoriously and be able to handle set-backs, then you have to maintain a very special relationship with the living Christ. His Holy Spirit will give you the assurance as well as the self-confidence, the strength and peace which pass all understanding.

People may obtain knowledge, but wisdom is a gift of grace which comes directly from the hand of God. (Bob Jones)

Master, thank You that You _____ me _____

Protection in temptation

"...but God is faithful, Who will not allow you to be tempted beyond what you are able, but with the temptation will also make the way of escape, that you may be able to bear it." (1 Cor. 10:13)

No Christian is exempt from temptation. Christ experienced it and those who follow Him, cannot escape from it. Indeed, it is by overcoming temptation that you are strengthened spiritually. That is why you need to thank God for temptation, because it offers you an opportunity to grow spiritually.

Temptation always comes either in a convincing or a delusive guise. The enjoyment of the present moment is accentuated, while the eventual tragedy – should you succumb – is hidden away. Nobody can prevent your being tempted, but it is foolish to let it brood in your mind. It is very easy to find an excuse why an enticing temptation cannot be withstood. You might regard it as very innocent; you know what you are doing and you are in control of the situation; though many others fell, it will never happen to you. These, and similar excuses, are offered by those who eventually gave in. Satan is a master in the art of disguising his fatal suggestions with a very attractive appearance. You are never more subtle than the father of lies, the great tempter.

The only safe action against temptation is to avoid it firmly. Even just the suggestion of a dishonest profit gained from a wrong action, must immediately be refused, without giving any explanation. The living Christ will give you the strength to do that, if you allow Him to control your whole life.

> Satan tempts us in order to destroy us; the Lord tests us in order to edify us. (Ambrosius)

Help me, God to _____ *temptations* _____

Control your tongue

"If anyone among you thinks he is religious, and does not bridle his tongue, but deceives his own heart, this one's religion is useless." (Jas. 1:26)

After a heated quarrel, when everything that could be said has been said, there is either reconciliation or division, peace or smouldering bitterness in the hearts of those involved. Perhaps things were said which could have remained unsaid and now there are hurt feelings or even thoughts of revenge.

Scripture teaches us that it is not easy to control the tongue. Every follower of Jesus Christ, at one time or another, experienced deep remorse because he gave his tongue free rein in a very aggressive manner. Perhaps a cutting remark or sarcastic word was expressed without first being thought about. The results could be far-reaching. The belief that that which is inside of you must come out, does not always have beneficial results. That which is inside of us is often not to the advantage of either the speaker or the listener at all.

The power to control the tongue is to be found in the spirit and your attitude. If you have a proud, selfish, bitter, haughty and un-friendly spirit, those qualities will always be revealed in your speech, regardless of how hard you try to exterminate it. It is also true however, that if your spirit and mind are filled with the love of Christ, negative and derogatory thoughts will disappear. Thus, they cannot find expression in your words. When the indwelling Spirit controls your life, He protects you against your own tongue.

> The most outstanding achievement in this life is to be quiet and to allow God to speak and act through you. (Meister Eckhart)

Lord, keep watch over what I say _____

_____

*𝒟*epend upon God

"But when they deliver you up, do not worry about how or what you should speak. For it will be given to you in that hour what you should speak; for it is not you who speak, but the Spirit of your Father who speaks in you." (Mt. 10:19, 20)

*𝒲*e are inclined to read many Scripture passages within historical context only. We then often have difficulty relating them to ourselves or the circumstances of our lives. In some parts of the world those who follow Jesus are experiencing persecution and adversity that are very real. When living in a Christian society we find it very hard to think that it is possible to be imprisoned because you are a Christian, to be challenged to defend your faith and sometimes even your life.

Nowadays it is more likely that you will be tested in your daily activities. Your test will come when you have to comfort someone who has experienced a tragic loss, to express words of hope to someone who threatens to commit suicide, or to ensure the invalid, who suffers constant pain, that God loves him.

Then it is important that you, as well as the one that you are ministering to, should depend totally on the grace of Jesus Christ. Open up your life completely to receive His Spirit and He will inspire you with the words you need to say.

> Testifying is the removal of the many obstacles of our self-love and to allow our fellowman to see Christ Who lives in us. (Paul Frost)

Holy Spirit, what a wonderful comfort _____

_____

*W*ith Christ into the future

"Do not be a terror to me; You are my hope in that day of doom." (Jer. 17:17)

*D*uring the first decade of the twenty-first century there are many people who worry about the future of the world. Breathtaking changes occur in every corner of the globe. For some people these changes are acceptable and for others definitely not. Whatever your attitude may be, the fact is that you are living in a world that is changing at a very fast pace and only God knows what the future holds for us.

History has proven that this is not a new or unique situation. Right through the ages people have experienced tremendous changes. Through the strength which they derived from their faith in God they managed to handle it and they survived. And it is the same God whom we still have with us today: *"Jesus Christ is the same yesterday, today and forever"* (Hebrews 13:8). He promised, *"I will never leave you nor forsake you"* (Hebrews 13:5).

If you want to experience peace of mind and tranquillity when looking at the future, it is important that you should put your faith in Jesus Christ. Surrender yourself unconditionally to His love and care. Allow Him to prescribe the pattern of your future and to lead you into the future.

Yes, you will experience problems and obstacles, but you will be assured of the safe journey which lies ahead. Your companion in these ever-changing times will be the living Christ who will be faithful till eternity.

The best thing about the future is that it only comes one day at a time. (Abraham Lincoln)

O God, abide with me _____

_____

Do great deeds through God

"He is your praise, and He is your God, who has done for you these great and awesome things which your eyes have seen." (Deut. 10:21)

The great majority of people conform to what others think of them. Because society expects nothing from them, they also expect nothing from themselves. They are merely individuals amongst a great throng of people who are willing to lose their identity in the masses. At times they are aware of deep stirrings in their spirit, which probably indicate that though they only form a minute part of the great human society, they must have something of eternity in them: one of innumerable masses, yet partakers of God's life-giving breath.

Each one who realises this amazing truth, starts looking for broader spiritual and mental horizons. They are dissatisfied with their present circumstances and long to extend their view of the future. However, they also experience the pull of the everyday, imperfect life. While they want to move forward, there are strong powers that want to hold them back. Many people get tired in their effort of fleeing from their visionless past and fall back into the shadows of the commonplace. Their hope has been disappointed, their dreams are shattered and that which could have been, is never achieved.

If God has given you a vision, you can be sure that it is going to take a lot of hard work and exertion to fulfil. History teaches that God usually entrusts people with tasks that are above their ability. It is only when you try your utmost, that you will know how much you can achieve through Him.

> Nobody knows what he is able to achieve until he has put in a lot of effort, and many will never try, unless they are forced to. (Basil W. Maturin)

Master, help me to discover _____

_____

*H*ave you lost your way?

" I am the way ... " (Jn 14:6)

*F*ew things can create a feeling of dreary despair faster than discovering that you have totally lost your way. There is nothing more frustrating than walking around in circles in an effort to find your way, while you don't have the vaguest idea of where you actually are.

How much worse the frustration must be when you discover that you've lost your way spiritually, that you are stumbling and groping around in what seems to be a never-ending wilderness, in an effort to rediscover your previous relationship – a relationship which had earlier brought you much joy, but which you've now lost.

The first disciples also expressed their doubt about finding their way to God. Jesus clearly explained to them that He is the way and that nobody can come to the Father, except through Him.

And still today the situation remains the same: to reach God, you need to have a first-hand, personal relationship with the living Christ. It is important that you walk with Jesus along life's path and through faith, have intimate fellowship with Him. To get to know Him better, you must use God's means of grace. Through faith, Bible study and meditation on the wonderful acts of God, you will walk in Christ with God. He will protect you from wandering away and the danger of getting lost.

Many people try to make peace with God, but it has been done already. God did not leave it to us to do; all we have to do is to accept it through Jesus Christ. (Dwight L. Moody)

Lord, when I go astray _____

_____

Christ cares for you

"Casting all your care upon Him, for He cares for you." (1 Pet. 5:7)

There are times when it seems as if everything is working against you: honest efforts end in dismal failure. It seems as though the burdens of life overwhelm you and as if all the blessings you've received are wiped out. At such times it is easy to become down-hearted and to stop trying to live a victorious life.

Strokes of ill-luck and problems become a terrible burden if you try to overcome them in your own strength and wisdom. You become spiritually and mentally fatigued and it's just a matter of time before you break down completely.

It might sound very brave to state that you can handle everything that life throws at you, but if your spirit is broken and your ability to recover has diminished, you need a relationship with God which is so real, that you will share your life with Him.

To consciously share the burdens of your life with your Father God, is to tap a source of omnipotence and power which will enable you to stand firm, even when the foundations of your life are being shaken.

The glorious truth is that in Jesus Christ and the Holy Spirit your heavenly Father cares for you. He longs to share your life with you. If you allow Him to do it, every burden and worry will be a new opportunity to extend your knowledge of Him. Accept this divine invitation and experience how God wants to protect you in the midst of adversity.

> How else, except through a broken heart, can Jesus Christ enter into a life? (Oscar Wilde)

Holy Father, it gives me strength and inspiration _____

_____

God hears your cry for help

"'I cried to the Lord because of my affliction, and He answered me.'"
(Jon. 2:2)

How often have you heard people complain that they have nowhere to turn to in their time of need, or that the person they went to, disappointed them? Someone has a problem, but feels there is nobody he can trust or nowhere he can look for help or advice. In the time of crisis the person they turned to was too busy and could not pay attention to them. This often happens in everyday life.

It seems as though the emergency services take very long to answer your call for help; as if travel arrangements are upset because of delays; and as if the person you are looking for is not available at that time. The list of examples is endless. The result is that the person who has the problem, experiences terrible fear and even total despair.

The joy of your Christian faith is the assurance that nobody cares for you better than Jesus Christ Himself, that He will be with you all the time and that He will never leave you, nor forsake you. Regardless of who and where you are, you are secure in the knowledge that God loves you and not only does He hear your cry, but He understands your needs better than you do yourself. Therefore you never call to Him in vain from the depths of your needs.

Never underestimate the power of prayer, or God's ability and willingness to answer your prayers. Perhaps you may not always understand His answers right away, but if you trust steadfastly in Him, He will guide you along His path. His path will always be best for you.

> Prayer is the unconditional requirement for everything God wants to establish in this world. (Andrew Murray)

Lord my God, in Your protective hands _____

God is your protector

"'Can anyone hide himself in secret places, so I shall not see him?' says the Lord. 'Do I not fill heaven and earth?' says the Lord." (Jer. 23:24)

Surely you have also experienced an inward shame because of something you've said or done. You can be certain that you are only one of many who experienced similar feelings. Indeed there are very few people who could truly and honestly say they don't fall into this category. Most of us have felt guilty about something some or other time in our lives, which even now fills us with shame if we only think about it.

There are two ways to handle this situation. On the one hand you could try to hide your guilt. However, you must realise that such conduct is doomed to failure. While trying to keep the secret to yourself, you experience feelings of guilt and self-condemnation which gnaw away at your peace of mind, causing great emotional, mental and spiritual unhappiness. Anyone with a sensitive conscience finds it impossible to cover up his atrocities in the futile hope that they will disappear by themselves.

The other method of handling the situation is infallible. Turn to God and bring your fears and feelings of guilt to Him in prayer. Confess with a contrite heart to Him your weaknesses and transgressions which torture you. Don't be afraid to do it, because Jesus Christ has already promised to forgive you by laying down His life for your sins.

Be open, honest and remorseful before Christ. You will experience the healing balm of forgiveness flowing into your life and you will know that you have been cleansed.

> The person who has truly received forgiveness and knows it, is the one who can also forgive others. (Martyn Lloyd-Jones)

Saviour, forgive me _____

_____

$\mathcal{S}$ave your inner strength

"... that He would grant you, according to the riches of his glory, to be strengthened with might through his Spirit in the inner man." (Eph. 3:16)

here is an area of your life which is only known to God and to yourself. Other people only see the façade which you present to them and they judge you according to what they see. You know that their judgement isn't always fair or correct, but you cannot blame them because they make an evaluation on face value.

To have a personality which is honest and true, it is imperative that the development of your spirit should be an important priority to you. Regardless of how pleasant and acceptable your personality might be, the fact that you are hiding a mean and petty spirit will eventually be revealed and that will destroy you.

Because of this basic truth, you need to protect your spirit against all derogatory influences which are trying to destroy it. This erosion of the spirit is very subtle and could be at work within you without your being aware of its negative power. It usually starts when you allow your spiritual life to be of lesser importance, prayer loses its quality and compromises weaken your relationship with God in a very disturbing manner.

Strengthening the inner man involves the acceptance of discipline which could be strenuous but at the same time rewarding. Nothing can replace prayer and Bible study as a means to strengthen your inner being. That involves praying even when you don't feel like it; claiming the presence of Christ – even when you feel very far from Him.

Love for Christ is the motivating force which gives you the strength to apply this discipline.

Growth is the only proof of real life. (John Henry Newman)

Saviour, increase my love for You so much that _____

The final reality

"He is not far from each one of us; for in Him we live and move and have our being." (Acts 17:27, 28)

All people are seekers. They may not always be aware of their search and it may seem as though they are quite happy with their way of life and all they ask is to be left in peace. Others seem compelled to seek for a purpose for living or to achieve success regardless of the cost. This inner motivational force to achieve success, is part of man's spiritual heritage which is revealed in a longing for or striving towards perfection. It is nothing less than a form of longing for God.

Many people may deny this truth, but the fact remains that regardless of how much people possess, they remain imperfect when they are without God.

God is the final reality. When you commit and surrender your life to Him, you experience a deep satisfaction and inner peace. Even though there may be many things that you don't understand yet, you can leave it in His capable and omniscient hands, because you know the One Who created everything. Living by faith in God means that you don't ask questions. Yet, at the same time it provides trust and guidance for those disciples who can't see beyond those unanswered questions which continually bother them.

The crucial truth which we need to accept and apply, is that the eternal God is the source of all good gifts. If you live within this reality, life becomes meaningful and manageable to you.

> God is called the Omnipotent because He can perfectly do all that He desires. (Thomas Aquinas)

Heavenly Father, I desire a life of _____

Winners in the power of Christ

"I can do all things through Christ who strengthens me." (Phil. 4:13)

In spite of the sophisticated times we live in and in spite of the progress man has made, it seems as if life is getting all the more difficult. People find that the demands made on them are in many cases more than they can handle. Pressure builds up and people bend double under the pressure of responsibilities piled on them and which need to be handled with success.

The human resources which are applied in the struggle for survival are multiple but not infallible. These methods may bring a measure of relief for some time, but are not the complete solution to the problems. This is the dilemma both adults and children face today.

Eventually there is but one successful way in which to handle the challenges of life up-front – through Jesus, the living Christ. Without Him you can do nothing, but with Him all things are possible. That is why Paul jubilantly says, *"I can do all things through Christ who strengthens me"* (Philippians 4:13).

Maintain an intimate relationship with Christ by spending time with Him in prayer and meditation. When you have established a unity with Him, you will find that His presence accompanies and protects you in every situation along your pilgrimage.

> The acknowledgement of our weakness is the first step on the road to recovering from our loss. (Thomas á Kempis)

Merciful Master, thank You for Your protection _____

_____

The Christian's trust

"Therefore will I look to the Lord; I will wait for the God of my salvation; My God will hear me." (Mic. 7:7)

This world is teeming with superstitions and strange inventions in which people put their trust when planning for the future. Many are convinced that their lives are ruled by the stars; yet others seek advice and guidance from fortune-tellers; and then there are those who don't dare to clinch a business deal on Friday the thirteenth. Such people come from all spheres of society – the poor and the rich, the narrow-minded and the enlightened.

These methods, regardless of how trustworthy they may appear on the surface, don't give complete confidence. Whenever we have to deal with the unknown, there is always the fear of insecurity or failure. The possibility that this fear may become an obsession, causes failure to become a much greater reality.

There is only one safe way by which you can go through this life with confidence, and that is through faith in God. Yes, you will still experience trouble and problems and when they do come, you will always have to deal with doubt. Nevertheless, remember that, in your darkest moment Jesus tells you what He told his disciples, *"In the world you will have tribulation, but be of good cheer, I have overcome the world"* (John 16:33). This trust in Christ overcomes all superstition and offers to you that peace which passes all understanding.

> Superstition is the cruellest thing in this world. Faith is to live in the sunshine. Superstition is to live in the darkness. (Katherine T. Hinkson)

Finisher of my faith, in confidence _____

_____

Your inspiration for life

"Now the Lord is the Spirit; and where the Spirit of the Lord is, there is liberty." (2 Cor. 3:17)

There are many people who are clearly disillusioned with life and are dissatisfied with life in general. They complain about boredom; they have lost interest in their work; time drags by for them and even their spiritual lives lack inspiration and meaning. They soon get depressed and life loses its sparkle.

If you should find yourself in a situation like this, you should not look for man-made solutions. It is true that there are many things that will bring temporary relief but it is important that you should find out where and how your problem originated. Once you have established that it won't be difficult to find a solution.

You will most probably find that either consciously or unconsciously you allowed your spiritual life to lapse into an uninspired routine. This then leads to a dull and colourless faith. It is important that you should open up your life to the inspirational influence of Christ the Lord and that you should have an intimate relationship with Him. If you do that, He becomes your partner in everything you do and all you undertake.

Once you are filled with His Holy Spirit, your life will be inspired and will have new meaning and purpose. And this is no temporary solution, because Jesus promised to be with you always if you are with Him always!

Spirituality actually means, "the Spirit at work"; an astounding action at work in the life of God's children. (Leon Joseph Suenens)

Lord Jesus, I rejoice that _____

_____

*S*afe in His hand

"But we are not of those who draw back to perdition, but of those who believe to the saving of the soul." (Heb. 11:39)

*I*t is very interesting to study people's reactions to the circumstances they find themselves in. In the majority of cases you will find that their attitude is determined by that which happens to them in their lives at a given point in time.

If the country experiences an economic slump, they immediately feel depressed; crime and unrest paralyse them with fear; personal set-backs create a feeling of hopelessness; sorrow drives them to despair. The end-result in many cases is that they simply give up. Suddenly life loses its meaning, its purpose and its joy. They are like people who have lost their way and they stumble along in darkness.

The one very important fact which we have to cling to in the midst of set-backs, is that Christ, through the Holy Spirit, is always with us and that He is holding us in the hollow of His hand. Indeed He is the One who came to give us life in abundance (See John 10:10). This implies that He wants what is best for you under all circumstances. In order for you to obtain that, Jesus has made the utmost sacrifice. And through that act He has overcome evil for time and eternity.

When circumstances seem dark and ominous to you, then remember that you are a child of God, that He loves you and cares for you; that He wants to, and can, protect you from all evil. Believe His promise that He will never leave you nor forsake you. Put your trust totally in Him and He will lift you from your depression and fear and will encourage you.

> Don't fear that your life will end in disaster: rather fear that it will never start. (John Henry Newman)

Loving Saviour, grant me _____

_____

*S*orrow in joy

"And Hannah prayed and said: 'My heart rejoices in the Lord; my horn is exalted in the Lord. I smile at my enemies, because I rejoice in your salvation.'" (1 Sam. 2:1)

*B*ecause man's warped nature is what it is, we are inclined to remember the problems and troubles that come our way much longer than the good things that happen. People pay a lot of attention to circumstances which precede and surround death; a financial set-back or devastating disappointment; calamity or disaster; guilt about a rash, thoughtless deed; or the failure of an important project. While people enjoy the sense of achievement and success as it occurs, it is soon forgotten and we move ahead to a new phase with new challenges.

One tried and tested way of dealing with set-backs and disappointments, is to think about the successes you have achieved and enjoyed in your life. Remind yourself of the goodness of God while you reminisce about how He guided and protected you in the past. Also consider the problems and disappointments you experienced and how He took your hand and guided you through them all.

Remind yourself again of the ways in which Jesus Christ provided for you every time you called out to Him for help; how He rid you of your fear and doubt and how He showed you the way out of the darkness into His marvellous light.

Regardless of how hopeless your situation may seem at this point in time, put all your trust in Christ, and through Him experience a life of joy and fulfilment.

> Joy is the unmistakable proof that God is present in your life. (Leon Bloy)

Lord Jesus, be my refuge _____

_____

God goes before you

"And the Lord, He is the One who goes before you, He will not leave you nor forsake you." (Deut. 31:8)

Many people are afraid to fulfil their plans because they fear the unknown which lies ahead. This was especially true of some spiritual giants in the Old Testament. One cannot help but wonder what course humanity would have taken had they been daunted by the challenges that were set before them. However, they moved forward in faith and did their part in executing God's great plan with humanity.

It was of the utmost importance that God's hand should be stretched out in protection over every person that He sent out in His Name. As a result of this and because of the steadfast faith of the Biblical heroes, much has been achieved for the kingdom of God. The most important fact is that they believed in the Lord. His view is perfect and eternal and He will never place you in a situation that will be harmful to you. He will be with you to protect you at all times, and to support and guide you.

Before putting your plans into action you need to lay them before God first and submit them to His will. Wait on His Holy Spirit to guide you. Walk intimately with Christ in prayer, meditation and Bible study and move ahead when and as He guides you. He knows what is best for you. Trust Him completely and never doubt the fact that He will keep you safe. He will grant you the fulfilment of your plans.

> The future of the whole of humanity depends on the measure to which the individual soul submits totally to the sovereign rule of the Holy Spirit. (Isaac T. Hecker)

Lord Jesus, with Your guidance _____

Trustingly into the future

"Behold, God is my salvation. I will trust and not be afraid. For YAH, the Lord is my strength and song; He also has become my salvation." (Is. 12:2)

Your attitude regarding the future determines your whole life. If you are fearful and worried, you will project those very things which you fear and wish to avoid into your future. Like Job you will then be able to say, *"For the thing I greatly feared has come upon me"* (Job 3:25). It is important that you go into the future with hope.

Unfortunately there are many influences which could undermine your hope. Perhaps you have long grown used to failure and now you cannot imagine how you could possibly achieve success. You might have lost your life companion and now you find it very difficult to make any kind of decision. Perhaps you have allowed your faith to be weakened, to the extent that you are not even sure about God any more. These, and many similar reasons, could destroy your faith in God as well as the faith you have in your ability to live a victorious life.

A very sure way of building your hope, is to work hard at maintaining a positive faith in Jesus Christ. Strengthen the ties that you have with Him in order that He can become a living, dynamic reality to you. You will find that the more real He becomes to you, the more your fears which have undermined your trust in Him, will change into a steadfast, constant faith in the Master.

To own Christ, is to be owned by Him. This enables you to venture fearlessly into the future. Through His Spirit He will lead you along His path.

In sorrow and suffering, go directly to God and you will be strengthened, relieved and encouraged. (St John of the Cross)

Holy Master, grant me an attitude _____

_____

THE FOUNTAIN OF GOD'S PEACE

> Peace is not made in council chambers or through treaties; peace is made in the hearts of men. (Herbert Hoover)

Gracious heavenly Father,
We worship You as the God of peace.
There are wars, hate and enmity, violence and confusion.
We plead: Lord, grant us peace in our time.
There are misunderstandings, suspicion and antagonism
and hatred fills the air.
Make me an open, receptive channel, always ready to be a
bearer of Your peace.
Let my eyes see what You see:
the beautiful, the good and the pure around me.
Let the words of my mouth testify of Your love in my heart,
Your light in my mind, Your peace in my soul.
O Prince of Peace, on behalf of a torn world I lift my
hands to You in prayer: Give us peace, O Lord!

April

Christ's peace – my inheritance

"Peace I leave with you, my peace I give to you; not as the world gives do I give to you. Let not your heart be troubled, neither let it be afraid." (Jn. 14:27)

This special inheritance is meant for Christ's followers through the ages. This world's peace is but a poor reflection of that which God assigned to His children who believe in Him.

In order to claim this inheritance, we first need to be in the right family relationship with the testator. We must become His children by accepting Him as our Father in faith (See John 1:12). We need to wholeheartedly long for and allow His sovereign rule in our lives. Then we also need to seek His perfect will for our lives, accept it, adapt to it and obey Him (See Luke 22:42).

The peace of God is the most outstanding peace imaginable: it enables us to live in peace with God, ourselves and our fellowmen. Christ's peace also has the highest distinction. It is unique and totally different from the world's so-called peace. It is complete and not partial. It extends across all areas in our lives.

The peace of God is constant and does not change according to our moods. It is real and not the kind which deceives like a mirage in the desert.

There are demands which need to be met before we can partake in the peace which Christ gives. It forbids worry, because that is the sabotage the devil uses to undermine our peace. It prohibits fear, because fear is the enemy of all peace. And above all it requires a steadfast faith in Jesus Christ, the source of this inheritance.

> When Christ came to this world, peace was sung about; and when He left this world, He left His peace behind. (Francis Bacon)

I praise and thank You for _____

_____

The power of Christ's peace

"And let the peace of God rule in your hearts, to which also you were called in one body." (Col. 3:15)

In the midst of the many changes that occur in modern life, there are numerous people who are upset, insecure and fearful. They long for peace and stability. In spite of all our achievements and technological developments there is still so much famine, poverty, violence and dissatisfaction across the world. The result is that sober, right-minded people become more and more anxious.

However, before a change for the better can occur, there first needs to be a change of heart. And that applies to all people, the victim as well as the oppressor. In order to restore peace and stability in the world, it is a prerequisite that people should open up their hearts to Christ so that He can change their lives.

The point of departure, of course, is vested with people like you and me and not with the high and mighty. If Christ is to get control over the affairs of mankind, it is important that you should first submit to Him and commit your life to Him. By asking Him to take control of your life and to acknowledge Him as your Lord and Master, submitting your mind, words and actions to His control, you contribute to peace on earth.

When surrendered to Christ, we look at life, people and situations through His eyes, and we can handle life through His strength. This is what creates that peace which passes man's understanding and this is where the solution to the world's problems is to be found.

> It is impossible for me to live in peace if even as much as a shadow of wilful sin exists between me and God. (George Eliot)

Your peace makes me _____

_____

Peace that calms the storm

"Be at peace among yourselves." (1 Thes. 5:13)

As the pressures and pace of life increase, people become more tense and grim. Many people, in many spheres of life, become more and more aware of the demands of our day and age. The more modern technology is geared to meet these demands, the more hectic becomes the treadmill of life.

Inevitably this tension causes people to snap. Obvious signs are irritation, moodiness, petty jealousy, and eventually the basis of our Christian faith, love, is destroyed. Of course Satan rejoices in this because anything which makes it impossible for you to love your fellowmen, will make it impossible for you to love God (See 1 John 4:20).

In order for us to handle the extreme demands of modern life, without losing our spiritual stability, an intimate spiritual fellowship with God is essential – and that on a regular basis. Open up your heart, mind and soul to the influence of the Holy Spirit so that He may control your life and your emotions. You will find that, in His power, you are able to handle the pressure without giving in to your human weaknesses. The Holy Spirit will fill your life with the peace of Jesus Christ.

In turn you will be able to let this peace flow through to others because you are a channel of God's love and peace. This is the only way in which the storm of tension and hurry-scurry can be calmed.

> Peace, like all rare and precious things, won't come to you. You have to go and get it. (Faith Forsyte)

Faithful Master, around me a storm is raging _____

_____

℘iety and peace

"In that day, 'Holiness to the Lord' shall be engraved on the bells of the horses. The pots in the Lord's house shall be like bowls before the altar." (Zech. 14:20)

℘iety is a word which, in our time, is going totally out of fashion – and when it is used, it mostly has a negative connotation. When someone is described as "pious", the impression is created that such a person is hypocritically virtuous. Nevertheless, piety is a virtue which is very close to the heart of God. True piety is not an act to impress people. It is conduct which flows from a life which is anchored in God, a longing to give expression to His will and allowing His Spirit to take the initiative in every situation.

This means that your life will become holy. Zechariah had a vision of piety when he prophesied that the common, everyday things will be engraved with the words, *"Holiness to the Lord."*

Many people find that this lifestyle does not attract them at all. However, for those who seriously strive to live for God, there is a rich reward. To consciously live in God's presence, sanctifies one's whole life. His guidance takes you along the paths which He has planned for you. The power which He imparts to your spirit, enables you to obey Him. The more intimately you love Him, the more you understand Him and the life He has called you to.

If you include God in every moment of your life, He will give you His peace. Then you will own a precious treasure which comes from God only.

> True piety contains no weakness, no sorrow and nothing that is forced. It expands the heart; it is simple and free and kind. (Francois de la Mothe)

Grant me, O Lord my God _____

The peace that strengthens you

"Now therefore, make confession to the Lord God of your fathers, and do his will." (Ezra 10:11)

Obstinacy and wilfulness are well-known and common characteristics of man. This often causes frustration and unhappiness. This is especially true where people know that they are wrong and find it hard to acknowledge or confess.

One of the greatest gifts that Jesus gives His children is peace. It is something unique in His being because it is a wonder cure for all our problems and hardships. The remarkable fact about it is that it is already available to you at all times. All you are required to do is to surrender your life to Christ and make Him the Lord of your life.

This sounds overly simplified. Furthermore, most people find it extremely difficult to surrender their lives unconditionally to Christ. If that is how you feel, then you will do good to compare the peace which comes from a life surrendered to Christ, to a life surrendered to this world. Read the Scriptures and see how often the peace of God sustains and carries people through. Even Jesus Christ was carried through difficult circumstances by this peace.

While you are trying to cope with the stress and pressures of modern society, openly acknowledge your complete dependence on God and submit yourself to the influence of His Holy Spirit. Then you will experience peace which passes all understanding and which will enable you to live victoriously.

We have five great enemies of peace within us: covetousness, ambition, jealousy, anger and pride. If these could be banned from our lives we would experience infallible, incessant peace. (Petrarca)

Lord and Master, let Your Holy Spirit control my life so that _____

eace through prayer

"Continue earnestly in prayer, being vigilant in it with thanksgiving."
(Col. 4:2)

here are many people in this world who are living under a cloud of anxiety, concern and fear. They might be concerned for themselves or for others. Their anxiety may be caused by fear with regard to the future of their country or the world. Their concern, anxiety and fear are increased by violence, unrest, terrorism, political and economic insecurity. How can one find peace in the midst of such situations?

The apostle Paul answers our question when he says, *"Be anxious for nothing, but in everything by prayer and supplication, with thanksgiving, let your requests be made known to God"* (Philippians 4:6). Then he adds in verse seven, *"And the peace of God, which surpasses all understanding, will guard your hearts and minds through Christ Jesus."*

In difficult circumstances it is especially true that you can do nothing in your own strength to solve your problems. Jesus, our Master, has said that we can do nothing of ourselves, but He also said that with God all things are possible (See John 15:1-8).

In spite of your difficult circumstances and regardless of how unsure the future might seem, your peace of mind will only be secured when you become still before the Lord in prayer. Prayer and meditation, in conjunction with praise and thanksgiving, is the only infallible method to ensure that you will be able to accept and overcome life's challenges. Do not rob yourself of this opportunity to find peace!

> Prayer doesn't change the God whom we pray to, but it does change the person who prays. (Søren Kierkegaard)

Even though the future is unknown, O Lord _____

God's peace is unfailing

"For who is God, except the Lord? And who is a rock, except our God?" (2 Sam. 22:32)

Every time people experience a need or a problem, they turn to someone or something for help or advice. They may look for advice or tangible help from a friend, they may look for relief in the form of some medicine or drug. Yet others will utilise the assistance of professional counsellors. Regardless of what the problem may be, they do require help in some form or another.

If you perhaps find yourself in a situation like this, you must never underestimate the omnipotence and love of God. In your efforts to handle your problems and relieve your difficulties, you should never forget the fact that the only true and effective remedy is to be found in the encompassing love and tender care that Jesus Christ bestows on all who turn to Him.

Regardless of the good intentions of every human effort it always falls short in supplying the complete healing which flows from an absolute and unconditional trust in, and surrender to, the living Christ. It doesn't matter what your problem is, the only lasting solution is to be found in the unfathomable love which God, through Jesus Christ, bestowed upon mankind.

Under no circumstances should you underestimate this glorious gift of grace. Never be too proud or too afraid to turn to Jesus. Lay all your problems at His feet. He gave His life to you and wishes to grant you the healing balm of His peace.

> If we do not have peace within ourselves, it is futile to search for it in external things. (Francois de La Rochefouchauld)

I want to hold on to You, Lord _____

_____

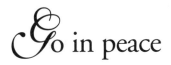

Go in peace

"Now acquaint yourself with Him, and be at peace; Thereby good will come to you." (Job 22:21)

It is a sorry sight to see someone who is at loggerheads with life. Such a person cannot think about anything good and can also not say anything good about anyone or anything. His whole outlook on life eventually becomes so negative and sour, that even his friends flee from him. The result is that such a person spends his life in solitary seclusion, feeling sorry for himself.

The tragedy that results from such an attitude is that the person who is guilty of it, eventually convinces himself that even God is against him and that God is responsible for everything that happens to him; that God is meting out some kind of divine judgement against him.

It is very easy to come to the point where one is at loggerheads with everyone and everything. If you are presently experiencing such emotions, it is imperative that you make peace with Jesus Christ, without wasting another minute. Spend time with Him in quiet. Meditate on your situation and your attitude. Talk to Him about your doubt, fear, anxiety and all the other things that upset you. Ask Him to remove these burdens from your shoulders and to fill you with His Holy Spirit. Try to look at life through His eyes.

Commit yourself and your time to doing this with great care. Soon you will find the peace of God descending upon your life. And this is the only way in which balance and harmony will come into your life again.

> Every time we say: "I believe in the Holy Spirit" we mean that there is a living God who is willing and able to enter the human personality and to change it. (J.B. Phillips)

Father, today I am guilty of _____

_____

An imagination that bears peace

"They continually say to those who despise Me, 'The Lord has said, 'You shall have peace;' And to everyone who walks to the dictates of his own heart they say, 'No evil shall come upon you.'" (Jer. 23:17)

Your imagination is one of the most powerful influences in your life. It is possible to create such strong emotional forces through your imagination, that the things you think and feel eventually become true in your life.

Thus your imagination (if it is under the influence and control of the Holy Spirit) can be an immeasurable force of good in your spiritual life. You can imagine yourself to be amongst the throngs of people addressed by Jesus at the Sea of Galilee; you can imagine that you are standing at Lazarus' grave, hearing the Master call, "Lazarus, come out!" An imagination under control of the Holy Spirit can cause the New Testament to come alive and be a vibrant experience.

The greatest blessing that can be derived from an imagination controlled by the Holy Spirit, is that the presence of Christ becomes a living reality. Christ promised that He will always be with those who love Him and therefore it is justified to imagine His presence. We do not know exactly what Jesus looked like in the flesh, but His reaction to human circumstances and people's reactions to His teaching give us a clear indication of His personality. Imagine yourself to be in His divine presence and experience the peace that only He can give.

When Christ has come to reign in the hearts of people, we will take Him along on the tractor, behind the desk, when closing a transaction or driving a car. (Alexander Nunn)

Lord and Master, please sanctify my imagination so that _____

Convictions determine relationships

"If it is possible, as much as depends on you, live peaceably with all men." (Rom. 12:18)

Nobody has a high regard for someone who always agrees with everyone. On the other hand it is also extremely hard to live in peace with a person with a brutal personality that always differs from everyone about everything that is said. There is no rational reason why he differs; it simply seems to give him great joy to differ from others.

The gift of maintaining strong convictions and yet keeping the friendship and respect of those who differ from you, becomes yours when you apply the basic principles of Christian love. It is wise and honourable to have strong Christian convictions, but it is unwise to elevate those convictions to a form of pettiness and narrow-mindedness. You must always be ready and willing to listen to the view-point of others. If your convictions are true and stable, you have nothing to fear from another person's convictions.

The key to happy and edifying relationships is not to be found in uniformity of thoughts. When love is the determining factor, it enables you to see good in those whom the world classifies as difficult people.

To have strong convictions which are reasonable and free from narrow-mindedness, and to reveal love in inter-human relationships, makes you a disciple of the Master and guarantees you His peace.

Religious convictions supply man with inner strength, spiritual insight and indelible peace. (Alexis Carrel)

Faithful Saviour, in my human relationships I long _____

The centre of Christ's peace

"Peace I leave with you, my peace I give to you; not as the world gives do I give to you. Let not your heart be troubled, neither let it be afraid." (Jn. 14:27)

Few people can honestly say that they haven't longed for peace of mind and inner tranquillity at some time or another. The general insecurity on life's stage today, sickness, death, dangers and unrest, create a deep-seated insecurity. The list is endless, yet the results are the same: unknown pressure and insecurity which border on despair.

Many of those who suffer seek professional help. The psychiatrist's couch and tranquillisers have become a common way of living. Others, who lack the willpower, indulge in drugs and liquor. Yet others give in to despair and live in a void where their lives have no quality whatsoever.

The only proven way to handle the pressures and tensions of life is through faith which is steadfastly founded in the living Christ. Your relationship with Him cannot only be a fleeting friendship or a matter of convenience. You need to permanently experience unity with Him. Under all circumstances hold on to Him, talk to Him, regardless of how desperate your situation might be, trust that He is always with you. Even though you may find it difficult to understand His peace, you will recognise it when it flows through your mind, overcoming all your fears.

Because fear has no reason, you should never try to reason with it. Only positive faith can dispel this dark danger and give you peace. (Marion Hilliard)

Prince of Peace, please help me _____

Peace that overcomes

"And the God of peace will crush Satan under your feet shortly ... "
(Rom. 16:20)

When problems clamp down on your life and you are upset and despondent, it is so easy to begin to doubt. It often seems as if one set-back leads to the next and you start to wonder if you will ever be able to move through the dark tunnel of depression. That is the time when you are most vulnerable and an easy prey to the plans of Satan. He is always ready and willing to lead you away from God onto the road of despair.

It is generally accepted that you must at all times keep your quiet times with God seriously and faithfully, thus strengthening your relationship with God. This is especially valid when your faith is being tested. When everything goes well with you it is fairly easy to maintain an intimate relationship with the Lord. However, when the set-backs of life hit you, the tendency develops to drift away from the Master. And that is fatal.

Whatever your circumstances might be, always remember that God loves you with an unfathomable love, a love that cannot be measured and which is perfect. He truly cares for you and invites you to turn to Him with all of life's burdens (See 1 Peter 5:7). If you would only cling to Him, believing His promise that He will always be with you, then He will fill your life with His heavenly peace, and Satan will be defeated time and time again in your life.

> The greatest joy of life is the conviction that someone loves us because of ourselves, or rather, loves us in spite of ourselves. (Victor Hugo)

Lord Jesus, You promised to _____

_____

Fight fear with love

"Behold, God is my salvation, I will trust and not be afraid." (Is. 12:2)

In times of personal danger, people are driven to survival or self-protection. Regardless of the nature of the danger, your immediate reaction is to protect yourself and to consider what is the best thing to do.

However, in times of danger, our mind is often confused because fear has taken over. Then it is difficult to think clearly or act logically. You are in danger of being overwhelmed by the problems that are facing you.

Then it is necessary to acknowledge with conviction that the love of God encompasses you. It surrounds you in *every* area of your life: *"You have hedged me behind and before, and laid your hand upon me"* (Psalm 139:5). He watches over you without stopping; He is always ready to listen to your cry for help; He is with you at all times and under *every* circumstance. If you are feeling far from God, you are the cause of that – not He.

Regardless of what might befall you, always remember that Jesus offers you His salvation. He gave His life in order for you to be saved. He gives you His Holy Spirit to guide you through all the problem areas of life. You will never be able to remain standing in your own strength.

When trials and tribulations come your way, never give in to the human temptation to snap. Open up your life for Christ. His perfect love expels all fear.

> Some people are so scared to die that they never really start living. (Henry van Dyke)

Lord, even though fear sometimes overwhelms me _____

_____

ℐn quietness and trust

"The work of righteousness will be peace, and the effect of righteousness, quietness and assurance forever." (Is. 32:17)

There are many diverse Christian and spiritual experiences. Some are exuberant and find expression in enthusiastic emotion. Others again are expressed in quiet service. Regardless what form your Christian experience might take, you must always make room for the experiences of other people. You must watch against being overly critical or condemning, or falling into spiritual pride by thinking that your experience is better than all others.

The Christian with a quiet disposition is often misunderstood and blamed for being spiritually lukewarm. Because of his introverted personality he avoids all forms of exuberance. In the presence of Christians who are extroverts, he often feels as if he lacks a very important spiritual virtue. And such a feeling is unfair. Some of the greatest followers of Jesus Christ were people with a quiet disposition.

External actions actually have very little value, because essential Christianity is an experience with God which occurs in the heart and is revealed in the life of the individual. The format in which it finds expression, depends to a great extent on the temperament of the disciple.

If you live for Christ, you don't need to compare yourself or your spiritual experiences to those of other Christians. Don't be jealous of others who serve God zealously. You may admire them, but because you give your best to the Master, and because your commitment is above reproach, you can worship in peace through the Holy Spirit who dwells in you.

> People will fight for their religion, write about it, die for it – everything, except live for it. (Charles Colton)

Father, at times I compare myself with others _____

_____

Peaceful tranquillity with God

"I will both lie down in peace, and sleep; For You alone, O Lord, make me dwell in safety." (Ps. 4:8)

Each one of us is a part of the world that we live in and the quality of our life should benefit our society spiritually and morally. The upsetting times that we live in are not really the main cause of our insecurity and restlessness. This grows from the realisation that we don't possess sufficient inner resources to meet the demands that are placed on us.

If God has revealed to you what you can become through the power of the indwelling Holy Spirit and you still cling to the conviction that it will never become a reality in your life, then you will experience an inner conflict which will rob you of your tranquillity and peace of mind. God's peace can only be experienced if you are willing to accept with joy all that He has planned for you. This acceptance has to take place according to His conditions. On days when you experience problems, sorrow and confusion, your faith needs to be strengthened through prayer and meditation.

In His Word, God has given you a pattern of what you can become and He has also supplied the spiritual material required to make it a reality. However, the responsibility to make your faith succeed in order for you to experience God's peaceful tranquillity, rests squarely on your shoulders.

By accepting the abiding presence of the Spirit and by staying close to Christ in prayer, you will experience the peace that only He can give.

> All people desire peace, but few are willing to work for those things that establish that peace. (Thomas à Kempis)

Make me willing, Lord _____

Jesus' steps of peace

"So it was, while they conversed and reasoned, that Jesus Himself drew near and went with them." (Lk. 24:15)

You must never entertain preconceived ideas of how Jesus Christ will come to you. If you regularly have your quiet time and wait upon Him, these will become precious times to you during which you will become aware of His divine presence. At such times it is almost unnecessary to say a word because you will know that Christ is spending inspiring moments with you and your soul is nourished.

The times come, however, when you have to take part in the activities of life and accept life's challenges. Even though your quiet time with God has provided you with spiritual and mental balance, the demands of your specific circumstances could make you forget that you have spent time with Him.

The way in which to maintain contact with Jesus in the course of a busy day, is by noticing Him in unexpected places. He may not be restricted to your quiet time with Him or to your personal prayer life. He can speak to you through the voice of your fellow-man. He might require your strength in serving another. He might look to you through the eyes of a lonely stranger, seeking companionship. You might see His beauty in the smile of a small child. A brief prayer for passers-by in a busy street might bring Christ very close to you.

Never be too busy to obey Him. As you obey Him in seemingly unimportant matters, He will become increasingly real to you and you will hear His soft footsteps at unexpected places and times.

> He who takes the basic principles of Christianity into everyday life, will change the face of the world. (Benjamin Franklin)

Help me to see You today in _____

_____

Peace with an instruction

"So Jesus said to them again: 'Peace to you! As the Father has sent Me, I also send you.'" (Jn. 20:21)

As the pressures and the fear-invoking pace of life increase, people become increasingly tense and more aware of the demands of our time. The more technology develops to meet these demands, the more the tempo of life's treadmill increases.

Unavoidably this causes people to snap which is seen in irritation, moods of anger, petty jealousy and eventually the breakdown of the basic foundation of our Christian faith – love! Of course this is a situation which suits Satan perfectly, because anything which prevents you from loving your fellowman, will also prevent you from loving God.

In order for you to meet the tremendous demands of modern life, you need to meet with God in quietness on a regular basis. There you find His peace and also His command to become a peace-maker for God. Allow the Holy Spirit to enter into your life and to control your emotions.

In His strength you will find that you are able to handle the pressure without snapping under tension because the Holy Spirit fills you with the peace of Jesus Christ. You can then pass this peace on to others and they will also start living under the influence of Jesus Christ's peace.

> Talk and move around in peace, as if you are in prayer. In true reality it is a form of prayer. (Francois de la Mothe)

Lord, the pressure has become so severe that I _____
_____

Anchored in the peace of God

"Trust in the Lord forever, for in Yah, the Lord, is everlasting strength."
(Is. 26:4)

When idols are mentioned we usually see in our mind's eye many of the gods that form an integral part of the life, culture and tradition of heathen nations. Through the centuries they have worshipped these gods. There were rain gods, fertility gods, war gods – the list is endless. People lived in fear and trepidation because it was possible that they could anger these gods and then the gods would avenge their going astray.

However, idols don't have a religious connotation only. These days people have elevated money into an idol and they are trying their very best to hoard riches. Yet others seek security in their earthly possessions, while others make liquor and drugs their idol in an effort to escape from the pressures of modern life. Covetousness, jealousy and lust are just as real to some people as idols are to pagans. Just like the pagan idols, they also create fear and anxiety in the hearts of those who worship them. They fear the loss of their earthly possessions, or they cannot cope without the crutch of drugs and alcohol.

Most people, if not all, intensely yearn for tranquillity and peace of mind. And this is to be found only with the one, true God. It happens when you surrender your life to the living Christ and when you love Him above all else. Live your life in Christ, open up your heart to Him. Spend time in His presence and draw your strength from Him. In that way His love will expel all fear and tension from your life and you will have a safe haven where you can live in peace.

> You can either win your peace, or you can buy it. You can win it by resisting evil; you can buy it through compromising with the evil one. (John Ruskin)

Lord Jesus, You alone are a safe haven against _____

_____

Peace in our country

"I will give peace in the land, and you shall lie down, and none will make you afraid." (Lev. 26:6)

The words recorded in Proverbs 2:22 are striking, " ... *the wicked will be cut off from the earth, and the unfaithful will be uprooted from it."* According to Solomon, we will receive peace if we stay on God's way and serve the Lord with a sincere heart.

In our time we have a deep yearning to be left unhindered, so that we can serve the Lord and sleep in peace. We long for the "wicked" and the "unfaithful" to be wiped off the face of the earth so that our country can be a safe haven of peace. We want to live our lives without worrying about wicked people or fearing criminals. This is something we can only achieve if we walk along the ways of the Lord: the way of light and truth, of prayer and humility, of faithful Scripture study where we seek God's revealed will for our lives. Through prayer the Holy Spirit opens up our hearts for the love of God in Jesus Christ. Where His love dwells, there His peace reigns.

Peace cannot come into our country unless it first comes into the hearts of people. Love must become visible in you and me, manifesting itself in our words, deeds and lifestyle. The peace in our hearts also creates peace in the area that surrounds us. From there it circles wider and wider until peace reigns in our country and in our world.

Therefore, we are personally responsible for the peace in our country. Unless we surrender our lives to the love of God, peace will remain only an empty dream.

> Peace does not necessarily mean the absence of war; it is a virtue, a way of thinking, an attitude of mercy, trust and righteousness. (Benedict de Spinoza)

Lord, I pray for _____

_____

The road to peace

"Perhaps everyone will listen and turn from his evil way, that I may relent concerning the calamity which I purpose to bring on them because of the evil of their doings." (Jer. 26:3)

When things seem to go smoothly, people are lulled into a false sense of security. This is true in spite of the lessons history teaches. Through the ages people have experienced acute needs and then made an appeal to the grace of God. However, once the crisis is over, they return to their previous self-centred way of life. They ignore the Lord and choose to go astray on the road of deception and disobedience. The troubled and confusing times we experience are ample proof of a world paying the price because people strayed from God, following their own, selfish ways.

Like everything else which is worthwhile in this world, peace and calm have their own price-tag. In order to achieve that in your life, you need to practise the discipline of obedience to Christ, committing yourself to His ways. This involves walking the road which He indicates, regardless of how appealing the road of your own choice might seem. You can, however, know without a shadow of doubt that you are doing the right thing by living according to God's will. This is also the only way in which you will become a partaker of God's peace – the peace which passes all understanding. You should really try it, the results will cause you to experience peace and calm.

As long as we walk according to God's plan, He will assist us. When we walk along our own path, He punishes us through failure. (Theodore Cuyler)

Lord, guide me _____

_____

℘eace and prosperity

"You will keep him in perfect peace, whose mind is stayed on You, because he trusts in You." (Is. 26:3)

*ℋ℘*hen our minds are stayed on the love and peace of God, we experience indescribable tranquillity and peace of mind. It is not in vain that the Master promised us, *"Peace I give to you; not as the world gives do I give to you. Let not your heart be troubled, neither let it be afraid"* (John 14:27).

When you set your mind on trusting God through every day and every sleepless night, calm and peace will descend upon your spirit. You will not only experience peace of mind, but you will also stop worrying about the well-being and prosperity of your loved-ones, because you have the assurance that they are safe in God's loving care.

By focusing on Jesus Christ and the peace and prosperity that He gives, you become calm and are set free because you know God is in control of your life. This creates the highest measure of prosperity man could experience. He leads you in paths of righteousness and there is no man or circumstance that can disturb your tranquillity.

Then He sets you free from anxious worry and tension, because the love of God enfolds you. And this love covers your dear ones as well. Thus you are completely redeemed from worries and stress. This freedom cannot be undone by anyone or anything – and all this because you put your trust in the Lord.

> Watch against being desperate about yourself: you are commanded to put your trust in God and not in yourself. (Augustine)

I want to trust You with _____

_____

Peacemakers for God

"Blessed are the peacemakers, for they shall be called sons of God."
(Mt. 5:9)

It is with shock that we take note of the violence, unrest, bloodshed and lack of peace in the world. We read about it in papers and magazines, we see it on television and hear it on the radio. Slowly but surely we become conditioned to accept it as part of life. We then become part of the problem instead of the solution. What are we supposed to do to contribute positively to peace? We can quietly bless everyone that we rub shoulders with, with a prayer for peace.

However, I first need to find peace myself. And the way to do it is to come to God with my storm-tossed life and become quiet before Him in prayer. Not only to speak to Him, but also to listen to what He wants to say to me through His Holy Spirit. In the time that I spend with Him, I need to get rid of all my fear, prejudices, anger and grievances against my fellowmen. I need to walk the road of forgiveness and reconciliation and allow His love to fill my heart. In the final analysis, it is love which brings about insight, harmony and peace.

I can become a peacemaker for Christ through praying honest prayers for peace. This will then be revealed through my life and actions, and like waves of light, peace will emanate from me in ever-widening circles. This will merge with the peace flowing from all of God's children praying for peace, and rise up to His throne of grace. He hears our cry for help and this will benefit the whole world.

> The world is full of faces, dark with anger, green with envy, red with shame, which could only be made shiny with spirituality and holiness through the life-giving power of prayer. (Samuel Henry Price)

Prince of Peace, I wish _____

*F*reedom and peace through Christ

"Whoever commits sin is a slave of sin." (Jn. 8:34)

*M*any people who brag that they are free, only experience supposed liberty. They are indeed slaves of destructive habits; they make no effort whatsoever to watch their language and they are leading a life which is directly opposite to their noble nature. And to add to their slavery, many people are driven by bitterness and unpleasantness, leading a negative and degenerating life. When sin controls a life, he is a harsh taskmaster and he robs that life of all beauty and liberty.

Unfortunately there are people who have accepted this type of slavery as a way of life. Because they've always lived an inferior spiritual life, they sadly don't know better and are blinded to the freedom and peace which Christ offers. The Word specifically says, *"Therefore if the Son makes you free, you shall be free indeed"* (John 8:35).

The liberty which Christ offers is essentially not a subject for theological debate. It is a unique experience during which man's spirit and body are set free from the destructive influence of sin. When you accept Christ as your Lord and Master, you enjoy a new freedom and a new pattern of life. All bitterness disappears in His glorious love. The Holy Spirit sanctifies your thoughts, words and actions. The single purpose of your life is to do the perfect will of God instead of obeying your own sensuous desires. The freedom which Christ gives, spans your whole life in a practical way and it is the only way along which you will find freedom and joy.

> We find liberty when we find God; we lose it when we lose Him. (Paul E. Sherer)

By doing Your will _____

Quietness with God

"Be still and know that I am God; I will be exalted among the nations, I will be exalted in the earth!" (Ps. 46:10)

We live in a fast-moving world. The more we give to life, the more it seems to demand from us. Eventually we are so tired and storm-tossed with all our efforts that we become frustrated and find it difficult to handle the pressure. When this happens, we lose perspective and it seems as if our world is falling apart.

One tried and tested method of controlling a life which threatens to spin out of control, is to set aside quiet times with God. This is what Christ did in the midst of the busiest times of His ministry. He withdrew from the multitudes to the quietness of the hills of Galilee in order to become still with His Father. If He needed that, it is infinitely more true of us.

We have a problem entering this quietness with God, because we lack focused concentration. As soon as you are alone and purposefully seek the face of God, superficial thoughts enter your spirit until you give up hope of even trying to enter into quietness with God.

It requires time and commitment to practise being quiet with God. You need to be patient with yourself, persevere and concentrate. Get to know God from His Word. Don't be in a hurry or lose patience. God is waiting to meet with you in the quietness and to impart His peace to you. Your responsibility is to calm down and to focus on Him with your spirit and your mind. It does require discipline, but you will receive the reward.

> When I am alone with God, my anxiety vanishes into the great silence of God. (Walter Rausenbusch)

Holy God, I come to You in quietness, to _____

_____

Your search for peace

"'This is the rest with which you may cause the weary to rest,' and 'this is the refreshing;' yet they would not hear." (Is. 28:12)

In times of tension, confusion and stress people generally show signs of fatigue. This is especially true in our world where so much is made of achievement, progress and results. People of all ages, from teenagers to the elderly, struggle with tremendous pressure. The result leaves scars on the spirits and minds of people and they yearn for rest and peace.

Yet, in the midst of our overly-busy life, Christ kindly invites us, *"Come to Me, all you who labour and are heavy laden, and I will give you rest"* (Matthew 11:28). It is remarkable that so few people respond to this invitation. We much rather look for man-made solutions to help us cope with the pressures of life. It is incomprehensible that people hesitate to turn to Jesus Christ and accept the only true peace. It is offered to us freely and promised with much love.

Regardless of how busy you are, it is imperative that you make time to withdraw from the demands of each day and spend time in quietness at the feet of the Master. Focus all your attention on Him and His love. In the quietness, become soaked in and loose strengthened by His peace. Make sure you do this regularly. Regardless of how demanding your life might be, you will experience a feeling of strength, peace and tranquillity while the Holy Spirit ministers His healing work in your life.

Quietness with God is like an underground river – it flees from the eyes of the world in order to see the eyes of God. (Thomas Carlyle)

I have such a need of Your rest, Lord _____

$\mathscr{L}$iving in peace

"Have salt in yourselves, and have peace with one another." (Mk. 9:50)

$\mathscr{I}$n the wild rush of modern life, people often experience an unmet need of stability. Competition in the business world is ruthless; young people are continually challenged to achieve higher levels of excellence in academic fields. Even in the field of sport the desire to improve achievements of the past becomes the motivational factor which encourages athletes to reach higher and more difficult goals. Many people work under such pressure that it often causes raw nerves, inflammable tempers and the blind and selfish desire to achieve success, regardless of the cost.

The highest and most noble objectives that have ever been achieved in the history of mankind, are to be found in a study on the life, work and ministry of Jesus Christ. In the face of jealousy and adversity, bitterness and hatred, He completed His God-given mission on earth in a quiet, humble and loving manner.

After His triumphant resurrection and ascension into heaven, He became for you, through His Spirit, the living Christ who is willing to take over your life and live inside you. If you desire to live a life of peace in the midst of a world that's in chaos, then simply open up your heart and life to the influence of His Holy Spirit. Strive to please Him – and not people. In this way you will live in peace with yourself and others and His Holy Spirit will assist you to do so on a daily basis.

People always expect to find peace in heaven, but the peace they will experience there has already been prepared. All peace which they could be blessed with, must be made here on earth already. (John Ruskin)

Lord Jesus, I long for peace _____

_____

The road to peace

"Then He said to the woman: 'Your faith has saved you. Go in peace.'"
(Lk. 7:50)

Worry, doubt and fear are all well-known for the decaying and negative influence they can have on a person's emotional and spiritual well-being. People who were stable and sound-minded are collapsing into confused wrecks through constant worry. It causes them to act contrary to their own nature and often to their own detriment.

How often have you been in a situation which you could not handle, simply because you could not think of a possible solution to your problem? Then you feel incapable and totally hopeless. It is in times like these that you are in danger of acting abnormally, putting your well-being on the line.

In order for you to remain standing strong in such circumstances and to avoid the potholes of foolish actions, it is important that you strengthen your faith in God. It is essential that you trust Him unconditionally and commit yourself as well as your interests to Him. Allow Christ to show you His path for your life.

Perhaps you think that such an action is above your ability – and you are totally correct in that. However, with God all things are possible. The closer you stay to the living Christ in every difficult situation, the more you will find that He lovingly guides you through every circumstance, along the path of His peace.

> Man cannot live without faith, because the most important require-
> ment for the adventure of faith is courage and the life force of courage is
> faith. (Harry Emerson Fosdick)

I believe in You and therefore I experience _____

_____

℘eace be with you!

"For the sake of my brethren and companions, I will now say, 'Peace be with you.'" (Ps. 122:8)

ℰxperiencing discord and dissension is always unpleasant. They often cause bitterness, hurt feelings and resentment which can cause immeasurable damage to human relations. The result is that people become unhappy and dissatisfied.

There are more than enough problems and worries in our world today which you need to struggle through. It is foolish to add to them by getting involved in bitter quarrels or by harbouring grievances in your inner man. Most people already have a hard time coping with the sweet and bitter which life offers. To be able to do that, it is essential that you live in peace with your fellowman; and you can only do that if you are living in peace with yourself. Any broken relationship will leave you confused and insecure and could easily be the cause of you acting contrary to your true nature – to your own detriment as well as that of others.

During His earthly ministry Jesus had to handle a tremendous amount of adversity and enmity. He endured mockery, hatred, humiliation, unfair criticism and rejection. Little attention or appreciation was ever offered for the good deeds which He did. Nevertheless, He never allowed circumstances to get the better of Him. And this was only possible because He was at peace with God, with Himself and with all people. Christ offers you His peace. Accept it and express it through your life and you will experience a life of harmony and peace.

> The world will only become a safe place where peace is provided when people accept the principles of Jesus Christ and apply them righteously. (William Pierson Merrill)

Saviour, because I found You _____

_____

God's peace has a calming effect

"Glory to God in the highest, and on earth peace, goodwill toward men!" (Lk. 2:14)

Of all the things people strive towards, the most important in our world today, are peace of mind and tranquillity. We live at a tremendous pace, in quick-changing and often fear-invoking times. The result is that people's discernment is not always sound, and thus poor decisions are made. Caught up in the rush of life, we are often inclined just to go with the flow. Often pain is inflicted upon us by the rocks of set-backs and we easily land on the desert island of despair.

In the same way that the birth of Jesus Christ brought a spirit of peace into the hearts of those privileged people who knew about His birth, so the rebirth of Christ brings peace into the hearts and lives of all who are willing to receive Him today.

While rereading the narration of the birth of Jesus Christ, you cannot escape the feeling of peace when you hear about the rough, hard-working shepherds who came from the fields of Bethlehem; or about the magi who travelled long distances over rocky places and through barren areas. Suddenly they find themselves in the presence of the Son of God and they are surrounded by an aura of peace.

The living Christ offers the same experience to you, regardless of your circumstances or where you may find yourself. Open up your heart to Him today and allow Him to take over your life. Your life will become a feast of peace.

Try all the roads to peace and well-being that you can think of, and you will find that not one will take you there – except Christ's road. (Matthew Arnold)

Lord, I lack tranquillity _____

_____

Jesus can help you

"But immediately Jesus spoke to them, saying: 'Be of good cheer! It is I; do not be afraid.'" (Mt. 14:27)

Many people find their lives being shaken to the foundations when set-backs come their way. A serious illness which involves long hours of suffering and anxiety; a change in lifestyle because of the death of a loved-one; approaching old age; or financial needs; confusion and worries about an unsure future: all these things can create a feeling of despair, despondency, hopelessness and futility in you.

More than in any other times of your life, you must turn to Christ and put all your trust in Him. The Lord who lived, died and rose for you, regards you as very precious and He cares for you tremendously. Your worries are His concerns too and He only wants what is best for you. Christ has assured you that He will not leave you nor forsake you and you can put all your trust in Him (See Hebrews 13:5).

In moments of weakness and despondency, when it seems as though ominous thunder clouds overshadow your life and when insecurity surrounds you like a dark shroud, remember that Jesus Christ is with you. Talk to Him; put your trust in Him completely; tell Him about your fears and anxieties. Ask Him to give you strength to carry your burden.

Trust Him unconditionally and you will suddenly discover that you can handle your problems. Jesus the Lord becomes a part of your life and He fills your life with His peace!

> With God in control of our defence, we will have inner peace. (T.T. Faichney)

With You by my side, Lord, I will _____

_____

THE FOUNTAIN
OF GOD'S COMFORT

God doesn't comfort us to make us comfortable, but to make us comforters of others. (John Henry Jowatt)

"O, help me to Your goodness, Lord, be with me in suff'ring. I cry to You, I cry again. I wait on your deliv'ring. Take my hand and comfort me – then will this dark hour pass me by." (See hymn 282:1)

Our suffering and pain are so different and yet so alike: confusion, bitterness and rebellion follow in breathtaking succession.

We cannot scale the walls of despair in our own strength. We cannot rationalise the sorrow – the pain within our broken hearts remains there all the time. Only with You do we find true and abiding comfort. Therefore we kneel before You, O God of comfort and plead that through the atoning offering of Jesus Christ and the comforting work of the Holy Spirit, You will grant us that comfort which is to be found with You alone. Your Word promises that You listen to the prayers of those who have lost everything; You will not disregard my prayer.

_ight in times of darkness

"Unto the upright there arises light in the darkness; He is gracious, and full of compassion, and righteous." (Ps. 112:4)

very believer who wishes to know God more intimately, must accept that while there will be times of sunshine along his pilgrimage, also there will be times when dark clouds of affliction will cover his path. For some time things may go well and one is joyfully aware of spiritual growth and progress. Then God is such a glorious reality to you; doubt doesn't have a chance to crawl into the heart and joy floods your life.

Unfortunately this condition is never permanent. Perhaps as a result of rebellious disobedience, or because of allowing your love for the Master to wane, the cloud of despondency descends upon your spiritual life.

When that happens, it is essential to re-establish in your mind the fact that God is unchanging. His love for you remains exactly what it always was. He is still calling His children to His heart and wants to have fellowship with us. He is still our Protector and our Guide. God never changes and even though we are in dark depths, His love will still surround us and keep us.

Experience has shown that the times spent in the dark valley, are never wasted. You may find it hard to accept, despondency might cover your life like a dark shroud, and God may seem far off and uninvolved. Yet, hold on steadfastly to the assurance that God loves you and that He cares for you. Never question His goodness or His purpose for your life. Fortunately, the dark times are also not permanent. You will step out of the shadows with new strength, and, being stronger and wiser, you will walk in His sunshine again.

Life with Christ is an endless hope, without Him a hopeless end.
(Anonymous)

I will trust You in the dark, because _____

*W*hen sorrow knocks

" I am with you always, even to the end of the age." (Mt. 28:20)

*S*orrow and sadness bring about a radical change in one's private world. Where previously one experienced love, companionship and understanding, there now exists a painful void which can only be understood by those who have experienced it themselves. Sorrow can come to you in numerous guises. The most common form is the death of a loved one. For many years you shared your life with such a dear one and now he or she is dead and you feel completely alone and totally lost.

Always remember that this sorrow is actually for yourself: it cannot possibly be because your loved one is with the Lord. If that person could speak to you, the message would be, "Don't cry for me; rather rejoice with me. In actual fact I am only really living now for the first time, and like never before." Don't grieve for those who went ahead of you, by mourning without end. They are now living in the encompassing love of God.

Sorrow can also destroy a family when the foolishness of one member brings shame upon all the others. This is always a very bitter experience and those who endure it feel as if the whole world is pointing a condemning finger at them. This however is not true. Many people are very sincere in their sympathy because they are only too aware of their own weakness and vulnerability. The majority of people forget easily. Can you still remember the scandalous headlines that were in the newspapers two months ago? The wise thing to do is to start reconstructing your life, without paying attention to what others say or think.

Death and shame are not issues which you should handle on your own. Christ had personal experience of both and He also triumphed over both.

> Sorrow, just like rain, creates roses and mud. (Austin O'Mally)

God, please enable me to _____

_____

An understanding Saviour

"For in that He Himself has suffered, being tempted, He is able to aid those who are tempted." (Heb. 2:18)

Never allow self-reproach to discourage you so much that you let go of all efforts to live the life Christ has intended for you. This can happen so easily. Perhaps you have a hidden moral weakness which you have been trying to overcome for a very long time. You are very sincere in your intention to break its bondage, but unfortunately you fail every time. Now you are hampered spiritually to such an extent that, every time you face this temptation, you are already convinced that you are going to fail again.

You may feel totally despondent because of your regular failures, but Christ knows you better than you know yourself and He still maintains His trust in you. He knows the intensity of your temptation, because He, just like you – and probably more so – suffered under temptation. He withstood His most severe temptations and triumphed over them and in His great love He wants you to do the same.

The fact that He understands doesn't mean that He condones your weakness. It simply means that He doesn't underestimate its power and influence in your life. He places a power at your disposal which ensures that you could overcome every temptation in His Name, thus living triumphantly.

This power is the gift of His indwelling presence which He gives when you love Him with your mind and your emotions. When your love for Him takes control of your whole being, you start living on victory ground. This is an immeasurable comfort for the storm-tossed human heart.

Satan tempts us to ruin us: the Lord tests us to crown us. (Ambrosius)

Saviour, obedience _____

_____

Comfort for the future

"Behold, the tabernacle of God is with men, and He will dwell with them, and they shall be his people. God Himself will be with them and be their God."' (Rev. 21:3)

In our day fear has cast a very dark shadow over the future. On the international scene there is ever-increasing tension; clashes between races and the seeming inability of leaders and politicians to handle even the most basic issues, cause people to wonder what kind of world is awaiting their children and their grandchildren. It is impossible not to personalise national and international affairs, because you are part of humanity.

To be sheltered in the living Christ, elevates your view above the temporal, giving you an exceptional appreciation of life. You realise that the times you live in, regardless of how tense and ominous they might appear, are still under God's control. The Lord God Almighty still reigns and has not rejected His creation.

If you do believe in the omnipotence of God and if your faith is built on a steadfast foundation, it will have practical results in creating a positive attitude in your life. You will not fear the extinction of mankind, but rather believe in God's redemptive work which will come to fulfilment in mankind.

To believe that God is working out His divine plan with us, in spite of man's sin and his going astray, enables you to maintain a well-balanced and calm attitude, even when the media sucks sensation from everything that happens. The choice is yours: you can look to the future without God and experience depression and fear, or you can believe in God's plan of redemption for mankind and approach the future comforted, and with trust.

> The only light on the future is faith. (Theodor Haecker)

Eternal God, I believe with conviction that _____

_____

Jesus also heals loneliness

"The ministry of reconciliation ... that God was in Christ reconciling the world to Himself." (2 Cor. 5:18, 19)

The good news of the gospel is that God, through Jesus Christ, has granted the whole world the opportunity to be His friends. There are many people from whose hearts the cry of pain ascends, because they are comfortlessly alone in this world; they have neither family nor friends; nobody loves them and there is nobody to love; nobody in whom they can put their trust or on whom they can rely. Unfortunately this is a condition which is common in our day because people are uninvolved and self-centred.

From this situation two vital factors emerge. Firstly, God's love for mankind includes everybody. His loving interest is available to you and all people. All you have to do is to turn to Him and make this gift of grace your own.

Secondly, people do accept that God is love, but believe that it is impossible for them to find Him. The answer to this is the fact that Jesus Christ is the only way to God. If you would only seek Christ, you will find Him in your everyday existence.

If you will serve Him among other people, by caring for them as He cares for you, then that is the exact place where you will, through Jesus Christ, find God.

When you have considered these facts, you will realise that you, through expressing Christ's love to others, will find the God of love. As you involve yourself in the ministry of love, you will discover that you are not lonely any more and that your own heart is being comforted.

> With Jesus, service to God and service to one of the least of his children, is one and the same. (Dietrich Bonnhoeffer)

Faithful Master, I serve You through _____

_____

$\mathcal{L}$et Christ light up your life

"The Lord will be to you an everlasting light, and your God your glory." (Is. 60:19)

$\mathcal{O}$n each of our lives there comes a time when we need encouragement and strengthening. Perhaps problems are weighing heavily on our minds; perhaps life seems to be empty and meaningless; our dreams may have caved in like a house of cards: plans may have failed and not been realised! That is the time when we search for something which will lift us up out of the quicksand of despair and despondency and add new meaning and purpose to our lives.

I can say to you without the slightest trace of doubt in my heart, that the solution to your problem lies in your acceptance of Jesus Christ as your Saviour and Redeemer. Christ came to this world as the Light and He lights up the lives of all those whom He touches. The healing power which flows from Him has brought healing not for the body only, but for the spirit as well. Those who came in touch with Him, have found their lives transformed by His divine influence. And in conjunction with that, they experienced tranquility and peace of mind.

If it seems to you that the light in your life has gone out, and you are plodding along in the dark, enquire after the living Christ. Seek Him in prayer and meditation, in His eternal Word, in creation and in the quietness of your closet. Gradually His power will flow into your life. His light will light up the shadows and shady patches in your life, and His peace will bring peace and calm into your soul. Christ offers you the real life in all its abundance (See John 10:10). Accept this and live in the Light!

> I have seen an ocean of darkness and death; but a never-ending ocean of light and love flooded the ocean of darkness and then I saw the unfathomable love of God. (George Fox)

Lord, guide me by Your light _____

*W*hen things go terribly wrong

"Because you have forgotten the God of your salvation and have not been mindful of the Rock of your stronghold ... " (Is. 17:10)

erhaps at this point in time, for some or other reason, you are going through a difficult time in your life. Perhaps you have lost your job and are searching in vain for another; perhaps you are in the process of getting divorced and it's causing you much pain; perhaps a very special relationship with a friend broke up; or perhaps everything is just going wrong for you. You might even be contending with God in a faith battle; it might feel as if you are groping around in the dark, disillusioned by the past, confused by the present and fearful of what the future holds. In these, and similar situations, man is inclined to look for something or someone to blame. You simply cannot understand how things could possibly have gone so very wrong and you are overwhelmed by a spirit of self-pity.

Perhaps you are presently experiencing a similar situation. Have you considered the possibility that perhaps consciously or unconsciously you've drifted away from God? In your preoccupation with your own disasters and problems, you have tried to set your life on track in your own strength.

In essence, the prerequisite for a life of happiness and fulfilment, is that you will allow God to take over. Put Him in control of your plans and actions. He knows what the future holds and only wants the very best for you. If you spend time with Him in prayer and follow obediently wherever He leads you, you will find that in the living Christ you have a friend who is a rock and a refuge who will never leave you or forsake you.

> Don't try to hold on to God's hand; allow Him to hold on to yours. Let Him hold on, while you trust. (William Peploe)

Lord, I am so weak, so helpless _____

For the dark days

"A little while longer and the world will see Me no more, but you will see Me. Because I live, you will live also." (Jn. 14:19)

Each of us goes through low-tides in our lives when our heart is heavy and we are inclined to become dejected. There is an arid barrenness which can have a decidedly negative influence on your spiritual outlook. Such a feeling is a common experience, even amongst the Master's devout disciples. It can be ascribed to a number of causes. The danger however, is that you might give in to this to such an extent that you find it extremely hard to restore your spiritual equilibrium.

The solution lies in acknowledging the fact that the living Saviour is always with you. Through His Holy Spirit, He offers you, as an integral part of your life, His guidance for the future; His comfort when you experience sorrow; encouragement when you feel discouraged and desperate; assistance which enables you to overcome the barriers in life; His strength and power to handle and overcome any obstacles life puts in your way.

If you feel discouraged or spiritually empty, go to Christ and place yourself, as well as your problems, in His capable care. Allow Him to control your life again and to guide you along the path which He has marked out for you. Go aside in private with Jesus, spending time in prayer and meditation until you feel one with Him again. Then see how your spirit is lifted up from the depths to experience new heights of joy and peace of mind. Then your heart will sing out, *"I am able to do all things through Christ who strengthens me"* (Philippians 4:13).

> Jesus Christ is a God whom we can draw close to without shame, and whom we can bow down before without despair. (Blaise Pascal)

Holy Jesus, the deepest joy of my soul lies in _____

$\mathcal{W}$hen you are on your own

" For He Himself has said, 'I will never leave you nor forsake you.'"
(Heb. 13:5)

$\mathcal{I}$t is essential for Christians to enjoy spiritual fellowship with one another in order to experience spiritual growth. Being part of a warm and loving spiritual community is a source of daily strength and inspiration for your day-to-day walk with God. Trying to walk our Christian pilgrimage on our own, without the support of a vibrant care-group, is to expose ourselves to the danger of spiritual loneliness.

If your spiritual viability depends upon enthusiastic and perhaps emotional meetings, the day will dawn when you might discover that you don't have a living faith, but only a mask of what true religion is. In your hour of crisis, this will leave you in the lurch. Then you will discover how essential it is to depend on Christ and not on people.

In each area of life you have to take responsibility for your own actions. Nobody else can do that for you. When you have made certain choices and taken decisions, then you alone must bear the consequences and walk along the path you have chosen. Therefore, choose wisely.

When you have to undertake life's last journey, you are on your own. Nobody can enter the valley of death with you. And yet, you are not alone, because the Master promised to be with you when you go into the vast unknown. As His follower you have the immeasurable privilege of knowing that you are enjoying the Master's companionship right through life, through death and for all eternity.

> Life is very much like a game of tennis: he who serves well, seldom loses. (Horatius Bonar)

I praise and honour You, my Lord _____

Comfort in crisis

"We were troubled on every side. Outside were conflicts, inside were fears." (2 Cor. 7:5)

Nowhere in the New Testament do we find that Christ's followers are offered an easy, care-free or comfortable discipleship. Though the Master offers love, joy and power, He also warns that His followers will have to endure persecution and carry their cross.

Resistance and opposition to the Christian faith can be very intense, and sometimes it seems that the harder the Christian strives to maintain faith, the more bitter it gets. When our faith is being pressurised, fear easily takes hold of us and doubt starts gnawing at our minds.

In case your Christian experience is presently at a low-tide and everything which you regard to be holy is being attacked, and you feel as if you are about to snap under the tension, then remember that the eternal values are unchangeable. It is possible that a feeling of loneliness may overwhelm you and you may be in danger of becoming despondent when your faith is under attack. Your spirit is bowed down inside you and you wonder if it is even worth your while to persevere.

In these times, when you feel least spiritual, you need to be active in confirming your faith. Say in steadfast faith that the living Christ is with you. Say to yourself with conviction, Christ is alive and triumphant and He is with me this very moment.

Initially it may not make any difference at all, but by repeating this inspirational truth in your spirit and mind, you control the despondency and loneliness. Thus your faith remains strong in the sure knowledge of Christ's presence.

> Christ changes the sunset-path into a radiantly bright day-break. (Clemens of Alexandria)

Saviour, please make Your presence _____

When life disappoints you

"Why are you cast down, O my soul? And why are you disquieted within me?" (Ps. 42:5)

Unfortunately there are people who feel that life has no meaning or purpose whatsoever. One dull day follows upon the next and sometimes people wonder whether life is even worth living at all: they feel they exist, without really living.

We must always remember however, that often this sad state of affairs was created by those people themselves. It is never the will of our heavenly Father that the gift of life that was given to you should be wasted on a useless way of life. He has given you life to utilise joyfully and constructively. Finding it boring and uninteresting is to deny His will for your life. It is when you live without a plan for your life that your days become aimless and frustrating. Therefore, the acceptance of a constructive plan for your life, is of essential importance.

When Jesus Christ said that He came to give us an abundant life (see John 10:10) and when we accepted His will for our lives, He gave us a challenge to enter into a new and satisfying life. That was not an emotional invitation, but an urgent call to accept the responsibilities of Christian discipleship.

Being a disciple of Christ implies a steadfast conviction of who and what Jesus Christ is. It means that you will have a firm and unyielding faith in Him. If your faith doesn't inspire constructive and positive service to Him, it has very little value at all. It is through serving your fellowmen that your life obtains purpose and meaning. Then it can also never stay on a low-tide mark.

> The church is a workshop, not a dormitory. Every Christian disciple is bound to serve. (Alexander Maclaren)

God who gives true life _____

"How great Thou art!"

"Come and see the works of God; He is awesome in his doing toward the sons of men." (Ps. 66:5)

We are living in a time of disillusionment and dejection and many people simply submit themselves to this spirit of despondency. They find very little that is good or worthwhile on the face of the earth. Their attitude is mostly that of futile resignation to what seems to them a hopeless future. In these cases their faith is not only weak, it is non-existent. They have become blinded to the glory and greatness of God because they are trusting in people's handling of worldly affairs.

In order for you to approach life with courage and steadfastness, and to ensure tranquility of mind and inner peace, you need to remind yourself constantly of the wonderful deeds God has performed in your life. Look at the beauty of creation again; think of all the conveniences which you just take for granted but which enhance the quality of your life; think of all the security you enjoy and the treasure of good health; and think about the marvel of your family and friends again. And above all this, meditate again on the comforting and strengthening presence of the living Saviour. Then you will probably think differently about your pilgrimage.

When you are tempted to discard this life as a failure, or when you find yourself in the company of prophets of doom, do not stop praising and glorifying God for the awesome wonder of life. Through your exaltations you will be elevated above the things which are wrong with the world while your eyes will be opened to the magnitude of the omnipotent Creator of heaven and earth.

> We must worship as if God is present. If my mind doesn't cooperate while I worship, I have not worshipped yet. (Confucius)

Creator God, I want to exalt _____

_____

*W*hen God is far off

"My God, my God, why have You forsaken Me? Why are You so far from helping Me?" (Ps. 22:2)

*E*ach one of us who has persevered on the spiritual road, undoubtedly experienced moments of darkness and doubt. It feels as though our spiritual life has been transformed into a desert and we derive no inspiration from prayer or meditation.

These times of spiritual drought and inability to pray or do Bible study, could be regarded as training schools for prayer. Without times in the dark valleys of life we cannot appreciate the mountain tops. It is the struggle to rise above the depths of depression which generates spiritual strength and stamina for the battle of life.

If you wish to grow into maturity, then the valley experience is imperative. We cannot live on the spiritual mountain tops permanently. It is of the utmost importance how you react in the valley. It is very easy to allow your vision of God to grow dim and to forget His earlier love and assistance. God's love for you never changes, regardless of how you feel.

Through all generations people's experience has proven that times spent in the spiritual valley can be beneficial, provided that you always remember that you are not going to stay there forever, that you are merely a sojourner. If God feels far removed from you at this moment, and you are deeply aware of your own short-comings, then stop for a while and re-establish His abiding presence and assure yourself prayerfully that He is with you. The darkness will gradually be transformed into light and you will be able to rejoice in the fact that your spiritual life has deepened.

> Only the strong grow through suffering, the weak only grow weaker. (John Dryden)

Thank You Lord, that You are always close to me _____

Comfort when you die

"And go quickly and tell his disciples that He is risen from the dead, and indeed He is going before you." (Mt. 28:7)

The disciples' beautiful dream was shattered in a cruel way on Good Friday; all the hope they had in their hearts was gone. Their Lord and Master had died on the cross and everything was over now. A small group of courageous and loyal women were going to the grave on Sunday morning with incense in their hands to pay their last tribute. How many people have not also experienced these same feelings after the death of a loved one? These women were mourning inconsolably, dejectedly and despondently as they performed this duty of love.

But everything was not over yet. Hope often springs from hopeless situations and broken dreams can be repaired. The message of life replaces the paralysis of sorrow. Jubilant joy filled the hearts of these women when they heard their Lord is alive; that the grave is empty; that He rose triumphantly; that death has finally been overcome; that the promise has been fulfilled and that God's love enables us to have eternal life (See John 3:16).

When you encounter the mystery of death, whether it's the death of someone close to you or fear of your own death, then remember Christ's glorious victory over death. Hold on to the wonderful truth that He expels our fear and ends our sorrow.

Do not fear. Physical death always leads to the eternal life that Jesus Christ has made possible for His children. Find peace and tranquillity of mind in the assurance that you and your loved ones are in the hand of the Almighty and that, after death, we will be with Him eternally.

Jesus has changed death into a narrow, star-studded road which connects the companionship of yesterday with the reunion of tomorrow. (William Jennings Bryan)

Source of salvation, grant me _____

_____

Fly with the wings of an eagle

"But those who wait on the Lord shall renew their strength; they shall mount up with wings like eagles." (Is. 40:27-31)

Life carries a heavy burden of human pettiness. Some issues are of little importance, but others are molehills which were allowed to become mountains. An insignificance that is blown out of proportion; an unwatched word which causes pain that was never meant to be. We so easily get bogged down by things that don't really matter. The vision of what you can be is easily dimmed by a narrow-minded view and petty spirit.

A positive Christian has the ability to rise above irritations by trusting in the Lord under all circumstances and by remaining conscious of His living presence. It is impossible to be petty and narrow-minded when the love of Christ fills your heart and mind. Spreading His love by the power of the Holy Spirit means to rise above petty narrow-mindedness and to reach those heights which the God of love desires all His children to live at.

Regardless of the circumstances that you live in, you must never allow them to claim your attention to the extent that you lose sight of spiritual realities. These are the very things that add depth, purpose and meaning, goal and direction to your existence. By developing a consciousness of the presence of the living God and by always trusting in Him, you will be enabled to fly like the eagles, thus seeing things in their right perspective.

> No man can fly with the wings of an eagle before he is filled with the power of the Holy Spirit. Only through the Spirit can we set the right priorities. (G. Campbell Morgan)

Holy Spirit, fill me _____

_____

God's abundance

"... and attaining to all riches of the full assurance of understanding, to the knowledge of the mystery of God, both of the Father and of Christ, in whom are hidden all the treasures of wisdom and knowledge." (Col. 2:2, 3)

Many people are unaware of, or ignorant about, the immeasurable generosity of God. Their own needs and dire poverty blind them and separate them from the One who could ease their suffering and transform their poverty into luxury, if only they would accept Him as their Saviour, and obey Him.

Scripture reveals to us the joyful fact that God is much more willing to give than we are to receive. If we would only pray and believe sincerely and in faith, we could receive that which we pray for. It is a fact that many disciples want to believe unconditionally and yet there are few who want to utilise the key which God makes available to unlock His abundance.

They know that God is able to give everything they ask for, but they also see their self-made obstacles which they've placed in the way of His answers. If you bring a request to your heavenly Father, make sure you don't harbour doubt that He won't comply with your request. Such an attitude creates distrust, prayers are not answered until doubt is replaced by faith.

The manner in which God answers your prayers is neither your concern nor your responsibility. A simple, child-like faith which looks to God, believing steadfastly that God indeed answers prayer, gladdens the Father's heart and usually produces a reply. God hears your prayers and will meet your every need from His treasure house – according to His glorious grace.

> The level of our faith is determined by the level of our prayer-faith; the power of our hope is the power of our prayers; the warmth of our love is the warmth of our prayers. (Carlo Caretto)

Holy Spirit, thank You for Your assistance _____

_____

When your burden gets heavy

"I loathe my life; I would not live forever. Let me alone, for my days are but a breath." (Job 7:16)

When you are feeling dejected or sad, it is good for you to go out and do something that will cheer up someone else who is down-hearted or lonely. It might sound like a senseless thing to you, but it is good therapy: it is impossible to make someone else happy, without easing the pain in your own heart. The danger of depression always lies in the possibility that you could focus all your energy and emotion on yourself.

Take a good look at the world around you: there is always someone whose burden is heavier than yours, whose sorrow is about to overwhelm him. Perhaps it is failure because of a mistake which is not that person's fault and it distorts his personality. Perhaps there is someone in your circle of friends who requires help which only you can give. It might just be possible that your own sorrow and grief served as preparation to equip you for greater and more effective service to others.

Regardless of what the cause of your despondency may be, God can use it to enrich the lives of others around you. Share your burdens with Him – He will never burden you with a cross which is too heavy for you to carry. Be ready to experience how He will lift the burden from your shoulders through your service of love to your fellowmen.

Never fall into the pit of self-pity. That is the death-knell of love towards others. If your love for God is true and sincere, you will love your fellowman and you will prove it by your service of love to those whom God sends across your path.

> They serve God well, who serve their neighbour well. (Caroline Norton)

Saviour, my neighbour _____

_____

Walk in the light

"This is the message which we have heard from Him and declare to you, that God is light and in Him is no darkness at all." (1 Jn. 1:5)

The things that are happening in the world today are a clear indication of a sick society in which people are either unaware of the evil forces that are at work, or they willingly subject themselves to them. People in their right minds and those who are sensitive, are shocked by the atrocities, scandals and other news events which we are confronted with daily. One of the most dangerous results of such a situation is that the average person feels inadequate to handle it. This again can give rise to an attitude of despair where people start believing that nothing can be done about it and that in this dark world of evil we can only try to make the best of a bad issue.

If you have a living faith in God and are willing to put your trust in Him unconditionally, believing that He can overcome all evil, you will soon experience the darkness in your heart clearing up. In the life of Jesus Christ here on earth, God's love broke through the darkest moment in history on that first Good Friday when He overcame the forces of evil and when He rose triumphantly from the dead on Easter morning.

Nothing in our modern world can be as appalling as the crucifixion on Golgotha. And yet the Light broke through. Regardless of how dark your circumstances, put your trust in Christ, follow Him and experience how His light expels the darkness from your life.

> No trials or temptation, no feelings of guilt or power of sin, no wounded spirit or guilty conscience dare drive us to despair. God's love, help and comfort are always available. (Thomas Scott)

Lord Jesus, in Your sight _____

_____

God is a Father who cares

"And in the wilderness where you saw how the Lord your God carried you, as a man carries his son in all the way that you went until you came to this place." (Deut. 1:31)

For most of us life is seldom an even road without any problems. There are times of peace and calm, alternated with experiences of frustration, disappointment, sadness, set-backs and irritation. These negative experiences cast a shadow of anxiety, fear and worry over our lives.

If you submit to the temptation of allowing yourself to be controlled by these feelings, you can be sure that soon your life will become empty and aimless. Depression, worry and even despair will control your emotions. You will find yourself developing a pessimistic approach, thus robbing your life of its joy, purpose and meaning. The problem which most people are confronted with is how to overcome these set-backs.

A thorough study of the Bible and of history, as well as a careful observation of things that happen in your life and in the lives of those around you, will prove to you that nobody is able to escape from the disappointments and set-backs of life. Some are more serious than others and have far-reaching effects. And that is a fact of life which cannot be wished away. Your research will prove that those people who had faith in the promises of God, always had the assurance that God was with them during those times, to help them through their difficult times by means of His supporting love.

When a crisis occurs in your life, the wise thing to do is to turn to God. After all, He invited us to do it: *"Casting all your care upon Him, for He cares for you"* (1 Peter 5:7).

> Often problems are the instruments that God uses to prepare us for better times. (Henry Ward Beecher)

God, in times of crisis _____

_____

*B*lessed assurance

"Commit your works to the Lord, and your thoughts will be established." (Prov. 16:3)

*P*lanning is an important aspect in every area of life. You plan for the future, for your marriage, for your money matters and for retirement. After that, often just as much time is spent on executing the plan as was spent on the planning. It would be interesting to calculate how much time and energy were wasted on useless planning.

There is however a method to prevent this waste of energy and to ensure that your planning will definitely be successful. It requires strict spiritual discipline to make it effective and it must be undertaken in true honesty. Then also it requires real faith and trust in God and in His promises.

Whatever your concern might be, lay it before God in prayer, trusting in Him completely. Talk to Him, submitting all the details concerned, tell Him about your expectations and fears, seek His all-wise guidance and ask Him for clarity and the gift of discernment and wisdom, to know and to understand when He gives you the answer.

Then you have to trust Him steadfastly, leaving the matter in His hands. In His own perfect time and way, He will show you the way. And when the Master does that, you need to move ahead obediently and gratefully, bearing in mind the glorious knowledge that He is with you every step of the way.

> I have never yet submitted even the most insignificant plan to the Lord, without having had reason to praise Him abundantly. (Anna Shipton)

Dear Guide, guide me to _____ *in obedience*

God keeps His promises

"Every word of God is pure, He is a shield to those who put their trust in Him." (Prov. 30:5)

God can be trusted to the utmost. With Him there is no shadow of turning and He faithfully keeps His promises, even though we become unfaithful. It should not be necessary to repeat such an unchanging truth, but when God seems far-off and it seems as if your life is tumbling down like a house of cards, it is of the utmost importance to be reminded of the steadfast faithfulness of God.

Right now it might feel to you as if God does not exist. You have prayed fervently and yet your prayers are just not being answered. That which you feared, did happen in spite of your serious pleas that God should prevent it. The result is that the promises of God are vague and unreal to you.

It is important that you should have a balanced understanding of God's promises. Many of God's promises that are recorded in Scripture, apply to a specific person in an unusual situation or at a specific time. There are, however, promises that became a reality the moment they were accepted in childlike faith.

When you realise your need of forgiveness, and you accept God's prerogative to forgive, in that moment, forgiveness is yours. Jesus, the Son of God, promised that His Spirit will dwell in those who are humble-hearted and who invite Him in. God's friendship and assistance are promised to all who will accept it.

The promises of God are sure and true. You can make them your own by knowing them, praying for them and then thanking Him for them.

> God's promises can be claimed through faith, hope and love. (St. Augustine)

Faithful God, through the guidance of Your Holy Spirit _____

Your life is in loving hands

"But as for me, I trust in You O Lord; I say, 'You are my God.' My times are in your hand." (Ps. 31:14, 15)

Some people are more sensitive to situations than others. They can quickly sum up a situation in the blink of an eye and then act constructively on it immediately. Others need more time to consider the circumstances before they are able to decide on any plan of action. This is the case in every area of life, and the spiritual life is no exception.

There are people whose spiritual intuition is very sensitive, thus enabling them to distinguish the truth and to act on it at once. Others again, gradually come to an understanding of the truth, but their reaction to it is no less sincere.

It is important to remember that your times are being determined by God's perfect timing. If you find it very natural to establish God's will, then you need to make sure that you don't unconsciously move faster than God intended you to. If you are more gradual in establishing God's will for your life, then you must watch that it doesn't become a smoke-screen for laziness or lethargy.

It is possible to be in perfect harmony with God's timing for your life. You will receive proof of this when you place your times in His hand, because His timing is always perfect. If you trust God unconditionally, there will be order in your life, instead of chaos. That is why it is so important to spend time with God in prayer. That is how the tempo of your life will come into perfect harmony with God's timing. And thus you will learn to really live.

> We trust as we love and whom we love. If we have much love for Christ, we will trust Him much. (Thomas Brooks)

Father, please fulfil my needs _____

_____

Everything will be fine

"Although I heard it, I did not understand. Then I said, 'My Lord, what shall be the end of these things?'" (Dan. 12:8)

D aniel's cry to God is one that most of us are only too familiar with. Especially in these unsure times, there are few people who don't wonder, or ask, where everything is going to end. Standards are being lowered, principles are being sold out and in many parts of the world it seems as if violence is the order of the day. Very little attention is given to those spiritual norms which are so important for a stable community.

It is understandable that people will be deeply concerned, insecure and confused. But we never dare lose sight of the fact that God is in control – even though the contrary sometimes seems to be true. Look back over the years – even the ages – to the beginning of time and you will find example upon example of the love and grace of God. Time and time again He redeemed mankind and the world from destruction.

It is true that at times there was great suffering, but remember Paul's immortal words in Romans 8:18, *"For I consider that the sufferings of this present time are not worthy to be compared with the glory which shall be revealed in us."* And also, *"And we know that all things work together for good to those who love God ... "* (Romans 8:28).

If you require unquestionable proof of this, it is to be found in the death and resurrection of Jesus Christ. He had to experience the humiliation of dying on the cross in order to rise as Victor from the dead. Put your trust steadfastly in God. He will not leave you or forsake you – and at His perfect time, everything will be fine!

> Hope never spreads her golden wings except than in troubled waters. (Ralph Waldo Emerson)

Loving God, through the grace there is in _____

_____

*D*on't fear the dark

"I am the light of the world. He who follows Me shall not walk in darkness, but have the light of life." (Jn. 8:12)

*I*t is only when you find yourself in the dark that you become aware of the tremendous impact that light has on your life. On a dreary, grey, rainy day, or when dark storm-clouds gather, a feeling of depression involuntarily descends upon man's heart. In the pitch-dark night you can easily imagine fear-inspiring ogres. A power failure not only creates irritation and a feeling of helplessness, but threatens to drive us to despair.

There are substitutes for sunlight. We use candles, torches or lamps, but they are just not the same and in any case their life-span is much shorter. Regardless of what shape it takes, or what the cause of the darkness might be, the absence of light definitely has a negative effect on the quality of our life, our mind and our health.

The same is true in our spiritual life. One moment we can bubble over with joy because everything is running so smoothly and prosperously. Suddenly things can change and we can be flung into dark depths.

This does not need to happen. Follow the road which Christ has planned. It is the path of Light – glowing with the love of Him of whom John said, *" ... God is light and in Him is no darkness at all"* (1 John 1:5).

> There is more light than that which we can see through the window. (George Fox)

Comforter, thank You that I can know that _____

_____

*H*ow do you handle worry?

"Casting all your care upon Him, for He cares for you." (1 Pet. 5:7)

*Y*ou cannot proceed far along the path of life before worry comes your way. Perhaps you are concerned about how you are going to meet all your financial commitments; perhaps a family member who has taken the wrong path is a source of great concern to you; it could be that you, or a relative, lost your job; you could be concerned about an insecure and dark future.

It is not possible for you to avoid worry or to escape from it, and neither is it a sign of lack of faith. On the contrary, the person who alleges that he never experiences worry, either doesn't speak the truth or he is self-centred and insensitive.

The way you react when you encounter worries is of the utmost importance. Worry can easily give way to panic and then you can act foolishly or impulsively. And that could have disastrous effects which could lead to deep regrets.

Determine the nature and cause of your worry in order to handle it in a constructive manner. Make sure that the thing which causes the worry is a reality and not a figment of your imagination. So many people are afraid of phantoms that don't really exist.

As a Christian you are not entering the future on your own. Share your worries and your burdens with the Master. Tell Him about your anxiety and fear and He will give you the strength and the wisdom to handle your problem successfully.

> When I think back about all my worries, I remember the story of the old man on his death-bed who said that he had so many worries in his life – and half of them never happened. (Winston Churchill)

Lord, I give _____

Realise who you are!

"What is man that You are mindful of him ... For You have made him a little lower than the angels, and You have crowned him with glory and honour." (Ps. 8:4, 5)

The opinion you have of yourself is of essential importance. It will determine your attitude towards life and also to a great extent determine whether you are a success or a failure. And your spiritual life is no exception to this rule.

In the life of every Christian there comes a time when he is deeply aware of his sinfulness. Before he met Christ, he lived according to his own imperfect standards and he sinned without any qualms or conscience. After he accepted the lordship of Christ in his life, a new relationship with the Father was established and now he realises that he is a child of God. Sin no longer has authority over his life and he experiences a spiritual liberty which till now was unknown to him.

Unfortunately it is true that many Christians, in spite of their new-found deliverance, cannot forget their sins of the past. They constantly remind themselves of it – and they also constantly remind God of it. Thus their previously committed sins still have an influential place in their lives, even though they rejoice in their new-found relationship with the Lord.

As a redeemed person you are no longer a sinner, but a person who, by the grace of God, has unlimited potential. You belong to God; you were created to live in fellowship with Him and to reflect His mercy in the world.

Therefore live like that. Then you become what God intended you to be.

> Forgiveness is man's greatest need and most glorious achievement. (Horace Buschnell)

Lord, I want to accept Your grace to _____

_____

Micah 7:1-10 ∼ 27 May

Equipped through faith

"When I sit in darkness, the Lord will be a light to me." (Mic. 7:8)

History has ample proof of the fact that mankind has experienced dark times through the ages, so much so that one period is known as the Dark Ages. There were times of economic depression; of devastating wars; of droughts, floods and famines; of plagues and other dark dangers. In spite of the scientific progress which modern society has made, there are still places where people across the world are living in fear and tension. It seems as though they are surrounded by a dark cloud of despair and the future becomes a dark, unknown wasteland.

In order to survive in these circumstances and to overcome pessimistic dejection, it is extremely important that your faith in the risen Christ must be powerful. Dark times are in actual fact the very times during which you must be able to look back and see how God has always, from the beginning of time, overcome the power of evil through His omnipotence and majesty. Pay attention to the Word of the Lord and you will see how He always transformed defeat into victory; how He made the weak strong; how He transformed the pitch-black darkness into radiant light.

All you need to do in your dark and depressing times is to remind yourself of Golgotha. Nothing could have been more devastating than the death of Jesus Christ on the cross, and yet, there is nothing more triumphant than His resurrection from the dead. Put your faith and trust in God and you will step from the darkness of your despair into the glorious light of His love. Equipped by faith you can live in the light.

Faith is dead to doubt, dumb to discouragement and blind to the impossible. (Michael J. Dee)

Lord Jesus, total trust _____

_____

$\mathcal{L}$ook beyond the cloud

"Now when He had spoken these things, while they watched, He was taken up and a cloud received Him out of their sight." (Acts 1:9)

$\mathcal{T}$he experience of Jesus' disciples on the day of His ascension is definitely not restricted to that time in history. However, in our case it is often clouds of despair, doubt, disappointment and anxiety which create the impression that the risen Lord is hidden from our sight. When this happens, we must never forget that the angels can also say to us, *" ... why do you stand gazing up into heaven?"* (Acts 1:11).

When it feels to you as if, for some or other reason, you have lost contact with Jesus, and He seems to be far away and isolated from you, it is important to remember this comforting fact: He is the living Christ! He is Emmanuel who is present in *every* life situation and who acts as guide for everyone who has accepted Him. It doesn't matter where you are or what your circumstances may be, you have the assurance that He is there.

In order for you to break through the cloud which mars and hampers your view, causing the image of your Master to grow dim, you need to pray earnestly for strength and guidance and then look around you. Try honestly to lend a helping hand where you see a need.

Support those who are less privileged than you are; show love and assistance to those who suffer. As Christ did, you need to go through the world doing good everywhere you go. Through the service which you offer others in His Name, the cloud will disappear and you will see the face of the living Lord again.

The world cannot always understand our confession of faith, but it clearly understands our service for Christ. (Ian Maclaren)

Spirit of God, I pray for the ability to _____

_____

Christ's invitation to you

"The one who comes to Me I will by no means cast out." (Jn. 6:37)

Many people hesitate to make a full commitment to Jesus Christ. They know that they should do it and even have the desire to do so. There are however factors which prevent them from making the irrevocable decision of surrendering their life to Christ. They consider all the things they will have to give up. They know that in their heart they cannot harbour both Christ and sin. When Jesus Christ says, "Come to Me!" He offers a complete and satisfying life which puts sin in its right perspective. An act of remorse as well as confession of sins is imperative.

Many people think it is embarrassing to yield to an emotional evangelical appeal and they don't want to be identified with it. Their attitude is a barrier of pride which prevents them from tasting the greatest experience that is humanly possible. People who advocate conversion may be mocked, but they still represent the greatest challenge man could respond to.

There are those people who have disappointed Christ so many times already, that they think it will mock His merciful invitation if they should try to follow Him again. Yet, at some or other time in his spiritual life, every Christian has experienced bitter disappointment. Regardless of the number of times that you have been unfaithful to the Master, remember that His invitation to return is still standing. He still says: "Come!" and if you come back to Him again, He will receive you heartily.

> When prodigal sons and daughters return home, great and wonderful things always happen. (A.A. Dowty)

I praise You, that I, like the prodigal son, can always _____

$\mathcal{O}$he compassionate Christ

"But when He saw the multitudes, He was moved with compassion for them, because they were weary and scattered, like sheep having no shepherd." (Mt. 9:36)

$\mathcal{C}$ompassion is one of the outstanding characteristics of the unique personality of Jesus Christ. It is not an indication of weakness, but indeed of His greatness. It was the core of His life and teachings.

Scripture tells us that ordinary people enjoyed listening to Him and that they covered long distances, making great sacrifices to come and listen to Him. The abridged version that we have of His teachings, reveals the depths of His wisdom and the uniqueness of His person. The attitude that He revealed when talking to people, not only stimulated their minds, but captured their hearts as well. They felt His love for them and reacted by showing Him their love in return.

Because the immortal Christ is still alive, His compassion for mankind today is just as real and true as when He walked along the dusty roads of Palestine. While we read the Gospels, our hearts are gladdened by the reality of His love for people: He healed the sick, opened blind eyes, opened deaf ears, touched crippled feet to walk again and even raised the dead.

If you are feeling that life has disappointed you, or that you have failed and despair threatens to overwhelm you, if you don't know where to turn to for strength and new inspiration, then remember the compassion of Jesus Christ. He is with you in all your distress and encourages you through the power of His love, to get up from the ashes and start building a new life. His compassion is your comfort and inspiration.

> He watched and prayed and cared for everyone. And He still does that today! (Oliver Goldsmith)

Saviour, may your love and compassion _____ *me*

An unfailing ally

"God is for us, who can be against us?" (Rom. 8:31)

Pessimism leaves a stain on man's soul. The effects are varying and far-reaching and can influence your life negatively. Your outlook on life can become narrow, growth is hampered, trust undermined and your whole life can stagnate.

If you are experiencing any of these emotions, it is imperative that you take a very close look at your life immediately in order for you to take steps to end this condition before it is too late. Otherwise you are robbing yourself of purposefulness and energy and you are in danger of living a futile life.

In spite of the most severe attacks of pessimism, there is one tried and tested method of preventing the decay that comes through these negative influences. That is to have intimate spiritual fellowship with God. Through Jesus Christ you can walk with Him daily. He has given you His unfailing Word that He will be with you always (See Hebrews 13:5). Why don't you accept this offer that is so rich in grace – thus making the living Christ your partner in each undertaking and experience of your life?

He is ready to share your success and failure with you. Allow Him to share in your sorrow and joy. Meet life on a daily basis with the sure knowledge that Jesus is closer to you than a brother. With Christ at your side you cannot help but walk through life with new confidence. This new-found assurance is established in your heart through the Holy Spirit. Face the future with that.

> Wherever you may turn, you will be forced to acknowledge your own ignorance and impotence, and the omnipotence of God. (Voltaire)

Lord, with You as my ally _____

THE FOUNTAIN

OF PRAYER

Daily prayer is the gymnasium of the soul. (C.E. Cowman)

To You O Lord, who answers prayer, all flesh must come.

You are a very present help in trouble and have always proved Your faithfulness.

We so readily want to pray according to Your will and we thank You that the Holy Spirit assists us in this.

We so readily want to practise a disciplined prayer life and we thank You that Your love enables us.

We so readily want to pray in faith and recognise and accept Your answers. Thank You that Jesus Christ was an example to us in this.

We so readily want to be powerful intercessors for our relatives, our church, the heathen, the spreading of your Word, our loved ones and our enemies.

Thank You, Lord Jesus, that we can enter this month knowing that You are our example and that we can follow You because the Holy Spirit enables us to.

Help us to pray in childlike faith in the glorious assurance that You determine what is best for us, and therefore we can say: May Your will be done.

June

Prayer is crucial

"Now in the morning, having risen a long while before daylight, He went out and departed to a solitary place, and there He prayed." (Mk. 1:35)

Some of God's most dedicated children are just too busy. It may be that they are involved with important matters which they regard as imperative for the building of God's kingdom. They become involved in numerous meetings and neglect their family in order to, as they see it, advance the Lord's work.

This kind of activity often serves as a smoke-screen to hide a spiritual void in their lives. Jesus Christ doesn't expect you to be so busy that you cannot prove your loyalty and allegiance to Him. He also doesn't want you to give in to all the demands that are made on your time in His Name. By His example and actions on earth, He stresses the importance of prayer.

It is impossible to achieve spiritual objectives without exercising the discipline of prayer. An aeroplane often travels at a very high speed and is often subjected to difficult and dangerous conditions, but is can only be controlled safely and effectively if the ground staff manage their maintenance and preparation tasks thoroughly and faithfully. You might be very active in the Master's service, but unless your activity is supported by the faithful practice of prayer, you are in danger of a complete spiritual break-down. Then you are flying around without having done sufficient preparation and somewhere, something is going to give, resulting in disaster.

Prayer is the infusion and inspiration of Christian service. It confirms the credibility and authority of everything you are trying to do in the Name of the Master and provides a deep satisfaction which cannot be achieved in any other way.

> Let us go forward on our knees. (Neesima)

Help me, faithful Lord, not to be so busy that _____

The main objective of prayer

"He shall pray to God, and He will delight in him, he shall see His face with joy, for He restores to man His righteousness." (Job 33:26)

There are many reasons why people pray. The urgent cry for help of a human being in dire straits is well-known to most of us. The prayer that pleads for God's blessing on an important undertaking is more common than the one begging for His guidance. To ask for guidance presupposes a willingness to obey the will of God.

The average prayer is filled with self-interest and self-centredness. Your desires are laid before God reverently with the sincere hope that your request will be granted. Nevertheless, while you are making your desires known to Him, you have this secret feeling that you won't receive that which you have asked for. And thus, doubt, rather than faith, is planted much more securely in your heart.

The real objective of prayer is not to use God as a very handy first-aid measure, but to pray when you really need Him. Honest prayer needs to be motivated by praise and worship. Because of the fact that in your prayer you have caught a vision of the beauty and holiness of God in your heart and mind, you are moved to worshipful praise by the Holy Spirit.

While you praise and worship God in prayer, you are filled with a deep desire to know Him better. And when this happens, your main objective is to submit to God's will for your life. Then you will act according to His divine will and prayer will become a glorious experience in your life.

> Prayer is not only the practising of the presence of God, but it is the consciousness of His glorious presence with you. (Joseph Newton)

Holy God, may all my prayers flow forth from _____

_____

ℬe diligent in prayer

*"So He left them, went away again, and prayed the third time,
saying the same words." (Mt. 26:44)*

𝓜any people, some of whom are true Christians, experience problems with prayer discipline. They reason that if God is omniscient, it is not really necessary to pray. Yet others feel embarrassed because it seems as if they are continually bothering the Lord with issues which He has known about all along.

Firstly: it is true that you may be aware of problems, but before your help is requested, you hesitate to get involved. If however you should be asked to help, you would be eager to react. If therefore you feel that your case is important enough for action, you ought to lay your request before the Lord without hesitation. Call upon Him and ask Him to handle the situation for you and to guide you as to what actions you should take.

Secondly: if you feel that something is worth praying for, you should not only handle it casually. Your prayer must reach out to God in all sincerity. Then, to the best of your ability, you should try to identify with the subject of your prayers.

Sincere prayer also involves the surrender of yourself, your time and emotions on behalf of someone or something else. God will never get tired of your prayers as long as you kneel before Him through Jesus Christ. A father knows what his child needs, without the child having to ask and the father also knows that he can do what the child asks him to. Nevertheless he wants to hear the voice of his child and experience his deep dependency. This is how it is with earthly fathers and also with our heavenly Father.

> Our prayers must mean something to us if we want them to have any meaning to God. (M.D. Babcock)

Lord, today I want to bring a special request to You to _____

_____

Continuous prayer

"Pray without ceasing." (1 Thes. 5:17)

The general idea is that in a disciplined prayer life specific times are set apart to pray, usually early in the morning or before we go to bed at night. These are then the times when we are alone with God. It has been proven beyond any doubt that such a routine has great benefits. A great number of people find that giving up this practice can lead to a serious loss which cannot be replaced by anything else.

The creation of a continuous prayer pattern is not a simple matter which takes shape very easily. Every sincere disciple who pays heed to the command, "Pray without ceasing" knows something about the feelings of guilt and frustration which develop when you discover that hours have passed, without your thinking of God once. The demands of life and the fact that you can concentrate on one thing at a time only, makes it impossible to consciously pray without ceasing every minute of the day.

Unceasing prayer is definitely not the continuous repetition of the same request, because that would indicate a lack of faith. And to have your problem constantly on your mind, could cause it to become an obsession. This again could prevent you from letting go and letting God take control.

The motive for continuous prayer is to be tuned in to listen to God and to be sensitive to His guidance. In the inner sanctuary of your soul you will become aware of His presence and experience His power. Wherever you are and whatever you do, you can always lift up your heart to God, even though it may only be for a moment, and you will experience the reality of His closeness.

Some thoughts are prayers. There are moments when the soul is on its knees, regardless what the posture of the body may be. (Victor Hugo)

Father, help me today to _____

_____

$\mathcal{T}$he essence of true prayer

"Jesus who, in the days of his flesh, when He had offered up prayers and supplications, with vehement cries and tears to Him who was able to save Him from death, and was heard because of his Godly fear." (Heb. 5:7)

$\mathcal{O}$ne of the tragedies of our modern time is that so many people regard prayer so lightly. For some it has degenerated into nothing but formality; for yet others it is little more than a panic button to be used in a time of crisis.

While there is definitely not the slightest doubt about the fact that God hears the distress call from the human heart and that He is always ready to answer, it is also true that we must be willing to spend quality time in prayer. If prayer becomes a top priority in your life, it will also bring about satisfaction and fulfilment in life.

Then it is also important that one should realise that prayer does not only consist of your conversation with God. On the contrary, you need to make time to become still before God and to wait on Him. You must be sensitive to the moving of the Holy Spirit and receptive to His guidance. Prayer is always a two-way interaction: your conversation with God, and your believing, listening to and obeying what God is saying.

Once you have taken this into consideration, you need to surrender yourself completely to God. Lay your desires, and those people whom you pray for before Him and then pray in self-denial that His will be done. In the same way that the living Christ discovered and obeyed the will of God, you will be enabled to do it too.

> Prayer is spiritual education. The one who prays, grows. The muscles of the soul expand to become iron bands. (F.B. Meyer)

Lord, You who hear our prayers, enable me to _____
_____

℘rayer obedience

"Lord, teach us to pray ... " (Lk. 11:1)

In its deepest essence, prayer is the soul of man reaching out to the living God. This is especially true in times of need and problems and it is instinctive. When circumstances and situations get beyond our control and we secretly hope that God will intervene through some or other miracle, then we pray – even though we have not spoken to Him, or listened to Him, for a long time. Of course God is able to do it. Yet, effective prayer places certain requirements on us – amongst others that we should listen to God and do His will.

True prayer consists of two components: you have fellowship with the living God, and He has fellowship with you, an insignificant human being. Unfortunately in our prayer life many of us are so busy talking, that we don't hear what God wants to say to us. Listening reverently to the voice of God is an important part of the discipline of prayer. He reveals His will to you through the working of the Holy Spirit – if you would only become quiet in His presence and receive His voice in your heart.

To be sure of His guidance, you must be willing to practise being obedient to His will, as revealed to you through the Holy Spirit. Too many people seek God's will and then sit back, waiting for God to act. Through our prayers we need to be inspired and motivated and an excited spirit of anticipation needs to take hold of us. As your prayer life develops and grows gradually in a disciplined way, you will become more sensitive to what God expects from you. Then you will find joy and happiness in just living for Him.

> Prayer is not a magic formula through which to obtain your desires from God, but it's the only way to become what God intended you to be. (Studdert Kennedy)

Lord, teach me to _____

_____

The power of prayer

"And the prayer of faith will save the sick, and the Lord will raise him up." (Jas. 5:15)

Never, in the case of illness, underestimate the power of prayer. Without minimising in any way the importance of fully utilising medical science, you should never lose sight of the wonderful fact that God still works miracles in answer to prayer.

Quite often prayers for the sick are offered to God in a don't-care or haphazard manner. Often no information is sought or given with regard to the nature of the ailment, or about the personality of the one who is sick. Yes, you are completely right. God does know it all. If however you should make a study of Christ's specific prayers for the sick, you will discover how He identified with them. He even felt power flow from His body during the healing process.

True prayer for healing is not an exercise of trying your luck. It was never meant to be tried as an afterthought. On the contrary, it requires the highest quality of faith and trust. Thereby the patient is submitted to the watchful grace of God. Yet, in the final analysis God's perfect will must be fulfilled in the life of the one who is sick.

Total involvement from the side of the intercessor and unconditional acceptance of God's will from the side of both prayer and patient, will establish the greatest miracle of all healing: the peace of God which passes all understanding.

> Prayer is the releasing of God's energy, because in prayer we ask God to do that which is impossible for us. (Charles Trumbull)

Lord Jesus, today I want to submit one who is sick to You _____

Pray even when it is difficult

"Then He spoke a parable to them, that men always ought to pray and not lose heart." (Lk. 18:1)

For many of the Lord's children, prayer is very natural and comes easy. Most of them however regard it as a discipline which they just never quite master. Their prayer life today is exactly at the level where it stood many years ago.

Yet, though they have made very little progress in their prayer life, they continue praying. They believe that, in spite of their weakness, there is a God who really cares for them. This is one of the basic components of the practice of prayer. You should however, never feel that God's caring love depends on your emotions. Even though you feel as if you are isolated from your heavenly Father, He is still as close to you as ever. God's love never varies and therefore your prayer life does not depend on how you feel. Faith always triumphs over feeling.

Keep on praying diligently, especially when you find it difficult. Persevere until you break through the arid desert of self-imposed inability into the light and love of the living Christ. Indeed it is not the will of God that you should feel far removed from Him. That is why He is approachable at all times. You must only be determined to reach Him in prayer.

There are certain ways in which you can be assured of a meaningful prayer life. Seek God's forgiveness for sins of the past; discipline yourself and wait upon the Lord; develop a consciousness of the presence of Christ.

> The act of prayer is absolutely the highest form of energy the human mind is capable of. (W. Coleridge)

I praise and thank You that in spite of my emotions _____

Prayer: the challenge

"And being in agony, He prayed more earnestly." (Lk. 22:44)

Contrary to popular belief, prayer is not always an uplifting experience. Of course there are those enriching moments when God becomes a glorious reality to you and you experience a feeling of intimate union with Him. At such times one derives a joy from prayer that is not easy to explain in words. If, however, this is the only aspect of prayer that you have experienced, then you have been missing the depth and quality of true prayer.

The great majority of Christ's followers never progress beyond the stage where their prayers are request lists laid before God. And when the answer is not according to their desires, they are disappointed, but not surprised – because they didn't really expect to receive an answer.

It is when you plead that God will let you grow, or that He will show you the right way, or use you in His service, that you will experience the full impact of the challenge of prayer.

Such prayers are essentially an issue between you and God, but you will soon discover that they involve other people as well. If you become aware of God's presence when you pray, you bring Him in contact with those who are in need: perhaps a child who went astray; a hungry, lonely person; or someone who is suffering and heart-broken – and many others that you are reminded of by the Holy Spirit.

As God lays these people on your heart, you begin to understand the responsibility of prayer. Sharing in this privilege, enables you to live in love towards God and your fellowmen.

> Prayer enlarges the heart until it is big enough to contain God's gift of Himself. (Mother Teresa)

Today I want to pray for _____

_____

*S*piritual growth

"But you beloved, building yourselves up on your most holy faith, praying in the Holy Spirit." (Jude v 22)

*P*hysical growth is natural and a matter of course and requires no help or assistance. Spiritual development on the other hand, requires concentration, time and discipline. However, this doesn't mean that you need to have a special level of intellect. It does mean though that you need to approach your spiritual life in the very special way that it deserves.

Because most of your time and energy are spent on executing your daily responsibilities, it could be that spiritual matters are low on your priority list. Most people only pay attention to their spiritual life when it is convenient for them or when they have time left on their hands.

It is God's will for us to grow spiritually. In order for this to happen, there are certain disciplines that you have to accept. The basic requirement is the development of a positive and meaningful prayer life. It must be a joyful experience whereby you get to know more about God because you are having fellowship with Him. Prayer is the most exciting and rewarding spiritual adventure one can experience.

While you are praying, you will form an image of your heavenly Father, and the Bible is an invaluable source of help to assist you in doing this. The Gospels reveal the character of God through the living Christ. While you strive to become like Him and to follow Him through the guidance of His indwelling Spirit, you will unconsciously, but surely, change into His image.

> If I should neglect prayer for one single day, I will lose a great deal of the fire of my faith. (Martin Luther)

Loving Saviour, please help me to grow by _____

_____

God is a refuge

"Is anyone among you suffering? Let him pray." (Jas. 5:13)

There are few people who immediately think about prayer when they experience a crisis. The sad fact of life is that prayer is usually a last act of despair when all other efforts have failed. Nevertheless, right through Scripture we are encouraged and admonished to turn to God and call on Him in prayer under all circumstances in life. Paul said to the Philippians, " ... *in everything by prayer and supplication, let your requests be made known to God"* (See Philippians 4:6).

Yet, in spite of repeated invitations, the average person always looks first for human solutions to solve the problems that cross his path, before giving any consideration to God's loving invitation. Time and time again He promises His assistance and grace to those who call on Him in their times of need.

However, Scripture does not only mention the Lord's many invitations, but there are numerous examples of the wonderful way in which He answered the prayers of believers. The history of mankind teems with examples regarding the power of sincere prayer.

Regardless of what the crisis or need in your life may be, lay your problem confidently before Him. He walked the same earthly road that we have to walk and therefore He will understand. Trust Him unconditionally and place yourself in His care. Believe in His ability to guide you along the road which He planned for you. Obey Him and He will transform your crisis into an opportunity.

> Prayer is not an effort to wake up God's interest: it is the indissoluble holding on to His loving willingness. (Richard Trench)

Father, I am experiencing a crisis _____

The challenge of true prayer

"And when you pray, you shall not be like the hypocrites. For they love to pray standing in the synagogues and on the corners of the streets, that they may be seen by men." (Mt. 6:5)

When you've allowed your prayers to be nothing more than a public show, it is no longer communion with God, but one big self-glorification. Of course there are times when groups or nations come pleading before the Lord. If they are humble and lay their petitions before God in repentance, He will hear their prayer. But public show is not the same as true prayer.

Personal prayer has many facets. It is a wonderful source of comfort. Once you are aware of the tremendous power of prayer you will discover your view of life being extended. Personal prayer enables you to remain calm in the midst of life's storms. The rewards for cultivating a positive prayer life are many and varied.

There is however a facet of prayer that is overlooked very often: it is the challenge of prayer which sooner or later comes to each one of us who is used to spending time with God. I'm referring to those times when God wants to reveal to you His will and desires for your life. Often God's expectations are at war with your own desires. You would much rather not listen to what God wants to say to you. If however you have the courage to persevere in prayer, not only will His will be revealed to you, but you will also develop a new programme for your life – and in conjunction with that the peace of God which guarantees to you peace of mind.

The secret of prayer is prayer in secret. (D.L. Moody)

Your expectations are contrary to my desires. Please help me to

_____

_____

Prayer and the future

"And when you pray, do not use vain repetitions as the heathen do."
(Mt. 6:7)

It is impossible to determine what the future holds and therefore it is wise to be prepared for the vast unknown that lies ahead. The only effective way of doing this, is to develop a practical prayer life. This means a prayer life which will give you strength in moments of weakness and comfort in times of sorrow. And this is not achieved in a fleeting moment of time, but is the fruit of sustained time spent in the presence of God.

A wise sailor doesn't start repairing his sails when a storm breaks. While in the calm of the harbour, he already takes care that they are in good, working condition. Thus the spiritual traveller becomes familiar with the art of true prayer when making time for it without the pressure of external influences.

Many people maintain that prayer is an instinctive action with man. This may be true, but powerful and fervent prayer is the result of dedicated discipline and the right attitude towards God. If your intentions are honest, you won't only pray when you feel like it, but you will find great joy and happiness in sharing every conceivable emotion and thought with your Master.

When the sun is shining, share your joy with God – and then, when an ominous storm starts building up around you, you will not become panic-stricken. You will have the conviction in your heart that God is even then in full control.

Daily prayer is the gymnasium of the soul. (C.E. Cowman)

When I think of the future, O Lord, _____

_____

*U*nanswered prayers

"But if you do not forgive men their trespasses, neither will your Father forgive your trespasses." (Mt. 6:15)

*S*ome people come before God with prayers which they should not be praying until they have first organised their lives to meet the basic requirements of prayer. You cannot just turn a blind eye to sin and ignore its detrimental effects in your life. God also doesn't ignore it! Anything which brings division between you and God, becomes a stumbling block to answered prayer.

God doesn't answer prayers of people who want to negotiate with Him: "Lord, if you grant my prayer, I will serve you for the rest of my life." God doesn't need to negotiate with us if everything in creation belongs to Him.

Meaningful prayer implies a willingness to obey God. Many people try to shift their responsibilities onto God. Perhaps someone wants a relationship to be restored and a prayer is made that God would do it – while all that is really required is to ask forgiveness. True prayer must also bear the mark of willingness to be jointly responsible for the answer to our prayers.

There are so many people who pray, saying, "Our Father" and yet their attitude is in total contrast with the concept of the brotherhood of people being implied in this prayer. If you maintain an attitude of antagonism and racism, you need to rid yourself from your prejudice and self-righteousness through the power of the indwelling Christ, before you can honestly say, "Our Father!" When you pray, make sure that your motives have been purified by the Holy Spirit.

True prayer is a spiritual attitude which creates a channel between the omnipotent God and insignificant man. Only man's sin can block this channel. (George Allen)

I confess that sometimes when I pray, I am not willing to _____

All-inclusive prayer

"For this reason we also, since the day we heard it, do not cease to pray for you, and to ask that you may be filled with the knowledge of his will in all wisdom and spiritual understanding." (Col. 1:9)

Without noticing, one's life can become self-centred. Only your own needs, your family and your friends are stressed. And it is so easy to forget the spiritual needs of others.

Every person has the need to be encouraged and uplifted through prayer. There is no person on the face of the earth who can lead a committed Christian life, except through the grace of God. Nobody is infallible and we are all exposed to temptations. Through our weaknesses we can easily fall prey to Satan, especially when we are dejected, moody, jealous, proud and selfish – to mention only a few.

For the sake of the church of Christ, it is of the utmost importance that we will remember others in our prayers. Pray for those in the ministry and the unique temptations they face; pray for those who are serving in the mission-field; members of church boards; those in special services; organists, vergers and everyone who must see to it that everything runs smoothly in a congregation. Pray for strength and guidance for those in youth-ministries, or who take care of the aged, for social workers and the staff in children's homes. In short, intercede with God for everyone who gives his or her time and strength to the church and who bears great responsibility. Especially pray for Christians the world over that the triumphal procession of Christ may be advanced and that His holy Name may be glorified.

> The man who has learnt to pray, is no longer alone in the universe. He lives in his Father's house. (Anonymous)

Father, today I want to pray for _____

_____

Effective prayer

"Now it came to pass in those days that He went out to the mountain to pray, and continued all night in prayer to God." (Lk. 6:12)

Nobody can grow spiritually without a continually developing prayer life. The Master illustrated to us the importance of long periods of time alone with God. The same requirement is valid for His modern day disciples if they wish to develop into spiritual maturity. Their faith can only be effective if they have a pulsating prayer life.

Man should have an overwhelming desire to pray. This fact is so self-evident that we actually shouldn't feel the need to stress it. Yet, very often prayer is the step-child of spiritual growth instead of being its foundation. Your prayer life can only be effective to the extent that you are utilising it.

Even though prayer is natural and self-evident, it doesn't easily develop into being the most important component of your spiritual life. It requires strict discipline and regular practice. There are times that you realise the importance of prayer, but perhaps are not really in the mood for it at that time. However, don't think your prayers are effective only when you are in the mood to pray. In actual fact it is when you don't feel like praying at all that you should persevere. If your prayer life is impoverished, you are the only person responsible for that.

Make sure that all your prayers are focused on God. Many prayers seem to accentuate the problem, instead of praising God for His ability to deal with it.

If you don't feel like praying, it is a sure indication that you should start immediately. (Billy Graham)

Lord, You who answers prayers, grant in my inner man _____

recious moments

"The Lord is good to those who wait for Him, to the soul who seeks Him. It is good that one should hope and wait quietly for the salvation of the Lord." (Lam. 3:25, 26)

hen we get unbearably busy, we have an urgent need of a moment of quiet so that our mind can just re-establish our values, putting them in the right perspective again. It sounds foolish to speak about peace and quiet when you are at your busiest. No person in his right mind would ever deny that there are times when we are just incredibly busy. A job needs to be done and it just doesn't feel right to withdraw into a place of quietude. Yet, it is equally foolish and delusional to think that you can always do your best without moments of constructive silence with God.

Our Master experienced that here on earth, and so did the Christians of the early church. Would you and I then imply that moments of rejuvenating and regenerating silence are not as necessary today as they were in times gone by?

Make time to meet with God. It doesn't have to be for long periods, but learn to treasure those moments and try to extend them. Those are moments in which you can say, "The Lord is with me and He blesses me and I am conscious of His divine presence." Such a time is an oasis during which your strength is replenished, a time of refreshment and of spiritual growth. It is also a battlefield where the power of Satan is broken.

If you do this conscientiously, you will return to your busy life with a feeling of balance and tranquillity of mind and the powerful assurance that God is always with you and that He grants you His wisdom, love and grace.

If you are too busy to pray, you are too busy indeed. (F.B. Meyer)

Loving Father, thank You for those precious moments when

*P*ray positively

"So Jesus stood still and called them, and said: 'What do you want Me to do for you?'" (Mt. 20:32)

*O*ne must never be vague and unsure when praying. Right through the Gospels we find that Jesus Christ calls people to pray, urging them to believe while they pray. He always accentuates faith. Yet, in spite of that we often find that prayers are made half-heartedly and even in a negative manner. In many cases people request intercession for themselves or others, without being specific about their requests.

Apart from the fact that Jesus was loving and patient, He was also very straightforward. Many instances are given where people were asked to give an explanation of what they specifically wanted Him to do. He would ask them directly if they wanted to be healed, wanted to gain the use of a limb or wanted to see again. And every time they responded to His questions.

Never be afraid to be positive and specific when you come to God in prayer. However, this doesn't mean that you can claim certain things from God, because we don't have the right to claim anything. When you stand before Him in the Name of Christ, you can tell Him exactly what you would like Him to do. At the same time you have to accept obediently that you will only receive that which is within the will of God. When you have done that, you can thank God that He has heard you (see Philippians 4:6) and for the assurance that He will meet all your needs. Then, with peace in your heart, you can wait for His answer, which will be according to His perfect will and timing.

> Nothing is outside the reach of prayer, except that which is outside of God's will. (Oswald Chambers)

O, Holy Spirit, help me to pray prayers that _____

_____

*T*rust when you pray

"Yet you do not have because you do not ask. You ask and do not receive because you ask amiss, that you may spend it on your pleasures." (Jas. 4:2, 3)

*O*ne of the most common laments we hear from churchgoers, is the often-heard complaint, "God doesn't answer my prayers." Some people regard it as a kind of punishment which God doles out for their iniquities. Yet others regard it as the clear proof of the futility of prayer. Regardless of what their attitude may be, the inescapable result is always powerless faith. Consequently prayer becomes relegated to a sheer formality where a flood of meaningless words is poured out repetitively.

In essence, true prayer is a personal experience of the presence of the living Christ. Not in your quiet times only, but right through the whole day. It is the joyous assurance that the Lord keeps his promise and that He lives in you and you in Him (See John 15:4).

The result of this is that prayer is a faith exercise which teaches you that, while you make your needs known to God, you must never imply that you want to know beforehand what His will is. Lay your prayers before Him and then ask Him that He will give to you that which you need according to His wisdom and that you will recognise and accept His answers.

When your faith in Jesus Christ is strong enough to make this commitment to Him, you can rest assured that He will give you what is best for you. Gratefully accept His will and then experience His perfect peace in your heart.

> The greatest problem in prayer is to let go and to let God. (Glenn Clarke)

Lord my God, it is with gratitude and humility that I accept

_____

_____

ractical prayer-practice

"Moreover, as for me, far be it from me that I should sin against the Lord in ceasing to pray for you." (1 Sam. 12:23)

he way in which you pray is of essential importance. It is so easy to retreat into habit: old, familiar phrases come to mind; arbitrarily you start thinking about those whom you intimately share your life with, your family and close circle of friends. Have you ever dared to venture into new prayer fields? In order to allow prayer to achieve its highest objective in your life, you need to become aware of areas that are beyond the restrictions of your own life and which will enhance your experience of true prayer.

If you wish to improve your prayer potential, you will discover that the daily newspapers provide ample opportunity. They reveal to you life as it happens. You can rejoice with those who rejoice and mourn with those who experience sorrow. You can thank God for a deed of self-sacrifice or for someone who managed to overcome his disability. Behind the most gruesome news report you can feel the heartache of innocent victims or, on the other hand, the hard-heartedness of the unrepentant sinner which can only be broken down through constant prayer.

Maintain a sensitive spirit while reading your daily newspaper. The Holy Spirit will spur you on to prayer. He will guide you as to how you should pray. Thus your newspaper can become a prayer manual and your prayer life an instrument in the hand of God to extend His saving grace in this sin-torn world. You could become a channel through which the grace and love of God can reach a sick world.

Let us not disappoint one another in our interest and care and practical help for one another. But most of all, let us not disappoint one another in intercession. (Michael Boughen)

O, Prayer-answering God, I pray for a prayer life that _____

Prayer leads to action

"What is the conclusion then? I will pray with the spirit, and I will also pray with the understanding." (1 Cor. 14:15)

At times we beg God to answer our prayers while we need to take action ourselves. There are many instances when, instead of pleading with God to supply a special need, we ourselves should be busy meeting that need. If you are lonely and constantly asking God for a meaningful friendship, you need to start by offering your friendship. Do you perhaps mismanage your finances to the extent that you constantly have to ask God to save you from debt – and yet you refuse to control your buying lust or draw up an achievable budget?

Every answer to prayer is a balanced approach to life. You will still have your problems, but if you handle them in a spirit of prayer, you will develop inspired common sense. If you are filled with the Holy Spirit and the attitude of Jesus Christ, He will give you guidance in your confusion and you will have the ability to act in accordance with His will and purpose for your life. He gives you the inspiration and the strength to achieve the seemingly impossible.

Prayer does not only imply a constant knocking at God's door for help. It implies cooperating with Him in the answering of your prayers and the development of your inherent potential. Prayer is that force which enables Christ's followers to tackle life with courage. It gives you the assurance that God's guidance and wisdom are always available for those who receive them with a sensitive heart and an open mind.

> Prayer, like radium, is a glowing, self-activating form of energy. (Alexis Carrel)

Living Saviour, I thank and praise You that I _____

_____

Prayer and Praise

"Is any one among you suffering? Let him pray. Is anyone cheerful? Let him sing psalms." (Jas. 5:13)

When a need arises in your life, you go to someone for help. You may require the service of an expert and qualified person. On the other hand you may go to a trusted friend for help or advice. Whatever action you may take, you go to that person in faith and with the expectation that he will be able to help you. Regardless of the outcome, you are always grateful towards your helper for the assistance he has given you. Of course you express your gratitude to him and most probably you will speak about him with great praise.

When you are experiencing a crisis in your life, you must never, in your confusion and anxiety, forget to take your problem to Jesus. He offers you His friendship and invites you to come to Him when you are tired and heavy-laden. Always seek Christ's comfort, advice and protection. He cares for you and understands your needs. Lay your problems before Him in serious prayer and supplication and you will experience the peace of God in your heart – that peace which always becomes the portion of those who put their trust in God unconditionally.

But don't just leave the matter at that. As the knowledge grows in you that Christ is now in control, you have to thank God for the blessed assurance that He cares for you and that His hand will guide you through the maze of problems in your life. Thus, while you are singing His praises, He leads you from the darkness into His marvellous light and love.

> Prayer crowns God with the honour and glory that He deserves and God crowns prayer with assurance and comfort. Those who pray most, have the most assurance. (Thomas Brooks)

I want to praise You because _____

_____

Prayer in your closet

"Therefore we also pray for you that our God would count you worthy of this calling." (2 Thes. 1:11)

Praying in private is a very special source of spiritual strength. Without that, nothing which is worthwhile is ever achieved. Through His teachings and example Jesus stressed the importance of personal fellowship with God. It is only when you experience His presence in seclusion that you can realise the great value of prayer.

However, prayer can be personalised to the extent that it becomes an indication of selfishness, "Lord, bless me and mine." "If You do this for me, I will do that for You." These and similar self-centred requests are in danger of making prayer nothing but a mockery.

To love, worship and appreciate God in private, is an enriching experience. However, while you are doing that, you become deeply aware of the world outside your inner chamber. There exists a desire for spirituality which can only be obtained through the ministry of persevering, believing prayer. The one who prays has a responsibility not only towards God and himself, but also towards the world.

Through prayer you become aware of the needs of people around you and you are compelled to lay those needs before God in prayer. There are times when you come before God, just you alone, but there are also times when you have to intercede for others. This ministry of intercession, or intercessory prayer, weighed very heavily on the heart of the Master. He practised it while He was on earth. Dare you and I then do less?

> If your prayer is selfish, the answer will be such, that your selfishness is reprimanded by it. (William Temple)

Dear Master, today I want to intercede for _____

_____

Prayer is boundless

"At Gibeon the Lord appeared to Solomon in a dream by night; and God said: 'Ask! What shall I give you?'" (1 Kgs. 3:5)

Many people get very irritated with verbose people who come with requests in a long-winded, round-about way. They obscure the real issue and get swallowed up in a flood of words instead of making a straightforward request. In the process they lose sight of their deepest need and also cause confusion and alarm in the person at whom the request is directed, because it is asked so awkwardly and with such verbosity.

A similar situation can arise in your prayer life. How often are you really totally open and clear about your needs when you come before God? A study of the Psalms and prayers of the prayer-warriors in the Old Testament clearly demonstrates the fact that they were completely open and honest whenever they spoke with the Lord. They did not hide or hold back anything. Their confessions were complete and revealing, their requests for forgiveness were real and humble.

Jesus Christ invites you to ask for that which you need, but if you don't make use of His gracious offer, you should not be surprised if it seems as if you don't receive an answer.

When laying your prayers before the Lord, don't be afraid of being specific, without however, demanding anything from the Master. Offer your prayers to Him in faith and accept His divine will for your life. Ask for the gifts of wisdom and discernment in order that you may recognise and accept His answers – and wait upon the Lord patiently.

> Prayer is not merely a temporary impulse when we experience problems: prayer is a way of life. (Walter A. Meuller)

I want to be completely open when I speak to You about _____

Pray when things go wrong

"I was sought by those who did not ask for Me. I was found by those who did not seek Me." (Is. 65:1)

There are always those who question God's existence when things go wrong. In the midst of chaos or personal disaster they cry out loudly, "If there is a God, how can He allow these things?" The brutality of war or the death of an innocent child is used as ground for an argument to deny the love of God. Often God is accused as the cause of the tragedy, or the love of God is denied, while cynical sceptics rejoice in the situation. It seems as if they find great satisfaction in using their distorted arguments to drive people even further away from God's merciful love. God's promises always were, still are and will always be that, if His children turn to Him in their need, He will hear them and respond to their call of distress. Jesus said, *" ... one who comes to Me I will by no means cast out"* (John 6:37).

Regardless of what your need or anxiety may be, regardless of how hopeless or desperate your situation may seem, turn to God in prayer and accept with praise and thanksgiving the help and deliverance which He offers you time and time again.

All of us have to deal with seemingly unsolvable problems. If we are faithful prayers, God will know and understand our need. Then we can go to Him boldly. It's not a matter of pressing a panic-button, but a continuing prayer programme which only increases in intensity in times of need.

Speak openly with God in prayer about your needs, your problems, even your fatigue in His service. You can never speak to Him too boldly or too openly. (Francois Fenelon)

I am tired and heavy-laden and I turn to You for _____

ℐt's never too late to pray

"He shall regard the prayer of the destitute, and shall not despise their prayer." (Ps. 102:18)

ℳany people rob themselves of experiencing peace with God because they feel they are unworthy. When they are in great need, they don't want to draw close to God because they have not spent much time with God in the past. Now they feel it is not appropriate to come to Him while experiencing a crisis.

Yet others are over-burdened with feelings of guilt or shame. They feel they may not address God. Whatever the reason behind their reasoning may be, they rob themselves of experiencing the peace of God which passes all understanding and which could fulfil the deepest need a human may have.

Jesus Christ promised that He will not cast out anyone who comes to Him. Categorically He declared that He did not come to seek those who are righteous, but to call sinners to repentance. Right through Scripture you will read about God's unfathomable love and compassion towards all people – the good and the bad; those who deserved it and those who didn't.

It is never too late for you to turn to the Christ who forgives, and to pour out your needs before Him. The murderer on the cross did just that in his dying moments and he received redemption. Christ will hear your cry of despair and will surround you with His love. Reach out to Him and expose your heart. Don't rob yourself of His peace and His blessing. The One who hears and answers prayer is available to you at any time and in any place, if you would only lift your voice to Him in prayer.

> If life pushed you off your feet, it's time to get on your knees. (Frederick Beck)

Holy God, I sincerely thank You, that with You, it's never too late to _____

_____

To be able to talk to God

"Righteous are You, O Lord, when I plead with You." (Jer. 12:1)

There are people who believe that prayer is nothing except their deepest desires which can never be fulfilled in their own strength, but that something supernatural could happen if they would only express it in the form of a prayer.

Unfortunately prayer can degenerate into little more than the spiritual counterpart of the psychologist's couch. There you can unburden yourself of all your problems, freely express your fears and talk about your doubts concerning the future. You will note that this kind of prayer is mainly self-centred and it seldom leads to the spiritual maturity where God becomes a glorious reality. If your prayers are self-centred, you are actually talking to yourself. Then you should not expect God to act, because you are hindering Him through your selfishness and self-interest.

When, through the power of the Holy Spirit, you focus your life on Christ, your prayers are rid of all self-centredness. When you speak to the Lord then, you are not merely expressing your own desires and generalities to and about yourself, but you are involved in vibrant, inspiring fellowship with the Lord.

When you rise above yourself, your shortcomings, your immaturity and your restricted spiritual view, you begin to understand and appreciate the magnitude of the Almighty. By speaking to Him in humility and by listening to the prompting of the Holy Spirit, your prayer life becomes powerful, meaningful and alive.

> Wishful thinking is not prayer. Prayer is a definite act of the human mind – an act whereby the human spirit reaches out to God through Jesus Christ. (William Taggart)

Jesus, I want to place You in the centre of my mind so that _____

_____

_____

Make your prayer life effective

"Continue earnestly in prayer, being vigilant in it with thanksgiving; meanwhile praying also for us." (Col. 4:2, 3)

The majority of people experience prayer as something of a drudgery. As a result, their prayer life is without power and colour – a repetition of hackneyed phrases. They pray to God only because they badly want something very special, or because their prayers originate from a habit of many years.

True prayer is an exciting adventure in your spiritual life and growth. It must never be taken lightly or allowed to stagnate. It is an experience that you share with God Almighty through Jesus Christ. Therefore, it should never become a flood of meaningless words.

God never gets tired of listening to your prayers. Therefore, your first priority must be to build your life around Him. Develop the very good habit of tuning your mind and emotions in to Him so that, when you fulfil your daily tasks, you are conscious of His divine presence all the time.

After praying to God and speaking with Him, it is of the utmost importance to discipline yourself in such a way that you will be receptive to the prompting of the Holy Spirit. In this way you will be guided to find His answers to your prayers, as He will reveal them to you in His own wonderful way.

The main factor, however, is that you should show your gratitude towards God. Never take for granted that He promised to answer your prayers. At all times thank God for the assurance that, in His wisdom and grace, through the living Christ, He will meet all your needs. Soli Deo Gloria – to God alone be all the glory!

> Worship rejuvenates the spirit as sleep refreshes the body. (Richard Cabot)

I want to bring honour and glory to You for _____

_____

⟲he challenge of Christianity

"Always in every prayer of mine making request for you all with joy."
(Phil. 1:4)

⟲eople react to your personality and the attitude you have towards life. You cannot live in a society without people reacting to who and to what you are. You may have hurt feelings because someone doesn't like you and you reacted antagonistically.

What you need to realise is that fundamentally, people accept you for what you are. The way they feel about you is therefore your responsibility. If you don't like people, you must not be surprised if they in turn, don't like you. If you hate people, you can never live constructively. After all, you are responsible for what people think of you.

The practical foundation of Christ's teachings becomes clearer when you realise this truth. He taught that love is always stronger than hate, that eventually love will triumph over all negative and evil forces. Jesus did not simply utter pious phrases that are remote from practical reality when He commanded us in Matthew 5:44, saying, *"love your enemies, bless those who curse you, and pray for those who spitefully use you and persecute you."*

When you start loving people and praying for them, a transformation occurs in human relations. Gradually your enemies will become friends. It is difficult to be antagonistic towards someone who loves you and prays for you. This is one of the biggest challenges of Christianity.

> If we love one another, God abides in us, and His love has been perfected in us. (John, Apostle of love, in 1 John 4:12)

Lord and Guide, grant me the courage to _____

_____

The burning bramble bush

"Take your sandals off your feet, for the place where you stand is holy ground." (Ex. 3:5)

Moses was tending the sheep of Jethro, his father-in-law, in the wilderness. It must have been a dry and arid scene and probably Moses himself was tired and exhausted. In this situation God revealed Himself to Moses in a wonderful way. Moses saw a burning bush that was not consumed by the fire and he went closer to look at the miracle. Then he received the command from God to take off his shoes because the place where he was standing was holy ground.

It is very unlikely that Moses had expected a revelation from God. Everything looked so commonplace, but the fact that God spoke to him made everything extraordinary.

Your life may seem boring and dull. The days just succeed each other, with no excitement at all. Perhaps you have already doubted for a long time that God wants to meet you in your everyday situation. The sad result is that the consciousness of God's presence has vanished from your life. You are no longer sensitive to His voice, you no longer see the beauty of nature, you no longer experience His conversing with you through a trusted friend, and you no longer enjoy moments of fellowship with your Creator. Yet, it is when everything seems so commonplace and dull, that God can reveal Himself to you.

The place where you are right now is holy ground if you would only acknowledge the presence of the living Christ. Stop what you are busy with for a moment and ask Him if there is something He wants to say to you. The result could surprise you!

> Prayer is the road signs through the wilderness to guide the pilgrim to the one, single great Light. (Douglas Meador)

Holy Father, help me to be conscious of the fact that every place

THE FOUNTAIN

OF GOD'S GRACE

In my own strength I'm unable to stand for but a single hour, without drawing fresh supplies of strength and grace from the Source of life. (John Newton)

Holy God, and in Jesus Christ, my heavenly Father, the grace You bestow upon me is amazingly great; a grace that accepted me, a sinner, and made me Your child and a member of the heavenly kingdom; a grace that sustains and nurtures me day by day and keeps my feet on Your path daily; a grace that will eventually lead me to the eternal heavenly home.

I rejoice in Your abundant grace which is new in my life every morning.

I sing Your praises to thank You for Your grace, because You always keep me from all evil and want to lift me from the dust.

Nothing of my own, it's all Your grace; I see Your goodness all around me, faithful Father, Your praise will continually be in my mouth.

(Adapted from Hymn 11:4, 5)

Grace – rich and free!

"The grace of our Lord Jesus Christ be with you all." (2 Thes. 3:18)

Where would you and I have been or how would we have handled the problems of life if it were not for the grace of God – especially in these ominous times that we are living in?

One of our best-loved songs speaks of "amazing grace". It tells about a "prodigal son – a run-away – who came back into the Father's house". John Newton, the writer of the song, says that he was spiritually blind and lost, but the grace of God touched and healed him. This song speaks of a redeeming God whose love is so great that He gave His all through grace.

And while you meditate on Christ's sacrifice, you are confronted with the highest deed of compassion and love that this world has ever experienced – that the Son of God took your guilt and mine upon Himself and sacrificed His life in order to redeem us from sin.

But His grace extends further than that. Man is untrustworthy and forgetful and therefore he turns away from God. Yet Christ waits patiently and lovingly for us to turn back to Him. This happens quite often when we encounter problems in our lives. But, through His boundless love He guides us back to the road which He has chosen for us – the road of obedience and love.

There is but one way in which you can express your gratitude for His boundless love, and that is by sharing Christ's love with others; by expressing to others the same grace and mercy that Jesus has bestowed upon me.

> The gospel doesn't consist of advice about what we can do for ourselves, but about what God is ready to do for us through grace. (James Beattie)

Your grace has _____ *me* _____

_____

*S*ufficient grace for you

"You therefore, my son, be strong in the grace that is in Christ Jesus."
(2 Tim. 2:1)

*M*any people are just not able to work through the set-backs that they experience. When a serious problem occurs, they collapse in a heap or snap. When they experience a personal crisis, they try to flee from the reality thereof. Fear has a devastating effect upon them. Anxiety and concern rob them of all peace and upset their equilibrium. This happens because people try to handle and solve life's problems in their own strength.

Scripture contains Christ's invitation to those who are tired and heavy-laden, to bring their problems to Him so that they may find rest for their souls. His Word also extends an invitation to you to bring your anxious cares to Him, because He cares for you. Right through the Bible you are called upon to turn to God in Christ so that in His omnipotence He can enable you to handle your problems with confidence and in a balanced manner. This is only obtained through Godly support.

Regardless of what your circumstances in life may be, regardless of how anxious you may be about seemingly insoluble problems, don't run away from them in panic and despair, but contend with them with Christ at your side. Receive your strength and confidence from Him. Regardless of how alarming the problem may seem, know for sure that God's omnipotence will be revealed in your weakness. Under all circumstances His grace will be sufficient to you so that you can deal with your problems in a new, confident manner.

No matter what man does to experience divine grace, the influence of God's grace is only due to the working of the Holy Spirit who draws us to God. (August Lang)

Father, I ask You for strength to _____

Chosen by God

"You did not choose Me, but I chose you." (Jn. 15:16)

For many people the conscious beginning of their Christianity dates back to when they acknowledged the sovereignty of Christ in their lives. In reality their Christian experience started when the Holy Spirit started working in their imperfect lives. Perhaps they were antagonistic towards Christianity at that point in time but they were inexplicably restless and nothing could give them the satisfaction that they yearned for.

The revelation of God's voice calling you – the fact that He chose you to serve Him – is usually accompanied by inner conflict and confusion. It is because you are not immediately willing to give what God is asking of you. Once you have committed yourself to God, such an inner struggle can be the beginning of a glorious spiritual ministry – as you open your life to the inflowing of the Holy Spirit.

You were chosen by God to serve Him and to live to the honour and glory of His Name. It may not sound very exciting to you and initially it may not really satisfy you. Those people, however, who submitted themselves unconditionally to the Lord when they heard Him calling, discovered that their lives gained new meaning and purpose. To be chosen by God for His service: what greater measure of grace could be shown to an insignificant human being?

> Just as the earth can produce nothing without the nurturing rays of the sun, so we can do nothing without the grace of God. (Vianney)

Lord and Master, You called me by grace. Therefore, please grant me _____

_____

To grow in grace

"You must be born again." (Jn. 3:7)

Spiritual rebirth is a scriptural truth and a necessary experience well-known to those who accepted Jesus Christ as
their Lord and Master. Many "new-born" Christians, however, don't
understand and appreciate the fact that people can go through
this wonderful and enriching experience in different ways.

Many experienced it during a revival service in which the Holy
Spirit worked in a mighty way. Yet others go through this experience
in the silence of their inner chamber. The living Christ is not bound
to work according to stereotyped methods. When a searching soul
yearns for God, He will meet that person regardless of where he
may be. The important fact here is not the method which is being
employed, but the fact that you are reborn spiritually and that you
know Christ as your Saviour.

In the spiritual life you need to grow in knowledge and in grace.
While you grow in the spirit and attitude of Christ, you can perhaps
look back to a time and place when this wonderful new life started.
However, you must never try to stay at that place and time. You
must grow in the grace and knowledge of the living Christ. If you
fail to do that, you will degenerate spiritually.

Growing spiritually is equally important to experiencing a new
spiritual birth. May both be your rich inheritance through the
overflowing grace of God.

> The earthly life is an apprenticeship. From this point of departure we
> must grow constantly and increase in the grace of God. (Robert
> Browning)

Lord, my God, I want to grow in knowledge and in grace so that

_____

_____

God speaks out of the whirlwind

"Then the Lord answered Job out of the whirlwind." (Job 40:6)

God utilises various methods to make His will known to us or to incite us to spiritual growth. And they are all part of His divine grace. Much stress is laid upon the fact that God can be known in silence. It is sheer grace that we can spend time with God in silence and experience His peace; to experience how the pressures of life ebb away and to see your priorities in their right perspective again. In the silence you experience God's guidance and a continuously increasing awareness of God's love.

If you are leading a life of pressure and tension, you will find comfort in the fact that God spoke to Job out of a whirlwind. In the hurly-burly of modern life where there is hardly any time between one project and the next, it is futile to suppose that God can reveal His will to you in the rush. Yet, He is the God of roaring activity as well as of consecrated silence.

God is willing to guide you in the midst of the whirlwind of life if you will only live in obedience and submission to His divine will. You can be conscious of His living presence at all times ... it is part and parcel of His endless grace to you. He is present in all circumstances to listen and to help. Feverish activity is no barrier to Him. If only you would turn to Him you will find that He is already waiting. Then the flurry of your life becomes positive and constructive and by His grace you are enabled to do everything to his honour and glory.

> If we could unify our actions and our religion, God will bless both through His grace. (H.G.J. Adam)

Help me, loving Master, that my activities _____

_____

A gracious sign post

"Who is the man that fears the Lord? Him shall He teach in the way He chooses. He himself shall dwell in prosperity." (Ps. 25:12, 13)

Our earthly lives can become extremely complicated. Especially in these sophisticated modern times where so many people find themselves caught up in a maze and they cannot see a clear way out. They are forced to make hasty decisions which influence them and their dear ones. Great multitudes of people simply cannot handle such situations and they are tossed hither and thither like driftwood across the sea of life. Their lives are controlled by the storms, the tides and the winds and, to their great relief, sometimes the calm.

Your life follows this pattern only if you allow it to. God is willing to accompany you along the way which He has ordained for you, if only you would be willing to follow Him obediently. Initially it may seem as if the things that happen to you are not in your best interest, but when you consider the end result, you will realise that God's way is the best for you under all circumstances.

Lay every decision that you have to make, whether big or small, before Jesus Christ in prayer. I'm not suggesting that you must dedicate your life to some mystical figure in order that he may solve your problems. It involves sharing your life with the living Christ in the sure knowledge that He, the Son of the omniscient God, will guide you along a safe path – a path along which He has already walked and which He will point out to you through grace. The alternative is too appalling even to consider.

> There is but one road to peace of mind and true happiness and that is to submit your life to God's guidance. (Epictetus)

I praise You, Guide, that I can follow You knowing that _____

Above every name!

"By those who come near Me I must be regarded as holy; And before all the people I must be glorified'." (Lev. 10:3)

It is an incalculable gift of grace from God that we may worship Him. Lately many people imply that they have come to such a new unity with the living Christ, handling their relationship with the Master with so much familiarity that the traditional believers stand in awe of their jovial relationship with God.

Expressions such as "the Boss" or "the Man upstairs" when referring to God, or "the Jesus Book" with reference to the Bible, cause many Christians to feel upset or uneasy because of the seeming lack of respect or formality which we are used to when we worship God.

As a disciple of the Lord Jesus Christ, your relationship with the Master is something personal and intimate and it is a relationship which exists exclusively between you and your Lord. Bearing that in mind, we must always remember that the same applies to other Christian pilgrims, even though their relationship with and attitude towards God differs drastically from yours.

However, what is of crucial importance in your relationship with God, is to ensure that, even in these modern and enlightened times, your attitude towards Him is always one of respect, love and worship, that you continually praise and thank Him for His grace, and that you will never allow your familiarity with Him to trivialise your worship. That would be a serious abuse of His great grace.

> Worship is the act through which we rise to a new consciousness of the presence of God which floods our soul with joy and wonder. (Rufus Matthew Jones)

Holy Spirit of God, please keep me from _____

Do you belong to God?

"... for you have found grace in my sight, and I know you by name."
(Ex. 33:17)

Apart from the fact that the Bible is the revealed will of God, it is also a report of the lives of very interesting personalities. Some of them were faithful servants, some rebelled against God and worked against Him, some disappointed Him very badly, but God knew them all by name. You have a heavenly Father who delights Himself in mankind. In modern society it may seem as if people's names are less important than numbers, but to God you are a one-of-a-kind, unique creation and He regards you as so important that you may be called His child.

If you are the kind of person who lives an extremely lonely life because you look upon yourself as inferior and unimportant, you have probably forgotten that your heavenly Father knows about you and loves you dearly. Perhaps you allowed your self-imposed loneliness to cause you to forget this glorious fact.

The fact that God knows you by name, causes you to feel that you have some worth. This can be cultivated through prayer and spending time with Him. This fellowship is accompanied by a deep sense of responsibility, because it is the epitome of the challenge of Jesus Christ. In your relationship with Him, the Master no longer speaks to the masses, but to you personally. He teaches you about love, righteousness, honesty, unselfishness and other wise ways about how to live your life. This is never done in general terms, but is directed at you personally.

The fact that He knows you personally by name, is sheer grace. You can only enjoy the benefit of this relationship if you have accepted Him as your Redeemer and Saviour.

> We are saved through grace, by someone who does for us what we cannot do for ourselves. (Donald Lester)

Father, I thank You for the assurance that _____

*F*ullness of life!

"I have come that they may have life, and that they may have it more abundantly." (Jn. 10:10)

*L*ife is what you make of it. You can choose to be happy or miserable. By meticulously setting objectives, you may obtain success, while a don't-care attitude regarding the future can lead to complete failure. The quality of your life depends on your own attitude and the way in which you approach and plan life.

This may sound like an ultra-simplification of a complex situation and you may question your own ability to handle life. If that is your position, it is important that you look at your faith in the light of God's Word. In His holy Scripture you will find numerous examples of people whose lives used to be useless and empty, but were transformed into inspired disciples. The prerequisite is that Jesus be allowed to reign in your life.

Christ specifically came that you may have life in abundance. Don't allow this offer to pass you by unused. Turn to Christ and walk your life's path in the company of the living Christ. Like Paul and many others you will become a new creature in Christ. You will discover a new self-confidence and develop abilities which can only be received from the Holy Spirit.

It is unnecessary that you should experience failure and loneliness in life. Christ is there for you to submit yourself to Him and to walk in obedience along the path which He has indicated to you. This is also "amazing grace"!

The glorious gospel of the grace of God is the amazing inheritance of the church and the imperative ministry to a lost world. (William E. Gilroy)

Holy Spirit of God, I plead that You _____

_____

ℐo accept God

"For by grace you have been saved through faith, and that not of yourselves; it is the gift of God." (Eph. 2:8)

It is strange that the simplicity of the gospel is a stumbling block for many who want to accept it. They never gain an insight into the grace of God. They get involved in good works, but in some or other way the assurance of the existence of God's grace always eludes them. After years of great effort they eventually give up with a feeling of deep disappointment.

God gives Himself as a gift to all who want to accept Him! All we have to do is to allow Him entrance into our lives. This divine gift of grace is not to be bought, to be begged for or to be borrowed. It is a heavenly gift which I can only accept in faith. It simply means to say with sincerity, "Lord, I open up my life to You," and then to believe that He will respond by surrounding you with His forgiveness and love.

Such an acceptance may or not be accompanied by a clear emotional experience. The important fact is that you have opened your life for Christ. As you reconfirm your dedication to Him daily, you develop a real consciousness of His presence.

When you have accepted God in faith, you should try to live like Christ. Then you become stronger spiritually, you become sensitive to the guidance of the Holy Spirit, your human relations improve. But most important of all, God becomes a reality to you and every day you see His grace revealed in your life.

> Three things are required for man's redemption: to know what he must believe; to know what he should desire; and to know what he should do. (Thomas Aquinas)

Lord, I open up my life to You _____

_____

God's triumphant march!

"Now thanks be to God who always leads us in triumph in Christ."
(2 Cor. 2:14)

In contrast to what some of Christ's disciples suggest, the Christian life can have its moments of depression and defeat. Such times can have devastating results if a follower of Christ allows them to cloud his spiritual view. When the songs of praise have stopped and the consciousness of Christ's presence has waned, you reach a point where faith and spiritual experiences can no longer inspire you.

Regardless of how dark and difficult the present moment may be, keep your eyes focused on Jesus Christ and always remember that in His power, you will overcome your weakness and victory will eventually be yours too. Remember that Christ is sufficient for you. Therefore you should not depend on your feelings or emotions, but on the faith that you have in His ability to hold on to you. Then you become victorious in spite of your emotions.

Be grateful that your faith doesn't depend on how you feel. It depends on what you believe about Jesus Christ. If you believe that He is what He says He is – the Son of God, that He lives today and that your future is in His omnipotent hands – then you can share in the grace of His victory. You have already overcome the powers that want to oppress and defeat you. Lift up your heart and remember whom you belong to and live triumphantly in His strength.

Thus, by the grace of God you become a companion of Christ in God's triumph through the ages.

Christ is the key to the history of the world. Everything not only harmonises with His triumph, but is also subjected to it. (Johannes van Müller)

Thank You that my discipleship doesn't depend on my emotions, but on _____

_____

Christ's way

"Good and upright is the Lord; therefore He teaches sinners in the way." (Ps. 25:8)

There are people who abandoned their Christian pilgrimage because they felt unworthy of it. How often we meet those who imply that the road is too steep and too difficult and therefore they deny their faith or let go of it? How many people get confused or disillusioned in their spiritual life and it seems as if they had lost their way? As a result, they wandered far from the road which Christ set before them.

Never lose sight of the fact that God loves you. His love is so unfathomable that in the birth, suffering and death of His Son, He assures you of forgiveness and redemption. Jesus, who was without sin, took our sins upon Himself to redeem and sanctify us. He willingly went to the cross and gave His life in exchange for your deliverance from the yoke of Satan. Such is the magnitude of His grace and love!

If God then was willing to pay such a great price for your salvation, it follows logically that He loves you tremendously. You are very precious to Him and He only wants what is best for you. Therefore the living Christ is always there to guide you through the dark passages of life on the paths of righteousness.

While you follow Jesus Christ's way, you will find peace and consolation. Your spiritual life will grow and the Holy Spirit will grant you the fulfilment of your deepest desires. There is no other way of finding this life – and it is part of God's endless grace to you personally.

> From the cradle to the grave man's greatest objective is to obtain peace of mind and spiritual security. This is only to be found in Jesus Christ. (Mark Twain)

Guide me along your way so that I _____

℘rayer is the key

"Attaining to all riches of the full assurance of understanding, to the knowledge of the mystery of God, both of the Father and of Christ, in whom are hidden all the treasures of wisdom and knowledge." (Col. 2:2, 3)

There are many Christians who are ignorant with regard to God's boundless grace. Their need or their poverty blinds them to the One who could supply their need if they would only trust Him.

Time and again Scripture reiterates that God is more willing to give than we are to receive. We are constantly reminded that if we pray and believe, we will receive that which we pray for. Prayer is the key which unlocks the treasure chambers of God. Many of the Master's disciples believe this but few actually use the key and enjoy the abundance of God's grace.

His believing children know that God can do anything that we ask, but many of them also see their self-erected barriers which obstruct His answers. When you bring a petition before God, don't at the same time start thinking how impossible it is that God will answer your prayer because there are so many obstacles in the way. Such an attitude births doubt and prayers cannot be answered where faith has been substituted by doubt.

How God is going to answer your prayers is neither your responsibility nor your concern. A simple, child-like faith which looks to God and believes unconditionally that He does answer prayer is the kind of prayer that God wants to answer with joy. Your prayer life is also part of God's unfathomable grace and if you use it in faith, God will give to you far beyond what you could think or pray for.

> Prayer moves the hand that moves the world. (John Aikman)

I thank You for the key of prayer with which _____

_____

Grace and peace to be found only with God

"I lay down and slept; I awoke, for the Lord sustained me." (Ps. 3:5)

Insecurity leads to uneasiness and confusion. If you are insecure about your future, if you are not sure at all about the next move of your competitor in the business world, if you are all alone in the dark of night, imagining that you've heard footsteps: all these experiences lead to the uneasy combination of anxiety, concern and confusion. Foremost in your mind is the importance of preparation and self-defence. How do you prepare yourself to handle any situation that could arise, in order that you may be relatively sure of a peaceful and safe life?

Right through history it is apparent that those people who had an intimate walk with God, were exactly those who found hidden resources of power to overcome their set-backs. Those who have an unflinching faith in the living Christ, will not waver or break under attacks. Those who put their trust in the all-surrounding love of Christ, will not give in to the icy touch of fear.

There is no magical power in these statements. The same Christ who hushed the wind and stilled the storm at sea when the disciples were panic-stricken, is calling out to you today, "Be strong and courageous; do not be afraid!" Put your trust in Him and experience for yourself how His love and grace cause the storms in your life to subside.

> With peace in his soul, man can handle the most appalling experiences. Without this peace he cannot even complete such a simple task as writing a letter. (Oliver Cromwell)

O Lord, I'm so insecure about _____

_____

Instruments of God's grace

"I will make a covenant of peace with them, and cause wild beasts to cease from the land; and they will dwell safely in the wilderness and sleep in the woods." (Ezek. 34:25)

Nowadays we often hear the prayer, "Lord, grant us peace, and start with me." In the midst of violence, anarchy and lawlessness which manifest almost world-wide, many wonder how serious and effective we are as peacemakers.

The Lord is a God of love who cares for His people, who protects His creation, and who came in the person of Christ Jesus to live amongst us as the Prince of Peace. Everything concerning Jesus speaks of love, peace and grace – even His terrible death on the cross. His mission was to bring peace into the world and to teach people the real meaning of love and grace.

The situation is no different today, because God still yearns for peace to reign on earth so that all people can live in harmony. The covenant which He made in the time of Ezekiel is just as valid today as it was then. The responsibility to implement this covenant rests on God's children.

There is an urgent need that all people should set aside their petty, personal preferences and act only within the will of God. Only then, through His grace, will this world know real peace.

Only if, in obedience to Christ's command, we spread the gospel, will we be able to fulfil the task assigned to us. And we can only do this if we walk intimately with Christ. Then we become instruments of His love and grace.

> Man cannot inspire his own soul with grace; just as a candle cannot light itself. (John Bunyan)

I so badly want to be one of Your instruments, because only then can I _____

_____

The gracious gift of prayer

"Continue earnestly in prayer, being vigilant in it with thanksgiving."
(Col. 4:2)

What value do you give to prayer? Do you regard it as a very special gift of grace from God, or as an almost unbearable burden? When some people move into the presence of God in prayer, they experience the sentiment of the hymn writer when he spoke of being "lost in wonder, love and praise". The sad thing, however, is that the great majority of people regard prayer as an unpleasant task which needs to be done. Therefore they pretend to pray, but all they are doing in actual fact is repeating well-known phrases like a recitation.

The privilege of prayer is a very special gift of grace from God. It is God's personal invitation to you to enter into His sanctuary and to talk to Him and listen when He has something to say to you. How grateful we are when someone in a position of authority manages to take off a few minutes to listen to us! Are you grateful towards the living Christ for the fact that He wants to speak with you and listen to you?

Prayer is a discipline which is more than worthwhile. However, it requires preparation and practice. Make time to become quiet in the presence of God. Focus your attention on Jesus. Make time to listen to God as well as speak to Him, thanking Him always for the gracious gift of drawing strength from the Source. That will enable you to live your life in an atmosphere of peace and trust. Neesima, the Eastern Christian author, said, "Let us go forward on our knees!"

> Prayer is not verbosity, but sincerity; it is not a definition of helplessness but a search for power; not a manner of speaking, but the zeal of the soul. (Hannah More)

Thank You for the privilege to _____ in prayer.

You are God's child!

"Behold what manner of love the Father has bestowed on us that we should be called children of God!" (1 Jn. 3:1)

When the truth of this Scripture becomes a personal experience in your life, a transformation occurs which brings meaning and glory into your daily life.

Perhaps you are feeling totally alone and lonely at this moment. You approach the future without any self-confidence and you make decisions about which you are completely unsure. Your salvation through Jesus Christ needs to transform this negative attitude into a positive approach to life. Because, by grace, you now call God your Father, and because you love and obey Him, it is your responsibility to make your life what God intended it to be. He requires of you total commitment so that His glory may be reflected in your life.

If the Lord's will is revealed through your life, a very intimate and strong bond will develop between you and Him. You will have the glorious assurance that He is really your Father and that you are irrevocably His child. This intimate relationship makes it so much easier to be obedient to the Father. The closer you live to Him, the more sensitive you become with regard to what He expects from you.

Therefore, live to strengthen these close ties with your heavenly Father. Do this through commitment and obedience. Thus the grace of God is established in your life every day, to His glory and honour and to your immeasurable benefit and joy.

> Nobody can teach you to be a Christian – it is in-service training of the highest quality. (Frank A. Clarke)

Thank You, Lord Jesus, for the joy of _____

The Christian's utmost desire

*" ... that I may know Him and the power of his resurrection and the
fellowship of his sufferings, being conformed to his death." (Phil. 3:10)*

All Christians experience some or other deep desire and the quality of that desire determines the strength or weakness of their spiritual life. If inferior influences have top priority in their lives, it is only a matter of time before their lives will wane and lose all purpose, goal and meaning.

It is important that true Christians should have pure desires to motivate them on their spiritual pilgrimage. The highest of all desires is "to know Christ and experience the power of His resurrection". When such a sanctified desire takes hold of man, all other surrounding perspectives fall into their rightful places. Without the urgent desire to know Christ more intimately, the spiritual life loses its motivational power.

"To know Christ" is much more than an emotional experience. It is an act of faith which opens up your mind to the influence and working of His divine mind. It enables you to walk in His steps. Knowing Christ so intimately, makes it impossible for someone with that knowledge not to reveal it in his everyday life.

Such a high standard of living would have been unattainable, if those who knew Christ didn't experience the power of His resurrection. It is that power exactly which enables them to live according to His will. And it is also just part of the unspeakable grace of the highest Majesty.

Our Lord wrote the promise of the resurrection not in books only, but in every leaf which opens up at springtime. (Martin Luther)

My deepest desire, O Lord, is to _____

Jesus provides spiritual wealth

"And you are complete in Him, who is the head of all principality and power." (Col. 2:10)

Right through the ages man has had the urge to gather belongings. He wants to provide for his life today and for the future. Such an attitude is praiseworthy and should be encouraged as a sign of maturity.

The danger doesn't lie in the gathering of possessions, but in the obsession to do it. When assets and luxuries become overwhelmingly important in your life, you fall prey to the destructive side-effects of covetousness and desire. Your efforts to live a life that is only to your own benefit, will mean that eventually you have no time to consider the needs of others. Worst of all is that you have no desire left to fulfil your responsibilities towards God.

Your top priority in life must always be the acceptance of the sovereign lordship of Christ. He must be in the centre of everything you attempt and are involved with. Your complete faith and trust must be put in Him at all times. Your persevering prayer must always be that you will remain sensitive to the prompting of the Holy Spirit.

If you live such a Christ-centred life, you will find that He meets all your needs. He will inspire you to serve Him amongst your fellowmen. Thus, through His rich grace you will live a life of the utmost fulfilment. Make sure that you are not so tied to earthly goods, that you become untied from Christ.

There is a burden of worry in obtaining riches; fear in the holding on to it; temptation in the use of it; guilt in the misuse of it; sorrow in the loss of it; and responsibility which will eventually be demanded of you for the use of it. (Matthew Henry)

O Lord, my possessions are busy _____

_____

The person you can become

"'Eye has not seen, nor ear heard, nor have entered into the heart of man the things which God has prepared for those who love Him.'" (1 Cor. 2:9)

There are two clearly identifiable sides to your personality: the person you are and the person you would like to be. If the first does not harmonise with the latter, you will experience bitter frustration and disappointment in your daily life. There is no harm in dreaming about the heights which you could rise to, provided it doesn't remain a dream only, but that you cause the dream to become reality. You must be able to plan anew daily to become the person that God wants you to be.

In your inner man lies hidden the potential for spiritual growth that is so great that you cannot fathom its depth. There are those singular moments when you become aware of a spiritual quality in your life which you did not know existed. When the old life reveals itself again, this moment fades into a memory and you wonder if it was real.

Spiritual greatness can be your portion if your life is lived in harmony with God. Then there must be no emotion of false pride. Your whole life must react to His love with joy and gratitude.

If such a way of life should sound too idealistic to be true to you, it is because your values are still based on your insufficiency and weaknesses. You have not had a vision yet of what life could really become when lived in harmony with God and you become what God intended you to be.

It is the essential nature of grace to inspire man to become that which God intended him to be. (Thomas Benton Brooks)

I beg for inspiration and strength to _____

Overcome temptations through grace

"No temptation has overtaken you except such as is common to man; but God is faithful, who will not allow you to be tempted beyond what you are able, but with the temptation will also make the way of escape, that you may be able to bear it." (1 Cor. 10:13)

If you really want to, you can overcome temptation! The problem with the great majority of people is that they want to be set free from their temptation, but they still allow this degenerative force to maintain its influence over their lives. God can only redeem you from temptation if you yourself desire it.

Such a desire is not cultivated easily. The Tempter is always there with his destructive powers, in the most acceptable and attractive guise. He works with you in such a convincing way which appears so reasonable. If this were not so, nobody would look at his diabolic commodities. In order to overcome temptation, it is imperative for the Christian life to be more attractive and creative than the temptation of sin. As soon as sin looks better to you than your personal experience with Jesus Christ, you are in danger.

In order for you to be strong enough in your spiritual life to beat temptation, and to overcome it through the grace of God, it is important that you should constantly live in the consciousness of Christ's presence. With the help and grace of your Saviour, you need not fear that temptations will triumph. Let us praise and honour the Lord for that.

> Temptation entices me to look up and plead for God's grace. (John Bunyan)

Loving Master, may my love for You always be stronger than

_____

_____

Our merciful God understands

"O Lord, You have searched me and known me. You know my sitting down and my rising up; You understand my thoughts afar off." (Ps. 139:1,2)

Often you want to help someone who has a problem but then are reproved for not understanding. In many instances this attitude is prevalent with people who sincerely want a solution to their problem, yet, they rather suffer than apply the discipline that will lead to the solution of their problem.

It may just be possible that you yourself may reveal this attitude when confronted with problems, when you are entertaining feelings of depression and self-pity. In such a situation you could easily complain that nobody understands you.

Regardless of how you may feel and in spite of others' seeming aloofness with regard to your problem, there is One who understands you better than you will ever be able to understand yourself. He knows you better than you know yourself. He knows when you are high and low, happy and sad, successful and failing, your strengths and your weaknesses – everything is known to the omniscient God.

Never be afraid or embarrassed to pour out your anxieties and fears before Him. Trust Him when you come to Him in prayer and share every worry of your life with Him.

Because He understands so well, He is always ready to listen and to remove the burden from your shoulders. Remember the words of 2 Corinthians 12:9, *"My grace is sufficient for you, for my strength is made perfect in weakness."*

> In this life there is nothing but the grace of God: we walk in it; we breathe through it; we live and die by it; it is the centre of our lives. (Robert Louis Stevenson)

Holy Lord Jesus, when I share my problems with You, I experience _____

*G*race for those who suffer

"But may the God of all grace who called us to his eternal glory by Christ Jesus, after you have suffered a while, perfect, establish, strengthen and settle you." (1 Pet. 5:10)

There are very few people who can honestly say that they have not yet experienced the torture of grief and sorrow. It might be from some or other physical defect, pain or ailment; it might have an emotional cause such as sorrow, heartache or despair; it might be spiritual because you have a deep feeling of guilt or because you are estranged in your relationship with the Lord. Suffering has many faces, but each one leaves its own scars of destruction on the sufferer.

Nobody has ever suffered more than Jesus Christ, and He went through that exclusively for your sake. He went through physical and emotional and spiritual suffering so that you could be assured of the eventual victory over the most severe form of suffering – the despair of death.

In your moments of despair and sorrow, turn to the living Christ, because His grace is sufficient for you in every situation in life. Allow Him to support and strengthen you and find your strength in Him. He has promised to open up the kingdom of heaven to all who believe in Him. Regardless of what happens in this life, the crown of life awaits those who obey and serve Him consistently.

God washes our eyes with tears until we see the unseen country where He Himself will wipe every tear from our eyes. (Henry Ward Beecher)

Gracious God, lead me safely through _____

_____

Know the grace of God and live!

"Grace to you and peace be multiplied." (1 Pet. 1:2)

In these modern times there are more and more people who are searching for the ability to handle the problems of our day with peace of mind. For many life has become extremely complicated and there are many traps and barriers along their way.

It is a commonly known fact that people are seeking man-made methods to handle their problems. Not the least of these is the addiction to drugs and alcohol. Here they find a refuge which wipes out reality for a little while. The fact of the matter, however, is that the problem does not disappear. On the contrary, the physical and mental ability to overcome, decreases. Added to that they end up with the discouraging feelings of guilt and self-reproach.

There is only one sure method of handling your life with confidence and assurance, and that is in the power of Jesus Christ. If you commit yourself and your life to Him unconditionally, then you can rest assured that He will grant you the grace to handle all the problems. Thus you will be blessed with tranquillity of mind and peace far beyond human understanding.

This grace and peace become a reality in your life only through Jesus Christ. Don't miss out on this because you have become detached from Him.

> Grace enters the soul as the morning sun enters the world: first there is dawn, then the bright light and eventually the sun in its full glory and shine. (Thomas Adams)

Loving Master, I thank You because, through Your grace You enable me to _____

The final objective of life

"... that the life of Jesus also may be manifested in our mortal flesh."
(2 Cor. 4:11)

There are those people who have their own hidden agenda for leading a good life. They see injustice and try their very best to set it straight. There are also many people whose dedicated service to their fellowmen is inspired by their commitment to Jesus Christ and humankind is enriched by such people.

Regardless of what form you express your Christian faith in, you must always bear in mind that service must only be the expression of an honest and deep experience with Jesus Christ. As a Christian you are not only called to do good works, but also to reflect the life of Christ in your thoughts and deeds – even though it may be in a very small measure.

The fact that you are called upon to be Christlike, offers a challenge which many people try to evade. Yet Christ often called upon His disciples to share their lives with Him. This wonderful fellowship and intimacy are the Master's gift to those disciples who love Him and have committed their lives to Him.

If Christlikeness is the goal of your life, it will give you a much better understanding of the needs and distress of your fellowman. The closer you live to Christ, the deeper your sympathy will be for those with whom you work. Commit your mental and spiritual faculties to becoming Christlike and people will see Him in your service to them.

It is a great gift of God to be found a faithful servant who spreads the image of the Master in the world. (Hugh Latimer)

Saviour and Lord, may Your beauty be reflected in _____

God's grace and your problems

"In all your ways acknowledge Him, and He shall direct your paths."
(Prov. 3:6)

Life can suddenly become filled with problems: some come charging at you very unexpectedly, but others are the product of your imagination. Regardless of what source they may arise from, they will control your life until you have found a solution.

Discussing a problem with a trusted friend often puts it in the right perspective, causing it to lose its overwhelming character. There is, however, a type of person who finds great joy talking about his problems, while secretly hoping never to find a solution, because then he won't have much left to talk about.

If you are experiencing a problem and sincerely seek a solution, direct your thoughts to God and don't focus on the problem. You cannot find a solution to your problem if you do not want to allow God to assist you.

Tell God about your problem, and continually confirm God's omnipotence. Allow Him to create order in the chaos and to give you the right solution. When you consider God to be more important than your problem, you will experience a feeling of deep satisfaction. You will be inspired with an unknown spiritual power, because God is then occupying His rightful place in your life and your life and circumstances will then be subjected to His grace. Thus you will find solutions to your problems and by His grace you will be able to live victoriously.

> The winds of Godly grace blow over us all. But we have to set our sails to become partakers of the breeze of grace. (Edward Payson)

Eternal God, I put You first in my life, knowing that You _____

To empty the bitter cup

"Put your sword into the sheath. Shall I not drink the cup which My Father has given Me?"' (Jn. 18:11)

Many Christians have good health, financial prosperity and social security as their priorities. They yearn for a life which is free from pain and suffering. The desire to obtain these things is natural and understandable, but it should never be the main objective of a Christian's life.

The Christian is called upon, by the power of the living Christ, to do the will of God. Experience has shown that doing the will of God brings about great satisfaction and joy. However, it might also be painful. The Master Himself proved this. The anxiety that He experienced in Gethsemane and His suffering on the cross, are clear proof of the fact that being a Christian is not an insurance policy against hardships and suffering.

However, the promise to everyone who loves and serves Christ, is His living presence under all circumstances. No Christian needs to go without Christ's guidance, or suffer alone, because Christ has promised to be with us at all times and never to leave us alone.

To venture into life in partnership with Jesus and to obey His will, is the summit of the Christian life. The circumstances that you may be finding yourself in, may not be your fault or choice and may have been caused by situations beyond your control. With His wisdom and wonderful grace and understanding, you will be enabled to empty the bitterest cup to the lees.

> It is through those who suffered, that this world is blessed. (Leo Tolstoy)

Dear Father, help me to, without complaining _____
_____

Hope for the future

"Yet He has made with me an everlasting covenant, ordered in all things and secure." (2 Sam. 23:5)

Many people these days experience life as over-burdened with worry and the future seems dark and unsure. Such an attitude can be the cause of deep anxiety while you are carrying the heavy burden of your daily responsibilities. Unless you have a strong and vital faith, it could have far-reaching effects on your physical, emotional and mental well-being.

The Son of the Most High God died and rose from the dead in order that you may be set free from this burden of care. God's love for the world was so great that Jesus Christ gave His life to redeem you from the terrible burden of anxious worries. It was to give you the assurance of forgiveness and salvation. Through His death and resurrection, Christ has given to all who believe in Him and who accept Him as Saviour and Redeemer, the glorious assurance that the reward of eternal life is waiting for them when they will be with Him for ever.

There is no doubt or insecurity about this Godly promise. You have the Word of the living God. Unlike those who have no hope, you are blessed with the assurance that the Saviour died in order that you may live. Regardless of the circumstances that you may find yourself in, this assurance should be a great comfort and encouragement. Hold on to it, because it is a covenant that God has made with you.

> No man should lay a cross upon himself or look for sorrows; but if a cross of sorrow is laid upon him, he should carry it patiently, knowing it is to his advantage. (Martin Luther)

I praise and thank You, Lord, that in spite of my circumstances I can _____

_____

One with Christ

"Abide in Me, and I in you." (Jn. 15:4)

The central truth of the Christian message is that of the indwelling Christ. He was crucified, He died and He rose again and He lives for ever in the hearts and lives of those who love Him. Their greatest desire is to grow into the likeness of His image.

For Christ to live in your life, you need to accept this glorious possibility in faith. He promised that He will do it, if you accept His promise and make it a reality in your life.

The mere thought of Christ living in your spirit, could be a highly emotional experience, and in most instances this is the case. But when the emotion has cooled off, the test lies in that which remains in your everyday life. Is His Spirit revealed in the sincerity of your motives, by honesty in your objectives, by unselfishness in your conduct and love in your actions? To speak of Christ living in you while refusing to allow Him to find expression through your life, is nothing but a caricature of the Christian experience.

It is both a humbling and challenging thought that the contemporary disciple is the only channel through which Christ can reveal Himself to this generation. It puts a great responsibility on all Christians. Many are scared off by this. The indwelling Spirit, however, supplements our human weaknesses. He meets our human inefficiency by holding us and strengthening us. We need only draw from the strength which Christ puts at our disposal.

> To be like Christ, is to be a Christian. (William Penn)

Holy Spirit of God, make my heart Your dwelling place so that

The greatest inspiration

"But you shall receive power when the Holy Spirit has come upon you." (Acts 1:8)

Inspiration is a wonderful asset and blessing in this life. When you are inspired you can accomplish more than is normally the case. Perhaps the source of your inspiration is listening to a great speech or touching music. While this is happening you feel like a newly created person. Someone with fluctuating emotions constantly needs inspiration to prevent depression. Often a vicious circle of inspiration and depression is formed and such a person seldom experiences the gracious gift of normality. True Godly inspiration is lasting and has the ability to overcome depression. It gives you the ability to function even when doubt threatens your spirit and mind.

The living Christ is the greatest source of inspiration through the indwelling of His Holy Spirit in all who accepted Him in sincerity as Redeemer and Saviour. This inspiration is not precarious. It is not subject to our changing moods. In the consciousness of His living presence, it has a lasting quality.

For inspiration to fulfil its true function, it must be revealed in practice – else it is nothing but a bubble, pretty while it lasts, but useless when it bursts. Unless that which inspires you is passed on to others around you, it won't last very long. Allow the Spirit of Christ to flow through you to inspire and to bless those with whom you come into contact.

When my spirit rises, my body falls on its knees. (George Lichtenburg)

Master, please let the inspiration of the Holy Spirit flow through my life so that _____

_____

God's love has no price tag

"May your money perish with you, because you thought that the gift of God could be bought with money!" (Acts 8:20)

here are always those misled people who think that money can buy them everything. While this may be true of material possessions, it surely does not apply to things like peace, tranquillity of mind, joy and fullness of life. These qualities have no price tags. On the contrary, they are God's gifts of grace which are available to rich and poor.

Everything we enjoy that is good and worthwhile, we enjoy by the grace of God. We don't deserve these things, we cannot earn them and we are not worthy of them. We are who we are and have what we have because of Christ's unfathomable love and grace towards us. This love has urged Him to sacrifice His life for us as proof of His majestic grace.

And for this very reason you should never take for granted the blessings which you receive from His hand. Regardless of how insignificant they may seem, always remember that they are gifts of God's endless goodness and a sign of His love towards you.

It is impossible to repay the Master sufficiently for all His goodness and grace towards you, for the simple reason that it cannot be calculated in monetary value. All you can do, and Christ expects you to do, is to share that with your fellowmen. By doing this, you will prove in a practical manner that the love and grace of God are at work in your life. Let us praise the Lord for His refreshing fountain of Godly grace.

God's grace is so amazingly great that it can cover all our sins. The healing stream of God's grace cleanses us from all sin. (Charles Wesley)

I want to thank You for the undeserved gifts that You _____

THE FOUNTAIN

OF GOD'S LOVE

God's love for wretched sinners is wonderful, but His patience towards loveless sinners is an even greater wonder of His love. (Henry Drummond)

"Our hearts rejoice that God is love! And we consider what love does: that He sent His Son to pardon our sin."
(Adapted from Hymn 74:1)

We worship You as the source of all true love: before we were born till the end of our lives we are surrounded by Your love. Your love carries us day by day as a mother carries and cares for her young. Your love gives us strength in our weakness, hope in our despair, peace in our anxiety, joy in our sadness and comforts us when we mourn. Your love is unfathomable and unchanging, independent of the ever-changing circumstances around us. We are safe in Your love as children are safe in the love of their parental home. "When my end on earth draws near, I will cling to my heavenly Father in my dying moments and to His love so wondrously great ... "
(Adapted from Hymn 226:5)

Then I will meet You face to face and bask in Your love for ever.

August

The cornerstone of your faith

"And now abide faith, hope, love, these three; but the greatest is love." (1 Cor. 13:13)

The Christian faith has many facets. People regard and interpret the teachings of Christ from various points of view. It is understandable because each person's frame of reference, tradition and personality influence his approach to Christ. Disaster enters your spiritual life when you deny the fact that another person's view-point could be correct even though it differs from yours. Such a denial is the result of fanaticism and pettiness and it will eventually destroy the beauty of your living faith.

The real test of your faith is the amount of love you have towards your fellowmen, especially those whose viewpoint differs radically from yours. Such a faith can only have its roots in a way of life that stays so close to Christ that His love starts flowing through you to others. It definitely doesn't lie in the denial of traditions and teachings endorsed by others. Your love for Christ includes all people who love Him, even though you may not be able to agree with them on an intellectual level about matters such as dogma and church government.

Love is predominant in your spiritual life. This love doesn't always mean peacefulness. There are times when it challenges and reprimands; it makes you feel humble in order that you may be carried to great spiritual heights; it empties you of yourself, of covetousness and pride, in order that you may be filled with the love of God. That is why it increases your appreciation of your fellowmen. If you love God and His love finds expression in you, you will of necessity love your fellowmen as well.

> All love must simply be stepping stones to the love of God. Thus it was with me and blessed be His Name for the magnitude of His grace. (Plato)

Lord, I pray that love will _____ through me _____

Love is a unifying force

"For this is the message that you heard from the beginning, that we should love one another." (1 Jn. 3:11)

Whether you want to acknowledge it or not, life requires us to make many adaptations. People adapt to their surroundings; you adapt in a marriage situation. Yet others make adjustments for the sake of comfort.

To make adjustments doesn't necessarily mean giving up your principles. Paul wrote to the church in Corinth, saying, *"To the weak I became as weak that I might win the weak. I have become all things to all men, that I might by all means save some"* (1 Corinthians 9:22). Nobody would therefore accuse Paul of compromising the lordship of Jesus in his life.

In the Christian life there are many disciples of the Master who hold such stereotyped viewpoints about the Lord, that they refuse to believe that others who are just as sincere in their zeal and love for the Lord, could hold another theological view of Christ. True followers of Christ should be able to adapt to the viewpoint of other children of the Lord, regardless of what their theological differences may entail. This is possible because the foundation of Christian brotherhood is our common love for God in Jesus Christ. Through Him love becomes a unifying force in our faith.

If you allow theological differences to cause division in your fellowship with other Christians, you have a restricted and marred faith which prevents the fullness of Christ's love from being revealed through you.

> The love of God makes all hearts to be tender. (George Herbert)

God, please let my love for my fellowman _____

_____

incere love

"Let love be without hypocrisy." (Rom. 12:9)

ew things in life are worse than falseness. Most people are repelled by others whose interest and care prove to be only superficial, those who switch on and off according to what is most beneficial for themselves. Their value as friends has no meaning whatsoever because their feelings are superficial. The tragedy is that when their falseness comes to light, innocent victims are hurt very deeply.

You need never at any time doubt the magnitude of God's love for you. Love urged Him to take on the form of a human being and to come to this world in the person of Jesus Christ; to be born in such simplicity; to suffer and die on behalf of us whom He loves. It was love that gave Him victory over death, which caused Him to rise triumphantly from death to ascend to heaven in order to intercede there for us with the Father.

It was love that urged Him to forgive your sins and to offer to you the gift of His Holy Spirit. Thus you are enabled to live a life of hope, conviction and assurance, even in the face of disappointment and set-backs.

This world will never know any love that is greater than that of God in Jesus Christ. He set us the example of sincere, upright love and now He calls us to love as He loved.

It may seem like an impossible task to you. Always remember that all things are possible with God. He will enable you to fulfil His command to love with sincerity.

The law of love is above every other law. God prescribed this law, and living according to it means living on the highest level of human experience. (Anonymous)

God of love, please help me _____

_____

What are you living for?

"To know the love of Christ which passes knowledge, that you may be filled with all the fullness of God." (Eph. 3:19)

*F*or many people life is nothing but a monotonous routine, a wild rat-race without meaning or purpose. Day in and day out they perform the same task without any enthusiasm and always wonder what the meaning of life is. Yet others are ambitious and try to reach the top of the ladder in their profession or field of study. In order to obtain riches and prestige, they often sacrifice precious time and honesty.

But there comes a time when every person starts seeking the hidden meaning of life. If monotony dulls your spirit and luxury leaves your soul sated, or when the ladder of social success is pulled out from underneath your feet, there comes a moment when you stop in your tracks, asking, "What is the meaning and purpose of my life?"

The most satisfying reply has a spiritual basis. Nobody with a sincere and vibrant experience with the living Christ ever asks this question. The simple reason is that they are too busy living a constructive life through the power of Christ.

The glorious truth is that man is born to glorify God, to worship and serve Him. It is only when God is in the centre of a life, that life reveals its deep secrets and God pours out His blessing upon dedicated hearts.

When living with the purpose of serving God and your fellowmen, you discover the deeper meaning of life. Monotony, frustration and feelings of uselessness vanish if your life is committed unconditionally to His love.

> It is not the owning of exceptional gifts which make us exceptionally useful, but committing what we have to serve God and our fellowmen. (F.W. Robertson)

Lord, I want to live to _____

To abide in Christ's love

"As the Father loved Me, I also have loved you; abide in My love."
(Jn. 15:9)

It is a disturbing thought that you could lose the consciousness of the Saviour's love. The Master loves His disciples, but how often do you wake up in the morning and thank Him for that love by telling Him of your sincere love for Him? What an inspiration it is to your spiritual life to wake up in the morning and to whisper, "Living Lord Jesus, I love You with all my heart!" This will cause your day to start on a very high note.

Jesus Christ has promised that if we realise our dependence upon Him, we will be enabled to do things which normally would be well beyond our ability. You can never reach your full potential until you are united with the living Christ in love. He reminds us that without Him we can do nothing, but by abiding in His love our vision is extended and our strength increased.

The great tragedy is that many Christians try to serve the Master without that all-important love which they need to have for Him. Then it is nothing but slavery. They are active in Christian service, but lack the inspiration which is derived from love for Christ and their fellowmen.

Start working diligently to develop a greater love for Jesus Christ, in order that you may be drawn closer to Him by the invisible but unbreakable cords of love. Then you become aware of His living presence and then you abide in His love.

> The most acceptable service to God, is to serve your fellowman lovingly.
> (Benjamin Franklin)

Living and loving Saviour, through fellowship by faith _____

To love one another

"Open your hearts to us." (2 Cor. 7:2)

Feelings of loneliness, rejection and isolation could have a destructive effect on a person's spiritual and emotional well-being. Only those who have experienced it can fully comprehend and understand the depths of depression that utter loneliness can drive one to. In many instances this has driven people to commit suicide because they couldn't handle the loneliness any longer.

The core of the Christian faith is founded on the love of God. It was His love for the world that urged Him to send His Son, Jesus Christ, to the world to die for our transgressions and sins. Christ's whole life was the epitome of love in concrete form. He indeed fulfilled the words that no man has greater love than that He lay down His life for His friends. The Son of God died for us out of love. It was Jesus who reiterated that the greatest of all commands was to love God and our fellowmen with all our heart.

If you are obedient to the commands of the Master, He will reveal His love through you. His Holy Spirit will urge you to seek out those who are alone in this world and to bring them comfort in the Name of the great merciful God. Allow Christ into your life and let His love urge you to serve those who are lonely in this world, and people will be able to see the Lord in you and in your actions.

Love is the cornerstone of your faith. Build upon it diligently and bring comfort and encouragement to others. By doing that you will honour and glorify God.

> The difference between "duty" and "love" is that the first represents Sinai and the latter Golgotha. (Richard Braunstein)

Lord, may Your Holy Spirit move me to _____
_____

God's boundless love

"A voice was heard on the desolate heights, weeping and supplications of the children of Israel. For they have perverted their way; they have forgotten the Lord their God." (Jer. 3:21)

Feelings of guilt are high on the list of main causes for mental, emotional and spiritual derangements. When people are oppressed by their feelings of guilt, they often become depressed and penitent to the point where they withdraw into themselves. Eventually they break down under the burden they carry.

To prevent yourself from throwing in the towel to the destructive effect of guilt, you must realise, acknowledge and accept that God, because He loves you so very much, has taken your sins upon Himself in Christ, and died on the cross in your stead. Thereby you received divine forgiveness and can be assured of redemption through the blood of the Lamb.

This however is by no means a free pass to a life of lawlessness. But it does mean that God's love for you is so boundless that He is always willing to listen to your confession of guilt and to take you back into the fold through His forgiving love.

Never be afraid or embarrassed to confess your guilt to Jesus. Plead for His forgiveness. You are assured of that. Because He died for you, you are very special and precious to Him. Why torture yourself with feelings of guilt while His unfathomable love through Jesus Christ is waiting that you should come to Him? There is only one way to answer to His love, and that is by loving Him in return. When set free from all your feelings of guilt you can live a life of love to His honour.

> We go to Golgotha to learn how to be forgiven, how to forgive others and to intercede for them in love. (S.J. Reid)

Christ of Golgotha, I thank You that I _____

_____

The extent of God's love

"'I have loved you,' says the Lord. 'Yet you say, In what way have You loved us?'" (Mal. 1:2)

There are many ways in which to love and if we should try to count all the ways in which God loves us, we would reach infinity and yet not nearly have managed to name them all. Nevertheless there are many people who, for a variety of reasons, still have a problem understanding God's love.

In the midst of personal set-backs and tragedies, in times of national and global disasters, in hardships and disappointments many people are inclined to hold God accountable for the situation they find themselves in. They question God's wisdom and love for allowing such a thing to happen to them. They repeatedly want to know, "Why?" In many cases people turn their backs on God as a result of the judgement they have passed on Him.

In this lamentable weakness of faith they totally miss the fact that all the disasters of this world cannot be ascribed to a lack of love in the Father or the Son, but to the foolishness of man. God gave us freedom of choice and in the final instance we are the people who selfishly misuse it.

The love of God is revealed in His abundant blessing, His all-powerful forgiveness, His mercy, His promise of eternal life, His comfort, His gift of the Holy Spirit and above all, the sacrifice of Jesus Christ on Golgotha. Do we need more proof than this? Dare we still question the love of God in Christ?

> I have never made a sacrifice. We dare not speak of sacrifice when we think of the "sacrifice" Christ made for each one of us on the cross. (David Livingstone)

Lord Jesus, I thank You for the privilege _____

Love is the key

"If anyone loves Me, he will keep my word; and my Father will love him, and we will come to him and make our home with him."' (Jn. 14:23)

So many people who call themselves Christians prefer to stand on the sidelines instead of entering the arena of faith to fight there with all their heart. They refer to supposed contradictions in the Word of God. They point out stumbling Christians who have made mistakes. They insist that unless all Christians are the perfect example of virtue and unless all their problems can be solved to their satisfaction, they are not willing to accept the Christian faith. Such people will never become real Christians, because their conditions cannot be met.

All Christians are sinners who try to be disciples of the Master according to the New Testament sense of the word. They don't pretend to be perfect, even though they follow Christ meticulously, striving to be like Him. They are not alone in their endeavour, because their Lord is always with them. He is constantly inspiring them in their efforts. His love towards His stumbling followers supersedes our human comprehension.

The acts and works of God can be analysed in minute detail by scientists; the beauty of His creation can inspire artists; theologians can try to fathom the depths of God, trying to penetrate the mystery that surrounds Him. But only a great love for Him can cause one to comprehend His Godly nature. Love is the key which unlocks the door into the holy sanctuary, where God reveals Himself to the sincere worshipper and where treasures of His grace are to be found.

It is only when people learn to worship in love, that they start growing spiritually. (Calvin Coolidge)

God, I plead in the Name of Jesus Christ _____

The reassuring love of God

"I love the Lord, because He has heard my voice and my supplications. Because He has inclined his ear to me." (Ps. 116:1, 2)

There comes a time in each of our lives when we urgently need reassurance. A fearful child looks to his parents for comfort and assurance. Even adults who are insecure need assurance. It is important for our peace of mind and the calming of our spirit. Regardless of how self-assured you may regard yourself to be, there will come a time in your life when you will realise and acknowledge such a need.

It becomes a problem however, when you realise that there is nobody you can turn to for reassurance. You are confronted with problems and hardships and you urgently need advice, yet there is nobody who can assist you in your crucial time. What are you supposed to do then?

The answer to this question is locked up in the psalm that we read from the Word of the Lord today. God is always there as a refuge and help in time of need. He is always there when you need Him, He always hears when you call to Him from the depths and you can be assured that He hears and answers your prayers.

When you turn to God through Jesus Christ in your times of need, wait upon Him patiently. In His own perfect way and timing, He will lead you along the right path and give you the reassurance of His constant love and care.

Of all earthly music that reaches the highest heaven, a heart beating warmly with sincere love is the most beautiful. (Henry Ward Beecher)

O Lord, my God, I love You with all my heart _____

The love without boundaries

"And when they crucified Him, they divided his garments, casting lots for them to determine what every man should take." (Mk. 15:24)

Even those who had killed Him, still wanted something from Him. In this instance the soldiers who had crucified Him, took his clothes.

People right through the ages have rejected Jesus. They have turned away from Him, denied and betrayed Him, and had no time for Him. Nevertheless, when they were in need or desperately needed something, they called upon Him and asked His help. This is especially true in our time of great haste where people can hardly find time for the Son of God in their busy programme – until problems occur!

The marvel of the Christian faith is that regardless of how you treat Christ, He still loves you. You can ignore or oppose Him, you can deny or betray Him, but when you call upon Him in your time of need, He lavishes His boundless love upon you and meets your immediate needs.

The crucifixion tells about the love of Christ which knows no boundaries. It is a love so sincere and pure that nothing can withstand it. Whether you are worthy or unworthy, whether you deserve it or not – this is the love that God wants to give to you through Jesus Christ. How is it possible that you can withhold your love from Him?

Christ is the bread of life for man's immortal soul. In Him the church has enough to feed the whole world. (Ian Maclaren)

Lord, I want to share in _____

_____

Be loving!

"And had no need that anyone should testify of man, for He knew what was in man." (Jn. 2:25)

People are particularly interesting beings. They differ so radically from each other that you will never find life monotonous, moving around amongst them. In your relationship with people it is an irrefutable fact that your attitude towards them will determine their attitude towards you. You may perhaps not be aware of this fact, but if you accept the truth of this statement, it will make life much easier and more interesting for you.

If you are constantly criticising your fellowmen, you are erecting a barrier which the spirit of friendship finds hard to overcome. If you regard others with contempt, you will soon taste the bitter fruit of loneliness. Your attitude towards others need not necessarily be expressed verbally, because people can feel intuitively what your attitude is.

For the sake of your own tranquillity of mind, happiness and peace, it is important that your attitude towards your fellowmen should be inspired and motivated by the Holy Spirit and the attitude of Jesus Christ. The most constructive way to live, is to love people. Bitterness vanishes, shyness is overcome and inferiority is replaced by self-confidence. The voluntary giving of your love does not only enrich your own life, but will draw people to you who will contribute to your quality of life.

When Jesus commanded us to love others, He did not speak to the religious fanatics, but to ordinary, busy, working people. Through the love of God you will understand the people around you better and serve them better too.

> Nobody will know what we mean when we say: God is love, unless we express it through our lives. (Lawrence Jacks)

Jesus of Nazareth, please teach me _____

The power of God's love

"The people will be oppressed, every one by another and every one by his neighbour; the child will be insolent toward the elder, and the base toward the honourable." (Is. 3:5)

Indeed the words of the prophet Isaiah have come true in our day. If you consider everything that happens in the world, you can see for yourself that this prophecy is being fulfilled. It seems as if chaos and anarchy rule in every corner of the world.

This however doesn't mean that people need to put up with the situation. Remember that Isaiah also prophesied the advent of the Saviour into this world. He brought light into the darkness of this world. God didn't reluctantly say, "It serves you right." In Christ Jesus He came to fight against Evil. He did this with the only effective weapon to overcome the forces of darkness. And it is just as powerful today – Godly love.

Even today God continues to shed His love on mankind. It is the Christian's privilege and duty to share this love with others by opening up his life to the influence of the Holy Spirit. We must allow Him to work in us so that we can pass God's love on to all other people.

There is just no other way of stopping the tide of evil that is threatening society today. Try to become a distributor of God's love. This is a watertight formula.

> The person who really loves with the love of Christ, creates a paradise on earth: he has God in his inner being, because God is love. (Robert de Lammanais)

Holy God, make me a _____

_____

Love is action

"Thus also faith by itself, if it does not have works, is dead." (Jas. 2:17)

If your Christian faith is not applied practically, you have not yet understood the full message of the living Christ. The Master was pre-eminently a practical person. He talked about feeding the hungry, clothing the naked, visiting the prisoners and working to the glory of God. It is important that love should find expression in service. The depth and quality of your love for and faith in Jesus Christ, will be revealed in the service that you render to others in His Name.

It is through a combination of love and service that faith is cultivated and strengthened. It cannot be inconstant or controlled by our emotions. We cannot only delight ourselves in it during moments of religious zeal. Acts of love must be rendered even when days are grey and boring and when your mood is heavy. Such times especially are opportunities for spiritual growth. If you persist in love and service regardless of how you feel, your spiritual life will increase in depth and zeal.

Love and service are the nutrients of a strong faith. When they feature, your faith is strong, but if they are absent, your faith wanes and fails in the function which it should fulfil. If you desire to have a stronger faith, you must love God wholeheartedly and serve Him with greater enthusiasm. Sincere love for God and inspired service combine to create a positive faith. It leads you into a deeper fellowship with the Master.

The things we did for ourselves, will die with us. What we do in love for Christ, is and remains immortal. (Albert Pine)

Master, please nurture my faith _____

*W*hen God's love possesses you

"Having predestined us to adoption as sons by Jesus Christ to Himself, according to the good pleasure of his will." (Eph. 1:5)

*I*t is impossible to compare the existence of the holy God with your own unimportant, insignificant and incomplete life. He is perfect while you can lay no claim to perfection and therefore it seems as if there is no common ground between God and you. It would have been true if the Name and character of God, as revealed to us through Jesus Christ, had not been love. But, because He is love, He calls you to Him and if you react to this love-call, your life is changed miraculously.

As the love of God becomes a reality to you, it controls your spirit and you become aware of your unity with the Father. It stimulates and inspires you. Yet, the love of God which is at work in you is not an entirely emotional experience that is stripped of all practical application. It is a way of life that involves *every* aspect of your life. The wonder of grace is that God gives Himself to you! As you open up your life to His life and influence, the Holy Spirit will enable you to live as He intended you to live: in His strength and in the consciousness of His living presence.

When the love of God fills your life and you become thoroughly aware of His divine presence, you experience a feeling of unity with Him. This is something that every person desires. This unity isn't something that you can earn through your own efforts. It is a gift from God. However, it only becomes yours when you appropriate it for yourself in faith and with gratitude.

> God often visits us, but most of the time we are not at home. (Joseph Roux)

Eternal God, Your unfathomable love _____

*U*nity through love

"Fervent lips with a wicked heart are like earthenware covered with silver dross." (Prov. 26:23)

*W*hen words are used in a religious context, they lead to various interpretations. This creates painful divisions in Christianity. There are thousands of conflicting voices who all maintain that they are preaching the truth. Some of them even imply that they are the only ones who have the full truth. Because they believe it, they develop a religious zeal which ignores the feelings and faith of other people. Their only goal is to recruit converts to their point of view. And this is the cause of petty religious fanaticism.

When an effort is made to explain Christianity in intellectual terms, it usually ends in disappointment and frustration. Christian unity can never exist as long as we are in favour of dogmatic and church uniformity.

Jesus Christ didn't come to preach a new religious theory to the world. He offered a new life to all who accepted His teachings. His way rose above religious differences, it avoided fanaticism and created respect and understanding for one another. This is the way of love and it is perfect. Jesus reiterated the importance of love for God and made it compulsory for His followers to love their fellow-men.

Even though people and organisations have different opinions and interpretations, when the love of Christ rules in their hearts, there will be no divisions in the spirit of their faith. In Christ they are bound together in unity – in spite of the differences in their words.

Authority can oppress, but love overcomes. He who forgives first, wins the laurel-wreath. (William Penn)

Loving Master, teach me to _____

_____

On God's loving protection

"And he said, 'O man greatly beloved, fear not! Peace be to you; be strong, yes, be strong!'" (Dan. 10:19)

Worry and fear can so easily become an integral part of your life and personality, thus robbing your life of its meaning and beauty. Worry necessarily develops into fear, then fear creates constant worry and the vicious circle goes on until joy and spontaneity vanish from your life.

If your life is being controlled by these negative forces, you urgently need to come to a fresh realisation of God's love. The fact that God loves you is not a vague religious speculation – it is a positive, constructive approach to life. Believing that God's love surrounds you and is waiting to be revealed through you, is the best antidote for foolish worrying and degenerating fear.

How is it possible to be constantly aware of God's love and to wipe out these negative influences? With the help of the Holy Spirit it is possible to rearrange your thoughts from negative to positive. Ask God to remove your fear and to replace it with the consciousness of His loving presence. Confirm to yourself continually that He is close and loves you.

Every time that the bullies of fear and worry want to enforce themselves on you, remember with gratitude that God loves you and that they have no more control over your life. Thus you will gradually become aware of the fact that His love for you is stronger than any demolishing force that tries to enter your life.

Only respectful fear of God can free us from the fear of man. (John Witherspoon)

Holy God, let Your love _____ me _____

Love is a trademark

"He who does not love does not know God, for God is love." (1 Jn. 4:8)

Through the ages Christianity has endured serious set-backs as a result of over-keen disciples who propagated their faith by means of clever-sounding Bible verses which were quoted incorrectly. In this century of instant everything, all ideas are portrayed in condensed, abridged format. Yet, Christianity must never be overly simplified to the detriment of its message.

The amazing truth that God is love, forms the core truth of Christ's message to this world. In order to understand Godly love correctly, the Christian needs to identify himself with God through our Mediator, Jesus the living Christ. Christ said, *"If anyone loves Me, he will keep my word; and my Father will love him and make our home with him"* (John 14:23).

To love God, means to love Him unconditionally and to open up your life for the Holy Spirit. This means to acknowledge Him as Lord and Master of every aspect of your life and to love Him above everything else.

To say, "God is love!" is not merely a sentimental expression of faith. It is a powerful confirmation of an irrefutable truth. Nobody can fathom the extent of God's love. Paul tried to do just that when he spoke about the dimensions of God's love in Ephesians 3, *"[that you] may be able to comprehend with all the saints what is the width and length and depth and height – to know the love of Christ which passes knowledge; that you may be filled with all the fullness of God."*

The true measure of our love for God, is to love Him without measure. (Bernard of Clairvaux)

Lord, please teach me the full extent of Your love _____

God loves you

"And we know that all things work together for good to those who love God, to those who are called according to his purpose." (Rom. 8:28)

It often happens that in the face of tribulation and set-backs people cannot understand why such things could happen to them. In many cases God is blamed and called to justice. Every set-back in life is then ascribed to Him.

One of the basic components of Christianity is steadfast faith in the love of God. This love has been proven undeniably in the gift of His Son to a lost world. That is why, in every situation of life, you need to put your trust in the wisdom and goodness of a loving Father. His knowledge spans your whole life, temporal and eternal – not only the temporal and predictable present.

No person can fully comprehend the magnitude of God's deed of love as expressed on the cross on Golgotha. The extent of His love towards sinners is unfathomable and incomprehensible. But without the gruesome events at the scene of the cross we would never have shared in God's pure love, and we would never have experienced redemption and deliverance. Through the death and resurrection of Jesus Christ, God has demonstrated His love to us in a crystal clear manner.

When you find yourself facing problems or set-backs, remember that your times and fate, are in God's almighty hands. Because of His great love for you, everything that happens to you in life has a purpose. In His own time it will be revealed to you. Your duty is to believe in God under all circumstances, to trust and obey Him.

The characteristic of true Christianity isn't so much freedom, but obedience. (Henri Amiel)

Jesus, in the darkest moments _____

God's saving love

"To them God willed to make known what are the riches of the glory of this mystery among the Gentiles: which is Christ in you, the hope of glory." (Col. 1:27)

There is a generally accepted idea that if we want God to love us, we need to live a good life. This finds expression in the well-meaning mother who says to her child, "If you are not good, the dear Lord Jesus will not love you!" It is accepted that God rejoices in the righteous person and that His Spirit enters our lives to change us to conform us to the image of Christ. But the wonder and glory of the Christian gospel is that God loved us while we were yet sinners. Without such a love we would indeed have still been lost.

Faith in the saving love of God is much more than a pious theological hope, or a dogmatic point for discussion. It is something that you respond to intuitively. Even though you are deeply aware of your imperfection and sin, you are aware that besides these things, there is a divine Omnipotence that is always calling you to a better and nobler life. You also know that you will never be able to reach these virtuous heights in your own strength. This realisation could cause you to lose hope, and then you do not treat your spiritual life with the earnestness it deserves.

If you are aware of the fact that because of your sins and digression, you don't have the ability to live your life as you should, it is important that you accept God's offer to re-create and reform your life. It is important that you allow the Holy Spirit to inspire you with the strength you need to walk God's way.

Redemption is free for you because someone else has paid the price for it. (Thomas Aquinas)

Master, I am sincerely grateful that _____

_____

The indisputable test

"He who says he is in the light, and hates his brother, is in darkness until now." (1 Jn. 2:9)

It is not difficult to generalise the teachings of Christ – people do so daily in every area of life. It is when the living Christ puts you to the test on a personal level that His claims and teachings become hard to obey. Perhaps you can easily accept the principle that you must love God. You could even derive great strength and inspiration from the fact that you confirm this love. To confidently declare that you love God, will always encourage and inspire you.

The problem arises, however, when your heavenly Father commands you to express that love in concrete form by loving those with whom you live, work and play. This immediately transfers your faith from the dogmatic and emotional level into the centre of the everyday world of human experience. This is indeed the place where it belongs.

This claim could create an impossible situation, because which one of us can love all those we come into contact with? But Christ has promised the gift of His indwelling Spirit to all who love and serve Him. Through the power of His Spirit, the impossible does become possible. An invisible cloak of love is revealed through your service, and it covers everyone that you come into contact with. Confirm your love for Christ and keep on loving your fellowmen and you will discover new depths and fresh dimensions of the love of Christ.

We must never be satisfied to be cleansed of our sins only; we must be filled with the Holy Spirit. (John Fletcher)

Holy Spirit, please fill my life so that _____

Incredible but true

"And now abide faith, hope, love, these three; but the greatest of these is love." (1 Cor. 13:13)

In these troublesome times when bitterness, prejudice and economic hardship are the order of the day, it is hard to believe that love is supreme.

For the Christian disciple all sin and depravity must be explained in the light that is radiated from the cross of Golgotha. All the forces of evil are concentrated with hatred on Christ. He underwent an unfair hearing and became the scorn of the Roman soldiers as well as the victim of the mobs. Then He was nailed to a cruel wooden cross. His disciples and faithful followers, in their despair, must have asked the same question which so often escapes our fearful hearts, "Why?"

The magnitude of Christ on the cross lies specifically in the fact that in the midst of public scorn and derision and unbearable pain, He prayed for those who crucified Him; that He gave to John the responsibility of caring for His mother, Mary; that He promised salvation to the sinner who was crucified with Him. These revealed His love in a practical way. His love surpassed all the powers of hatred. Three days after His death, love triumphed gloriously over all things.

When murder and crime make a mockery of everything that Jesus Christ lived for and taught, then remember Golgotha. You cannot escape the afflictions which ravage society, but your spirit and attitude, elevated by the Holy Spirit, will bind you to the principle of Godly love. You will have peace and calm which will make you aware of the immortality and invincibility of love.

> Godly love is a sanctified flower which, in its budding stage is happiness and in full bloom it is heaven. (Louisa Hervey)

God, I plead that love will be _____

_____

We worship a God of love

"For He has not despised nor abhorred the affliction of the afflicted; nor has He hidden his face from him; but when he cried to Him, He heard." (Ps. 22:24)

One of mankind's most general shortcomings is that we lose track of the fact that God is a God of love. When families are met with disaster or disappointment, when cruel deeds are committed, after set-backs or failures – God is often blamed for many of these. Then we complain, "How could a God of love allow such a thing?" or "Why must something like this happen to us? After all, we do love God."

Of one thing we can be very sure and that is when problems do occur, they have not been planned by God. They may be the result of wilful actions by ourselves or a result of our own foolishness. God will never do something to harm or injure His children. He loves us so much that He sent His Son to die for our sins.

If you find yourself in a tight spot at the moment, or if it seems as if your whole world is falling apart, you need to consider the role which you yourself have played creating the situation. Did you go to the Lord with your burdens and problems, asking Him in all honesty to indicate to you where you had gone wrong? Do that, even though the truth may be painful.

If you truly love someone, you will never ignore him in trouble but much rather help. Remember therefore that God feels exactly the same way about you and wants to do the same for you, if you only allow Him to.

Happiness is not a reward – it's an effect. Suffering is not punishment – it's a result. Both are such because God is love. (John Dryden)

Dear Saviour, Your gracious love _____

Our most glorious life-experience

"To know the love of Christ which passes knowledge; that you may be filled with all the fullness of God." (Eph. 3:19)

For many of us it will be a difficult choice to decide immediately what our most glorious experience in life has been. Some people will say it was that mystical moment when they met their life companion and knew immediately that they were meant for each other. Others again will recall those memorable incidents that have caused them excitement, satisfaction and fulfilment.

If you regard your spiritual life highly, you will remember that wonderful moment when the love of God became a glorious reality to you and you will know that it was the most wonderful experience of your life. It might have been sudden and dramatic, or it could have happened gradually. But the moment when God became a loving reality in your life, will always be precious to you.

When the love of God entered your life and started to find expression in your life, you received a small but important part of God's nature, because God is love and through the expression of love, you are in a sense like God. The realisation that God loves you and fills you with His Holy Spirit, is an unforgettable experience which increases in riches and depth as time goes by. The influence that God's Spirit has in your spirit is not a one-time experience. It is the sharing of yourself with the God of love, moment by moment through prayer, Bible study, meditation and positive witnessing about His love.

> To love abundantly is to live abundantly; to love eternally is to live eternally. (Henry Ward Beecher)

God of love, I praise You _____

_____

Love is indispensable

"Looking unto Jesus, the author and finisher of our faith." (Heb. 12:2)

Two of the most important characteristics in the life of the Christian are power and simplicity. Over time many contradicting view-points developed concerning the person and work of Jesus Christ. Today there exist literally thousands of interpretations of who He was and what He taught. There are many people who would like to know Him, but they don't know what to believe about Him. It seems as if confusion exists even in church circles.

However, the confusion is not nearly as big as it seems. The fact of the matter is that the majority of Christians acknowledge that He is Lord and that He is their Saviour. If they cannot make this simple confession of faith, they don't qualify to be called Christians. The living Christ is the unifying factor amongst His followers. People from divergent theological perspectives give their love and allegiance to Him. It is tragic however, that so many people don't admit that their love for Him should rise above their dogma.

To love Christ places the responsibility upon you to love your fellow believers – even those whom you differ from intellectually. *"By this all will know that you are my disciples, if you have love for one another"* (John 13:35). It is possible to love in spite of our differences.

When the Holy Spirit is at work in a person's life, the sincere desire exists to obey God's will. The basic command that the Master gave His disciples is that we must love one another. All dogma and theological discussion are of no use if there is not love.

> Where there is love, there God is too. (Leo Tolstoy)

God of love, let my love _____

_____

Speaking the truth in love

"The lips of the righteous know what is acceptable, but the mouth of the wicked what is perverse." (Prov. 10:32)

Some people are very careless with regard to what they say. They couldn't care if what they say is appropriate or whether it deeply hurts the person they talk to. They take pride in the fact that they are straightforward people who honestly say what they think. However, it is nothing less than impertinence. They tread on the feelings of others with spikes on their feet. These people normally live a very lonely life because others steer clear of them as much as they possibly can.

People who are aware of the powerful impact words have, use them to help, encourage and heal. Unpleasant truths sometimes have to be expressed, but do so with firmness and tenderness which will alleviate the pain that necessarily follows. When, as a Christian, you are required to speak frankly, it will be wise to spend time in quiet meditation first. Pray for the guidance of the Holy Spirit in order that you may receive the grace to handle an unpleasant task with sympathy, dignity and love. As a "righteous" person, willing to say the "right thing" in a difficult situation you can trust the Holy Spirit to assist you in your task of love.

> One of the most serious tests of friendship is to point out his mistakes to your friend. To love someone to the extent that you cannot bear to see a stain on him, and to express the painful truth with loving words, that is true friendship. (Henry Ward Beecher)

Lord, guide me to tactfully _____

_____

The greatest gift of grace

"And yet I show you a more excellent way." (1 Cor. 12:31)

The Christian faith reveals itself in many ways. It changes lives in a radical manner, it reforms attitudes, it heals the sick, it makes God a reality to ordinary people, it reveals in many ways that the teachings of Jesus are more than a romantic philosophy – that they form the basis of a practical way of life.

Because, as a devoted Christian, you love and serve the living Saviour, it is possible that you are constantly searching for signs to confirm your faith. You may be yearning for one of God's special gifts so that you may do great things for Him and to the glory of His Name. The gifts of speaking in tongues, healing, teaching, working of miracles or the power of discernment are but a few of God's spectacular gifts. You might feel that if you could only receive one of these gifts, you will achieve the ultimate spiritual experience.

God's very greatest gift is the gift of love. Loving God with all your heart, all your mind and all your strength should be to you the ultimate of all spiritual experiences. Regardless of which other gifts you desire, they will have no essential value if the love of God is not revealed through you. It is only love which sanctifies the common, everyday things and surrounds even the most humble gift with a halo. It reflects the Holy Spirit of God in its purest form.

> The true disciples of Christ are not those who know most, but those who love most. (Frederich Spanheim)

Glorified Saviour, please grant me _____

_____

*L*ove brings life

"We know that we have passed from death to life because we love the brethren." (1 Jn. 3:14)

In the teachings of Jesus Christ, love is all-powerful. Everything He was, everything He taught and did were manifestations of love. He made it a condition for discipleship and stated very clearly that man cannot serve or glorify God without love.

People who are not in harmony with His teachings simply cannot understand such a strong accent on love. Their concept of love is that it is an emotion which operates in response to every passing mood. They just don't understand that the power of love overcomes hate, that love can offer years of service without counting the cost. Love is a God-like characteristic which enriches everyone who allows God to reveal it in their lives.

It is possible to have a first-hand experience of the love of God and to allow your life to become a channel of God's love. This is the wisest way of life there is for man. The opposite of loving is to hate. This is the path of bitterness, dissension and broken relationships.

When the love of God is a powerful influence in your life and His love reaches out to others through you, your personal life is enriched in a way you never dreamt possible. It is impossible to love without being enriched in your mind and spirit.

Love is the door through which the human soul enters, moving away from selfishness to service, from loneliness to fellowship with mankind. (John Randolph)

Lord God, through Your Holy Spirit please do the impossible

The test of true discipleship

"As I have loved you, that you also love one another. By this all will know that you are My disciples, if you have love for one another." (Jn. 13:34, 35)

There are many Godly laws that govern your life and it is very easy to stress one to the detriment of another. When that happens, your life gets out of focus and your image of God gets twisted. Then you only see one characteristic of your heavenly Father and you become sectarian instead of being a balanced disciple of the living and always loving Christ.

Christ loves you completely and in return He expects you to love Him completely. He loves all people, regardless of how sinful they may be or what their theological view may be. He also expects this quality of love from you because you are His disciple. Pride, self-righteousness, fanaticism and other forms of spiritual perversion parade before the people, claiming their attention and admiration, but they have no place in the life of a true disciple of Christ.

If you understand the teachings of Christ and realise that He expects self-sacrificing love from you, everything else becomes less important. The most high-sounding and most logical religious theory crumbles when there is no love. All the good works done in Christ's Name lose their motivational power if they are not sustained by love.

According to Jesus Christ, the living Lord, the test of discipleship is the love that you have for Him. As His committed disciple you will love your fellowmen, regardless of their teachings.

> Love is the highest gift of grace to mankind, the holiest right of the soul, the golden link which connects us to service and truth, the redemptive principle which determines whether we are disciples of Christ. (Daniel A. Poling)

Lord Jesus, help me _____

_____

All-surrounding love

"The Lord is my shepherd, I shall not want." (Ps. 23:1)

To the Palestinian shepherds their flocks of sheep and goats were very precious. In most cases they were the life source of the people and everything depended on their well-being. These animals provided milk, meat and cheese, as well as wool and skins for clothing. Therefore the shepherd took very good care of them. He took care of them by providing them with pastures and water, by protecting them against attacks, by keeping them safely on the right path and searching for the ones that went astray and were in danger of getting lost.

For Jesus Christ His children are also very precious. That is why we got to know Him as the good Shepherd. He cares for you by providing for your daily needs, by protecting you, by showing you the path of righteousness and by searching for you when you go astray. Then He lovingly brings you back to the safety of the flock.

However, there is one crucial difference between the Palestinian shepherd and his relationship with his flock and the good Shepherd and His children. And this difference is what makes the Christian faith what it really is. In order to enjoy the care and protection of the shepherd, the flock had to provide for the material needs of the people. Jesus Christ, the good Shepherd, however, offers you His protection and immeasurable love, and only asks that you should love Him in return. Is this a price too high to pay for a love which exceeds all other loves by far?

Commitment is to give to Jesus a blank page to complete, with your signature at the bottom. (H.H. Miller)

Good Shepherd, thank You _____

Unconditional love?

"Love bears all things, believes all things, hopes all things, endures all things." (1 Cor. 13:7)

This life consists mainly of giving and taking. Nevertheless it seems as if the majority of people do the taking and the minority do the giving. In spite of that it seems as if the ones who give, are happier.

Unfortunately some people claim things which cannot be given. Love cannot be claimed – it must be earned. Parents cannot claim love from their children only because they gave birth to them. Love creates love, and as a child is nurtured in love, he learns to react with love.

Elderly people, though they usually are understanding and friendly, are inclined to fall prey to self-pity; instead of giving love, they claim the impossible. If they would only develop an attitude of love and pray for those who serve them, others will provide for their needs with great joy.

Many of the beautiful things that enrich our lives, come from ordinary people who learned to love their neighbours. Even though their love is often accompanied by sacrifice, the joy they experience exceeds the sacrifices by far. A person who loves his fellowman gives expression to that love by taking an interest in and having concern for them. Those who are inspired by the love of Christ, serve the world around them with the love which fills their hearts, asking no reward for their service of love.

Those who lay claims and ask for rewards, may enjoy temporary benefits, but those who give in the spirit of God's love, discover the rich and permanent blessing which God meant for them.

> The best way of getting to know God, is to love your neighbour. (Vincent van Gogh)

God of grace, thank You that I can unconditionally _____

THE FOUNTAIN

OF GRATITUDE

You have already given me so infinitely much. Please give me one more thing: a grateful heart. (George Herbert)

Oh, heavenly Father, could I sing to Your glory with a thousand tongues – how I would joyfully draw close to You, bringing my song of thanks, O Lord! I would sing Your praise and glory, telling about Your innumerable, wondrous deeds. (Adapted from Hymn 59:1)

Your goodness and grace are new upon me every day and You surround me daily with Your love and faithfulness. Your love spans my past, my present and my future; how will I ever express my gratitude in words?

I thank You for all the good You have done in my life, but also for bitterness and sorrow; by that You always draw me to You.

I can only praise You through a life of gratitude as worked in my inner being by your Holy Spirit.

I thank You for Jesus Christ who died for me and by His blood washed me from my sins.

I thank You for the Holy Spirit who guided me to be reborn and daily brings me to repentance.

September

Gratitude

"Giving thanks always for all things to God the Father in the name of our Lord Jesus Christ." (Eph. 5:20)

*M*any Christians find life hard and demanding. Wherever they turn they experience only opposition and discouragement. It seems as if their human relations are in a mess. Nothing they attempt seems to work out to their satisfaction.

Unfortunately many Christians have lost the art of practising thanksgiving. They are so overwhelmed by set-backs and problems that a cloud of depression has descended upon their spirit and mind, so that they can find very little to thank God for.

When a Christian loses the gift of thanksgiving, he has lost a source of great inspiration and spiritual strength which can hardly be replaced by anything else. First and foremost you must thank God that He loves you and cares for you. The thought of God's compassionate love should inspire you to have a spirit of sincere gratitude.

Thanksgiving is a powerful factor in your spiritual life. It can replace inferiority with trust and dispel the dark clouds of depression and down-heartedness. The only way to establish the power of thanksgiving is to practise it every day. Make sure to lift it out of the rut of your Sunday worship. Start every day with a sincere prayer of appreciation to your heavenly Father for the gift of life. You will discover that by doing this, you will have a guideline for the day that will cause you to live in victory.

> Every grateful thought directed towards heaven, is a prayer in itself. (Ephraim Lessing)

Holy Lord Jesus, I praise You because _____

_____

Praise the Lord!

"One generation shall praise Your works to another, and shall declare Your mighty acts. I will meditate on the glorious splendour of Your majesty, and on Your wondrous work." (Ps. 145:4, 5)

In these eventful times where the voices of the prophets of doom seem to rise above all other voices, and like Job's comforters, are casting a heavy gloom over life, very little gratitude is expressed towards God for the assurance that this is still His world. That He still controls it and still determines the fate of mankind.

When problems strike and the future suddenly seems unsure and ominous, man so easily forgets the mighty acts of God. Time and time again in the past He saved man in his time of need and kept the world back from the chasm of destruction.

The Bible speaks of the mighty acts of the Most High and history mentions numerous occasions where God's hand helped when man's foolishness drove him to the brink of extinction and anarchy. In every catastrophe He saved the world.

When those who are in favour of doom and despair start doing their death-dance, it is time for the Christians to praise and thank God for everything that is good and noble. Then it is time to call on the living Christ and to plead that He must fill you with His Holy Spirit. The Spirit will strengthen your faith and cause your hope to burn high. Negative thoughts can be wiped out by reminding yourself with gratitude of the mighty acts of God and by remembering that He cares for His creation. Be grateful to God for His nurturing love!

> If children owe their earthly parents gratitude, how much more should the great family of God not be grateful towards their heavenly Father? (Hosea Ballou)

I thank You for Your greatness and omnipotence _____

_____

Gratitude glorifies God

"I will praise You, O Lord, with my whole heart; I will tell of all Your marvellous works." (Ps. 9:1)

Whatever you do, never allow a situation to develop where your faith makes you arrogant. Religion is a serious matter, yet some of God's most dedicated servants were high-spirited, happy people. A religion which is void of humour, can hardly express the spirit and attitude of Jesus Christ.

One of the most beautiful things we read about Jesus, is that ordinary people enjoyed listening to Him and that children were at ease in His presence. Could this have happened at all if He had constantly expressed an attitude of heavy-heartedness? His personality must have emanated a deep peace. Happiness, joy and quiet humour enabled Him to love and appreciate people.

Your sense of humour, enriched by your gratitude and love, undoubtedly is a gift of God. It is difficult to think that a God, who reveals His beauty in the setting sun, who confirms His eternity in the freshness of day-break, who causes birds to sing and children to smile, does not have a sense of humour.

While, in the attitude of Jesus Christ, you learn to thank God with joy, you will make the exciting discovery that there is true joy in His service and that gratitude and gladness can glorify God much more than verbosity and arrogance could ever do.

Joyful gratitude is the sign of a noble soul. (Samuel Johnson)

I am so grateful for _____

_____

𝒪he power of thanksgiving

"To console those who mourn in Zion, to give them beauty for ashes, the oil of joy for mourning, the garment of praise for the spirit of heaviness." (Is. 61:2, 3)

𝒪hanksgiving and praise have life-changing power. Yet there are many committed disciples of the Master who believe that it must only be expressed when our emotions run high and when everything goes well. However, nothing could be further from the truth.

When the storm-clouds of life obliterate the sunshine of God's love; when doubt threatens to destroy our faith in the goodness of God; when it seems as if life itself is falling apart – then, more than ever, it is necessary to resort to praise and thanksgiving which originate in the depths of our being.

You may very well ask how one can thank and praise God if you have nothing to thank Him for. Regardless of what you may feel at this very moment, you are still irrevocably God's child. He loves you with a very special love and cares for you very much. The Master is still with you, even if you are not conscious of His presence.

Remind yourself of this steadfast truth and, in spite of what you may feel, thank God for it. Thank Him for the fact that He is greater than any problem you may struggle with and any frame of mind you may find yourself in. In the clear realisation of His greatness you will find that your life is being elevated above all destructive influences and then you will have the ability to thank and praise Him.

Thanksgiving and praise create a spiritual force which enables you to lead a well-balanced life in all circumstances. Learn to exclaim, "Praise the Lord!" in every circumstance, even in abnormal situations.

> Worship requires only one person and God. (H.W. Vaughan)

O Lord, teach me to rejoice in spite of _____

_____

_L_ive life to the full

"For with You is the fountain of life; In Your light we see light." (Ps. 36:9)

_N_ever allow life to become an unbearable burden to you, because it is God's greatest gift to you. He only gives to you what is good and you should be exceedingly grateful for that. Unfortunately it is possible to make your life an unbearable burden through degenerative and negative thoughts and by the total neglect of your spiritual life and principles.

If you want to lead a full and blessed life, there are certain principles which must be accepted. One of the most important principles is that you must be grateful for your life because it is the best thing God has given you. Of course this doesn't mean that everything must always be plain sailing, but when you accept the goodness of life with gratitude towards God, you will stop fighting against it. When you start cooperating with life, you become a collaborator with the almighty Creator.

When you accept that life is good, you become aware that it has a clear goal and plan. This acceptance removes all impatience and frustration, and life becomes an exciting and satisfying experience.

But, in order for you to understand the great plan of life, you need to know the Planner. This knowledge requires a positive faith and courage. You accept the fact that God exists and you allow your life to be controlled by Godly principles, until eventually you become an expression of those plans.

When you have this experience and make it your own, you possess a unity with the Creator and more and more your life is filled with the fullness of God. How can you possibly thank and praise Him enough for this in one lifetime?

Gratitude is a course from which we never graduate fully. (Fred Beck)

Creator God, I thank You that in Jesus Christ I _____

God is great

"You are my God, and I will praise You; You are my God, I will exalt You." (Ps. 118:28)

From time to time you will meet a person who will state that he is self-sufficient. You hear about people who maintain that they are self-made and totally independent, that they don't need help from anybody and that they trust themselves completely for everything they want to do or need.

While we may possibly admire these people, it is however an irrefutable fact that nobody can honestly pretend to be self-sufficient. This becomes evident when they are met with set-backs and suddenly find themselves defenceless.

It is a fact that God is in control of everything and only He can provide for you, protect and guide you. When things start going wrong in your life, you can be sure that you strayed from the Lord or that you acted directly contrary to His will. If however you put your trust completely in Him, He will use even your negative experiences to your benefit.

An honest study of Scripture will prove how God has done that in the past. The greatest example of this is how He used the awfulness of the crucifixion to establish the glory of the resurrection. Thereby victory was achieved over sin and death for all time when His love triumphed over Evil.

Never cease to praise and thank God, even under appalling circumstances. You can always count on the wonder of His love. He will care for you and never leave you or forsake you. We worship a mighty God who deserves all our praise and thanksgiving.

> Gratitude is not merely a memory, but it is worship from the heart, dedicated to God for all His goodness. (N.P. Willis)

I want to praise You for _____

_____

Spontaneous thanksgiving

"Your way, O God, is in the sanctuary; Who is so great a God as our God? You are the God who does wonders." (Ps. 77:13, 14)

We have a wonderful God and King! Unfortunately we don't always succeed in keeping the vision of His greatness in mind. The result is that we lead petty, unfulfilled lives. Instead of allowing ourselves to grow through meditation of Him, we try to keep Him on our level.

God is great and the one consistent theme of Scripture is His invitation to us to share in that greatness, together with all others who love and serve Him. This invitation to spiritual greatness starts in your own spirit, because this is where God is present. We will never find God until we have found Him in the inner life of our soul. Jesus promised to dwell in those who love Him and to be revealed through them in our world. This creates spiritual greatness in those lives where fanaticism and pettiness used to run riot. To be conscious of the presence of the indwelling Christ, requires a steadfast faith in His promises and the courage to live as if those promises have already been fulfilled – as is indeed the case.

The consciousness of God living in you creates a new approach, and a new attitude towards life. Trust takes the place of inferiority; love overcomes hate; compassion overcomes bitterness. The consciousness of your gratitude for the glory and beauty of daily life grows from an honest acknowledgement of the greatness of the indwelling God.

Thanksgiving to God causes even temporary blessing to be a foretaste of heaven. (William Romaine)

Wondrous God, because You dwell in me through Jesus Christ

℘raise the Lord in gratitude

"Yours, O Lord, is the greatness, the power and the glory, the victory and the majesty. And You are exalted as head over all." (1 Chr. 29:11)

℘he words quoted above appear in a very touching prayer of gratitude by David. When the Christian comes before his Lord, much time is spent in intercession. Requests for the one who is praying and on behalf of others are brought to the foot of God's throne of grace. Worries, fear and anxiety are brought to God while seeking His assistance and guidance. Indeed, many people's prayers to God consist of personal requests only.

Don't make the mistake of neglecting to praise and thank the Lord in your prayer life. Remember all the love He has shown you in your life; take note of the blessings which He lavishes upon you; remind yourself of all the instances when Jesus helped you to overcome obstacles and how He provided in your everyday needs. And for how many years has He been doing all this? Do not belittle these blessings simply because they are common and everyday.

Never for a moment think that God doesn't need your praise and thanksgiving. By faithfully worshipping you will find that in your spirit you are constantly drawn closer to the risen Saviour. Your worship, praise and gratitude should not be lip-service only, but should flow sincerely from your heart.

While you are praising God's holy Name and thanking Him, you will find yourself being surrounded more and more by His love, until you eventually experience that unity with the living Christ which is the deep desire of every true disciple of the Master.

> Learn that there can be worship without words. (James Russel)

Today I worship and praise You as _____

_____

We worship a magnificent God

"And my speech and my preaching were not with persuasive words of human wisdom, but in demonstration of the Spirit and of power." (1 Cor. 2:4)

One of the greatest dangers which threatens the church today, is the great number of people who attend worship services to listen to a popular speaker rather than to the eternal Word of God. Such an attitude could easily develop into a situation where people go to church to be entertained. Above all else, it must be an opportunity to meet with God and to reach out to fellow believers.

When founding the early church, Christ mainly used simple people with little or no education. Through the ages many of the spiritual giants had very little schooling, but still brought thousands to salvation. God often uses simple instruments.

This again serves to stress the fact that it is the Holy Spirit, and not a human being, who moves people to commit their lives to Jesus Christ. In all preaching it is the honour and glory of God through Jesus Christ, which must be accentuated. Christ not only needs to be the centre of all preaching and worship, but the whole message must glorify Him. In your grateful worship you must always seek the guidance of the Holy Spirit. If you have prayerfully wrestled a message from Him, you will feel compelled to submit yourself to His service as a form of gratitude for His great sacrifice. Then you will know for sure that you are worshipping in spirit and truth and with a heart filled with gratitude.

He who worships with his lips only, only worships partially. The full, grateful worship comes from the depths of the heart. (Alexander Pope)

I want to worship You because You _____

_____

The highest goal in life

"While I live I will praise the Lord; I will sing praises to my God while I have my being." (Ps. 146:2)

God's highest goal with creation was His honour and glory. What place does this have on the agenda of your life? There are many who serve God sacrificially and unselfishly, staggering our imaginations with their inspirational deeds.

Yet, often the most noble deed man can render doesn't seem important or exciting at first sight. Singing the praises of the almighty God has been watered down as a religious duty for too long. Many people regard it as totally remote from our everyday life. When praise and worship are mentioned, the average person thinks of hymns, Scripture reading, corporate prayers and sermons. These things do play an important role in our worship and in the fellowship of believers because in most congregations the members have a need of them. Corporate worship is definetely not out of fashion yet.

Nevertheless, worship and praise are much more than a religious practice: it is a way of life that is inspired by the living Christ. It is not sufficient to restrict praise and thanksgiving to a few hours per week. It must be practised every hour of every day, during our week of work and on the sports field. Praise and thanksgiving are the power and inspiration which touch the common things in life, making them holy. Everything must be done to the glory of God. Praise and thanksgiving empower and elevate and they are the hidden motive behind every worthwhile noble deed worthwhile.

There is no duty more urgent than to praise and thank God. (Ambrosius)

Lord, my highest goal in life is _____

_____

$\mathcal{T}$he power of thanksgiving

"Heal me, O Lord, and I shall be healed; Save me and I shall be saved, for You are my praise." (Jer. 17:14)

$\mathcal{T}$he person who has not yet lifted his heart and mind to God in an act of grateful praise, has missed out on one of the greatest experiences of life. Unfortunately most people experience the time of praise and worship as a time of gloominess, something to be endured rather than enjoyed.

Psalm 47 appeals to all people with the following words, *"Oh, clap your hands all you peoples! Shout to God with the voice of triumph!"* (Psalm 47:2). It is impossible to clap your hands and sing exultantly to the honour of God and still be gloomy. The speaking of praise is a powerful inspiration. If you are feeling down-hearted at this moment and it seems as if nothing is working out well for you, then start praising and thanking God now. It might sound foolish to you but you can thank God that He is with you in your present situation.

True praise and thanksgiving to the almighty God should not depend on your feelings. When you are down-hearted and depressed, these are the very moments that you need to praise Him. Then you will experience the wonderful, elevating power of praise and thanksgiving. It is the key which God provides you with to open the treasure chambers of life in Him. It is also the way in which you can overcome the degenerating influences which continually haunt you.

You don't need an organ or the church choir to truly praise and thank God. The simple lifting up of your heart to Him, brings you into His presence immediately and you cannot help but sing His praise and glory, with the angels surrounding His throne.

A grateful heart is the only door which gives entrance to the presence of God. (Joe Orton)

I want to lift my heart and mind to You and _____

_____

Practise the prayer of thanksgiving

"Is anyone among you suffering? Let him pray. Is anyone cheerful? Let him sing psalms." (Jas. 5:13)

Whenever you have some or other need, you turn to someone for help. You may need the help of someone who is qualified in a specific field, or you may only need the help of a trusted friend. Whoever it may be, you go to this person, trusting that he will be able to help you. Regardless of what the outcome may be, undoubtedly you are grateful. You express your gratitude towards this person and probably you will testify about him with great praise.

When you are confronted with a problem, in the midst of your anxiety and confusion, never neglect taking your need to the One who, through grace, is offering you His friendship. The One who invited you to come to Him with all your burdens. Lay your problem down at the foot of the cross and hand it over to Christ in prayer.

However, don't stop there. Thank God for the assurance that Jesus is in control now, that He really cares for you and that His hand now guides you through your maze of problems. He will lead you out of the darkness of your situation into the marvellous light of Christ's love.

Prayer is the channel connecting you with the living Christ and only through prayers of thanksgiving do you release the omnipotence of God in your life as well. Believe that God put this power at your disposal in order that you may live on victory ground – and thank Him for it daily.

> Prayer is the unconditional requirement for everything God wishes to establish in this world. (Dr. Andrew Murray)

Father, I want to come to You with _____

_____

The challenge to surrender

"He who says he abides in Him ought himself also to walk just as He walked." (1 Jn. 2:6)

One of the great dangers in the Christian's experience is that he can become so emotionally involved in religion that he disregards the practical claims of the Christian faith. In the excitement of a spiritual experience, it is easy to forget those who are hungry and thirsty, or to restrict your Christianity to the people who think as you do.

The challenge which Christ sets before you, requires the total commitment of every aspect of your life to Him. The minute you exclude some part of your life, regarding it as an area where the Christian ethics don't apply, your commitment to Christ is incomplete. Then your faith also becomes ineffective. The challenge of the living Christ is that He must possess you totally if you wish to grow into His image and attitude.

Your commitment to Christ must never be dependent on your fluctuating emotions. It's not what you feel, but what you are that counts in your Christianity. It must be established as a reality in your practical world. You cannot be one with Christ if you are not like Christ or don't act like Him. It can no longer be "Christ and I", but "Christ alone!"

Thus the challenging question is, Can you commit yourself to Him totally and can you trust Him with your life? You can if you seriously desire it and if you are truly grateful for being redeemed by the living Christ. If you do that, you will taste something of the pure joy derived from commitment and submission to Christ your Lord.

> To believe in Christ is initial faith; to accept Him is redeeming faith; to strive to become like Him is active faith. (Corneluis Woelfkin)

Today I want to accept the challenge of total commitment by

*B*e thankful in everything

"Better is a little with the fear of the Lord, than great treasure with trouble." (Prov. 15:16)

he Christian faith creates great expectations in many people. Inspirational phrases such as, "Expect God to do great things," or "We serve a miracle-working God," or "Nothing is impossible to those who believe," and many similar expressions stress the greatness of God. However, it seems as though the average Christian derives more inspiration than practical experience from these sayings. He steadfastly believes that they are true, yet in his personal life he still has to get to know the great deeds of God.

One of the main reasons for this is that he is so anxious to look for a revelation of the miracle-working God, that he is not able to see God at work in the common, everyday matters. Perhaps we find it difficult to believe that all the good and beautiful things that happen to us all the time as small and inconspicuous blessings, are indeed given to us by a gracious God.

It is when you have learned to appreciate the small blessings from God, that you are able to see how God is at work in your life. The wonder of true friendship, the basic goodness of people, an understanding heart that opens up to you when others misunderstand you, the marvel of joy and laughter – and many other important things in life – are all expressions of the greatness of God who bestows His blessings upon us.

Therefore, decide now that from today on you will not take anything for granted. Thank God for blessings as you become aware of them. By doing this, you will unlock a treasure chamber of God, which will add new beauty and riches to your life.

Gratitude is when the heart remembers. (Samuel Johnson)

I praise and thank You, gracious Lord, for the small things _____

Joy in the Lord!

"Rejoice in the Lord always. Again I will say, rejoice!" (Phil. 4:4)

Many people experience their religion as a sombre burden which they feel compelled to bear. They feel compelled to attend church services and to worship and when they don't do it, they feel very guilty. Bible study and prayer have become a form of duty to them which they have to do in order to please a formidable God. The result is that their submission to the Christian teachings and objectives is a colourless habit which doesn't have any deeper meaning to them.

This approach is a total misrepresentation! There is nothing colourless or boring about Christ's life here on earth and there is nothing dull in the abundant life which He offers us. As with everything else in life, it depends on what you make of it, and if you experience a colourless spiritual life, you should take a serious look at yourself.

Jesus Christ invites you to become part of His life. He wants to become a part of your life, in order that, as He Himself said, " ... *and your joy no one will take from you*" (John 16:22). Then the joy of Christ becomes full in our lives. The whole Christian experience is one of great joy because Jesus overcame sin and death.

With such a rich inheritance to look forward to, can you do otherwise than to rejoice in the Lord – and to do it in such a way that the whole world will know who your Saviour and the Source of your joy is? Let us stop cursing the darkness and rather light a candle of joy, thus helping dispel the darkness.

If there is no joy in your Christianity, it means that you have a leak somewhere in your Christianity. (W.A. "Billy" Sunday)

O Lord, I rejoice in _____

_____

We are His children

"Behold what manner of love the Father has bestowed on us, that we should be called children of God now we are children of God" (1 Jn. 3:1, 2)

This heading may seem smug to many people, while others may find it somewhat sentimental. In reality it is one of the great evangelical truths which causes Christians to be grateful, happy people.

God's children are to be found in every area of life. A few fill high positions which carry much responsibility, many have a lot of authority, but millions spend their lives in humble obscurity. Regardless of what area of life they move in, they have the assurance that the eternal God is their heavenly Father. This knowledge brings indescribable joy and happiness into their lives – something which the non-Christian can never understand.

To accept the Fatherhood of God and to rejoice in it, brings joy and beauty into your life. You become aware of the fact that God is your guide. You remain sensitive to the prompting of the Holy Spirit. It is an exciting and satisfying adventure which creates a wonderful sense of partnership with the Father. Calling God your Father implies that you will live in harmony with Him. If you co-operate with Him in unity, life unfolds for you in a wonderful way.

Regardless of what humble position you may hold in life, you can hold your head high when you realise Whom you belong to. Such an attitude isn't the cause of spiritual pride. It causes a Godly dignity to be added to every earthly task, because everything you do, you do as a child of God – to His glory! Life can hardly give greater joy than this to any human being.

True Christianity is the highest form of being. (Edward Young)

To acknowledge You as Father, gives me _____

Show your gratitude

"Then the Lord said, 'I am Jesus, whom you are persecuting.'"
(Acts 9:5)

There are many people who, when they read the report of Jesus Christ's life in the Gospels, stand amazed at the attitude people had towards Him here on earth. He was a person who emanated goodness, compassion, sympathy and love and yet, through His whole ministry, He had to deal with opposition. The religious leaders of His time hated Him and continually looked for ways and means to destroy Him. When He was eventually crucified, people humiliated Him and His most intimate friends denied Him.

In our time people in their right mind stand dismayed at the treatment which the Prince of Peace received, while He only wanted what was the very best for everyone. Nevertheless, believe it or not, even in our day Christ is still being persecuted.

Every time you turn away from the Lord, when other people or things are more important to you than your relationship with the Master, when you turn your back on Him by participating in activities which grieve Him, when you don't notice the needs of your fellowmen – then you are involved in subjecting Jesus Christ to persecution in the same way others did centuries ago.

Through the sacrifice of His life the living Christ gave you salvation. All He requires from you in return is to surrender your life to Him unconditionally so that you may enjoy the complete joy of life in Christ. How can you ungratefully reject such an offer?

> There is but one important virtue: the unceasing sacrifice of the self. (George Sand)

Saviour and Friend, I want to prove my gratitude by _____

Appreciate your life

"I will offer to You the sacrifice of thanksgiving, and will call upon the Name of the Lord." (Ps. 116:17)

There are times when man's enthusiasm wanes and life loses its dynamic quality. This unfortunate situation can overcome you very unexpectedly. You suddenly realise that the positive and meaningful life you once led, is something of the past.

To really appreciate life, enthusiasm must be renewed all the time. The gift of life must never be taken for granted, or it becomes common and boring and you lose your sense of anticipation and vision for the future. You must always make time for something to look forward to. Enjoying and appreciating the beauty of life must be an integral part of your life.

Do you regard the love and support of your family as your right?

Can you still marvel at the rising of the sun?

Have you become so used to the suffering around you that it no longer moves you with compassion?

Can you still laugh without embarrassment about a funny situation, or do you find it hard to believe that humour is one of God's gifts to you?

Your daily existence can so easily degenerate into drudgery, like a donkey which walks in a never-ending circle around a watermill. If you practise the art of appreciation, you can change your life into a beautiful and exciting experience. If you allow God to form the centre of your life and thoughts, you will discover that by appreciating your life, you are continually moving closer to Him, the Source of all real life.

No man lives to the full who doesn't live to the full spiritually. (W. Marshall Craig)

Father, I appreciate _____

_____

Grateful obedience

"Serve the Lord with gladness; Come before his presence with singing."
(Ps. 100:2)

Strange as it may sound, most people experience their worship as a heavy burden instead of pure joy. They feel that they have to lay down so many things that are precious to them and that they enter into a life of seriousness and hardship. They forget the fact that when they lay down their old life and start a new life in Christ Jesus, that it is a life of indescribable joy and gladness. When God asks us to lay down our old life, we can be confident that He will replace it with something much better.

Don't believe for one moment that when God requires total obedience from you, that your life will lose its joy and gladness. God probably finds it easier to use an obedient, happy person in His service than one who is overwhelmed by the idea of the heavy responsibility he believes it takes to serve the Lord.

He promised to bear our burdens if we obey and trust Him. If He calls you to obedience, trust Him completely so that the morbid experiences of depression and unnecessary concern will vanish under the influence of a positive and cheerful faith.

Many of God's servants have great responsibilities, but they don't bear them on their own, because they are thoroughly aware that His everlasting arms are supporting them.

If God has called you to a special responsibility in His vineyard, don't become despondent to the point where your life becomes a burden. Rejoice in the Lord and in His omnipotence and accept your duty with gladness and gratitude.

> Obedience to God is the most infallible proof of true and total love for Him. (Nathanael Emmons)

I want to accept my task with gladness, Lord, because _____

_____

Fight depression

"Create in me a clean heart, O God, and renew a steadfast spirit within me." (Ps. 51:10)

When you feel depressed and it seems to you as if life has lost its sparkle; when your outlook on the future has become bleak, it becomes extremely difficult for you to believe in God's compassion and love. If someone tries to cheer you up by telling you that God loves you, you become irritated and you feel as if you want to reject your faith in Him altogether.

At such times you need to stop and stand still in the barrenness of your spiritual desert to look back into the treasury of your memories. Recall those happy times when God was a living reality to you, when He guided you along difficult paths and touched you in your sorrow with His comfort. Remember those times when it seemed as if your whole life was falling apart and He upheld you with His loving hand. Recall those times and start thanking Him for them.

Perhaps you spent too much time in the valley of despair and sank into self-pity. You were only aware of your defeats and failures, and the negative influences of "what could have been" totally overshadowed your mind. Now is the moment to start to thank and praise God for His grace in the past and His help in the present. Re-establish your trust in Him. It is indescribable what praise and thanksgiving can do to a contrite and depressed spirit. Accept the challenge and experience how, in His goodness, He can lift you up from the dark pit of despair!

True joy and gladness are not derived from comfort or riches or the praise of people, but from giving praise and thanksgiving to your Creator God. (Sir Wilfred Grenfell)

I want to thank You for those times in my past when You ___

$\mathscr{S}$trive for God's honour

"That in all things God may be glorified through Jesus Christ, to whom belong the glory and dominion forever and ever." (1 Pet. 4:11)

$\mathcal{W}$hen you are involved in the work of the church of Jesus Christ, it is very easy to become so enthusiastic that you become so involved that you exclude everything and everyone else. Regardless of how praiseworthy such total commitment may be, one must be very careful to ensure that in the first place your commitment is to God and not to a task.

If you are so absorbed in the task that it receives preference above everything else in your life, watch out for danger signs. You may just be following your own will for your life, and not God's will. Such a situation unwittingly leads to self-gratification rather than a desire to serve the Master.

Before you undertake any task on your Christian pilgrimage, make very sure that it is the task which the Lord has called you to do. Then open up your heart and mind for the Holy Spirit. You must allow Him to lead you along His path. Then He will give you the ability to fulfil the task.

In everything you do for Him, you must only give your very best. Always remember that the praise and honour must always belong to God alone. His honour and glory depend on the way in which you serve Him as his disciple. It is not without reason that Jesus taught us to pray, *"For Yours is the kingdom and the power and the glory forever"* (Matthew 6:13). Our highest goal is the glory of God the Father.

I started by asking God to help me. Then I asked if I could help Him. I ended by asking God to glorify Himself through me. (Hudson Taylor)

Help me to do my work in Your church in such a manner that

Experience the joy of the Lord!

"Then the children of Israel, the priests and the Levites and the rest of the descendants of the captivity, celebrated the dedication of this house of God with joy." (Ezra 6:16)

There are two attitudes towards the Christian faith which can cause immeasurable damage to your worship of God. The first is to regard your faith as an unpleasant duty. The second is to become so blasé that you lose sight of the mystical wonder of God.

Commitment to and the worship of God are not merely a duty, but also a privilege. In everyday life it is usually very hard to get an appointment with a very important person – if you can manage it at all. To enter into the presence of God, the King of all kings, all that is required of you is to turn to Him in prayer. Indeed, through the living Christ, He is willing to come into your life and become a part of your existence if you invite Him to do it.

Familiarity can so easily develop simply through the habit of "going to church". Regular attendance of services or places of worship must never be allowed to make you into a passive spectator. Remember that you are essentially in the presence of the most holy God during times of communal worship. Like Moses, you are at the burning bush of God's divine presence.

Enjoy your pilgrimage of following Christ. Allow Him to become part of your everyday life. Then you will discover the fullness of life which He offers you in John 10:10, *"I have come that they may have life and that they may have it more abundantly."*

Don't forget that even your work can be worship. To be joyful is also a form of worship. (Robert Louis Stevenson)

Please keep me from empty ceremony so that I _____

_____

Count your blessings

"So that he who blesses himself in the earth, shall bless himself in the God of truth." (Is. 65:16)

There are so many people who go through life moaning and groaning. Their view of life is totally negative. If anyone should dare speak a word of praise about a project or a person, they will always mention some or other fault or character flaw.

The person who has developed the habit of counting his blessings, is extremely happy. He believes there is a solution for every problem and won't rest until he has found that solution. In the darkest moments he maintains a spirit of hope and optimism because he believes things will work out well.

To the optimist the simple things in life are a constant source of joy – the gift of unrestrained bursts of laughter, the sympathy and understanding of a loved one, the bright rays of the sun.

The fact of the matter is that, the more you count your blessings, the more it will seem as if God pours them upon your life, even though you are not worthy of them. At such times your heart and mind will overflow with gratitude for God's charity. Counting your blessings is of course more than an emotional experience. It has a practical application for every one of the Master's disciples. When life becomes a burden to you and it feels as though you are living under an ominously dark heaven, recalling such blessings is a sure method to restore your spiritual equilibrium. Make an effort to notice God's abundant blessings in your life, appreciate them and thank Him.

Learn from David the gift of gratitude. Every furrow of the book of Psalms is covered with the seed of gratitude. (Jeremy Taylor)

Father, how will I be able to express my gratitude in words? You bless me with _____

_____

Start your day giving thanks

"Rooted and built up in Him and established in the faith as you have been taught, abounding in it with thanksgiving." (Col. 2:7)

It is of the utmost importance that we, as children of God, must maintain a positive and constructive attitude towards life. Lack of sufficient rest can however cause you to be irritated to the extent that you develop a wrong image of what your life can and should be. Poor health can influence you negatively so that you become difficult to live with. Yet, numerous invalids are channels of blessing for those who take care of them. Your attitude towards life is of the greatest importance to yourself and those whom you live with.

A healthy approach and positive attitude towards life is not something that comes naturally to the average person. When we wake up in the morning, we are subjected to the whims of our emotions. If we didn't have sufficient sleep, we tend to look at life from a jaundiced point of view.

When you wake up in the morning your first responsibility is to take positive control of your thoughts and to thank God for the privilege of giving you a new day. Many of your fellowmen do not enjoy the privileges that you do. Recall some of the blessings which you take for granted: your home, your friends and loved ones, your job and many more things.

Gratitude brings your heart into harmony with your heavenly Father. If that happens, then every day is filled with true gladness in the Lord. However, it requires an act of your will to start every day with true thanksgiving – but it is worthwhile.

> Gratitude is not merely the memory of the heart – it is also the heart of worship. It is offered to God for His goodness. (Nathaniel Parker Willis)

I want to start my day by thanking You for _____

"Search for a blessing!"

"Therefore, whether you eat or drink, or whatever you do, do all to the glory of God." (1 Cor. 10:31)

Your daily task can either be a blessing or a curse, depending largely on your attitude. If you are one of those unhappy people who needs to drag yourself through every day and only comes to life when your day's work comes to an end, the time has come for you to reconsider your attitude towards your job.

Does your job in any way add to the well-being of your fellowman, even though it may be in a very small measure? If your daily work is to the detriment of another person's well-being, you cannot possibly ask God's blessing upon it. The result is that you are robbed of a source of blessing and inspiration. If you have the ability to look beyond the temporary financial gain and to make an essential contribution to the society that you live in, then you can dedicate what you do to God, praying for His blessing upon you and your work.

If you are able to bring your daily work as a sacrifice to God, you will add a new dimension to your life. There will no longer be any division between that which is secular and that which is holy. Everything in life will be filled with the power and purpose of your heavenly Father. God then becomes your inspiration and your source of motivation. Tasks which previously were dull and meaningless, then become interesting and meaningful.

Whether your daily work is humble or high, if you do it to glorify Him, it will be elevated above what is earthly and will be enriched because you know that God is your ally. Then you will be inspired by His Spirit to seek only that which will bless your fellowman and to give God all the glory.

Blessed is the man who is too busy to worry during the day and too tired to worry during the night. (Charles Dickens)

I want to ask your blessing upon my daily work so that once again it _____

Bear one another's burdens

"Bear one another's burdens, and so fulfil the law of Christ." (Gal. 6:2)

It is very easy to become self-centred in your spiritual life. When this happens, everything you do is motivated by selfish self-glorification and satisfying your own ego. Even your good works are then done with a selfish motive.

When you become a disciple of Jesus Christ, the centre of your world moves from yourself to your Master. You live only to please Him and you forget about yourself. This includes having a loving interest in people – especially those who suffer under heavy burdens. Because you belong to Christ, you also belong to those who need you and you try to help them in the Name of Christ.

This kind of service can be very demanding and often requires more from you than you think you can give. Always remember that the Master will give you the support and strength which you need for the task. The Master never calls you to do a task in His Name, then leaves you to yourself to do it in your own strength. He is renowned as the Great Bearer of burdens and if you will allow Him, He will be your partner in your efforts to carry the burdens of others.

Becoming the Master's partner in such a big task, will strengthen your bond of unity with Him. It is impossible to cooperate with Him without getting to know Him more intimately. Thus, the bearing of other people's burdens becomes a rich blessing and inspiration for all who are willing to cooperate with Christ – and as a result the world we live in becomes a better place.

> Next to love, sympathy is the most sacred passion of the human soul. (Samuel Taylor Coleridge)

When I carry the burdens of others, please teach me to _____

Think and thank!

"I thank my God upon every remembrance of you." (Phil. 1:3)

When the path of life becomes steep to you and when dark clouds of depression ominously cover you and threaten to suffocate all inspiration, it is time to come to a halt and consider the way along which God has led you thus far, to remember all His abundant blessings.

Undoubtedly there were moments when you thought that you would bend double and break under the stress and strain. Then God unexpectedly sent someone into your life to bring you new hope and strength. There were times when disaster loomed and you felt that everything was lost, but by the mediation of one of God's children you were able to rise from the ashes of failure.

Once again you realise that there was a blessing for every negative and degenerating influence.

The key that unlocks the door to a creative life is gratitude. In everything that happens to you, look for something to be grateful for. Thank God for all the good people He allowed to cross your path of life, for opportunities He created for you, for the wonder of friendship and, above everything else, for the assurance of His eternal presence at all times.

When this truth becomes your personal experience, you will approach the future with God-given confidence and the assurance that in the Name of Christ and in His strength, you can triumph over every situation.

> The true test for character is seen in the measure and strength of our gratitude. (Milo H. Gates)

Loving Master, I recall the blessings of the past _____

The joy of grateful service

"For though I am free from all men, I have made myself a servant to all, that I might win the more." (1 Cor. 9:19)

Most of us strive to achieve independence. Children dream about the day when they will be adults, employees yearn to start their own enterprises in order to answer to themselves only. And so we can name many examples of people who strive to be in control of their own lives.

Even though it is self-evident that the ordinary Christian will never consider being separated from the authority of Christ, we must watch against the danger of submitting ourselves totally to the will of another person. In order to serve God as we should, we need to be able to act independently of human pressure and influence, as long as it is not contrary to the will of God.

Nevertheless, if you want to witness effectively for Christ, it is important to willingly make yourself available to your fellowman so that you can lead him as the Holy Spirit leads you. Even though it is not comfortable for you, you must at all times give yourself as a sacrifice in order to be an instrument for God's peace and a channel of Christ's love and compassion.

Undoubtedly it will encroach upon your time and in certain situations it can be extremely frustrating. But the joy of winning souls for Christ through grateful service, will more than compensate for anything you may suffer. Put this to the test and discover the truth for yourself.

> Even though I am the lowest and most insignificant, let me be eternally counted amongst the number who are really free because they discovered real freedom in your service. (John Greenleaf Whittier)

Master, I am willing to _____

The joy of faith

"But he who is joined to the Lord is one spirit with Him." (1 Cor. 6:17)

Joy and gladness are not the main goals of the Christian's faith, but an important by-product of it. The beginning and the end of a dynamic faith is the Master Himself. When you have experienced the inflowing of His life-giving Spirit, the joy of a Christ-filled life becomes yours.

To be united with Him and to share in Christ's life, presupposes that you will have a relationship with Him which rises above all dogma and that you will experience the peace and power of His indwelling presence. Such an experience is much more than an emotion because it is founded on a living faith of someone who has accepted His forgiveness and only lives to portray Christ in the midst of life's harsh realities.

Forgiveness which goes hand in hand with a Spirit-filled life, gives tremendous joy to all who strive to live "in Christ". But the summit of this joy is to be conscious of Christ's living presence.

Such moments may be few and far between, but they create a blessing and joy that last for a long time. You find yourself in fellowship with Him at all times and in every place. The more you become aware of His closeness, the stronger and more meaningful your faith gets. Then you realise that your faith is in actual fact your personal relationship with the living Christ.

There is no way in which we can express this pure joy in words – except to live in gratitude for His glory and to serve our fellowmen as He had done.

> Joy is the echo of Christ living in us. (Joseph Marmion)

I want to express my gratitude to You for your closeness by

_____

_____

*S*erve the Lord with gladness!

"Serve the Lord with gladness; Come before his presence with singing."
(Ps. 100:2)

*L*ord, my God and my Father, with the psalmist I want to confess jubilantly, *"Praise the Lord! Oh, give thanks to the Lord, for He is good! For his mercy endures forever!"* (Psalm 106:1).

I praise and thank You as Creator, Father because You created me and you re-created me as Your child; for the wonder that I may call You my Father. I thank You for creation through which You speak to me and in which I can come so close to You in worship.

I bow before You in gratitude for Your Son, Jesus, the living Christ. That You sent Him to this sin-torn world to save sinners and make them children of God. Thank You, Lord Jesus, for Your suffering, death and triumphant resurrection and that I can be a part of Your triumphal procession through the ages. I stand in awe because of the gift of the Holy Spirit who led me to Jesus and worked the rebirth in me. I thank You for the guidance of the Holy Spirit.

It is with gratitude that I praise You for Your Word, which, through the Holy Spirit, reveals Your divine will for my life. I thank You that this Word is the light for my path and the lamp for my foot. Help me to study it faithfully.

I praise and thank You, my Father, for abundant blessings: for my life's companion, my family, my friends and all the things which make my life worthwhile. Give me a grateful heart always, O Lord, that my life may be a song of thanksgiving to your honour. *"For the Lord is good; His mercy is everlasting, and his truth endures to all generations"* (Psalm 100:5).

> Learn from David to be jubilantly grateful for everything. Every furrow of the book of Psalms is covered with the seed of exultant gratitude. (Jeremy Taylor)

I want to sing to the Lord's honour as long as I live because _____

THE FOUNTAIN

OF FAITH

The Christian faith offers us peace in a time of war, comfort in sorrow, strength in weakness and light in the darkness. (Walter A. Maier)

Eternal Father of love and grace, when I read in Your Word about the mighty deeds of the great heroes of faith, it seems as if faith came to them so easily. I so badly want to believe like a little child, not only to receive eternal life, but also to be firmly convinced here and now that You are present to guide me in every moment of insecurity and confusion; to comfort me in every moment of sorrow; to strengthen me in every moment of temptation, uncertainty and doubt. Help me, through Your Holy Spirit to be sure of my salvation through Jesus Christ my Saviour; that nothing and no one can separate me from Your love; so that I can fearlessly, and with courage, deal with the demands of every day. And Lord, sometimes when unbelief eats at my heart – please help my unbelief and give me more faith, O Lord. Help me to live on the victory ground of faith. I pray this in the Name of Jesus the Christ.

Faith: fact or fiction?

"If you have faith as a mustard seed, you can say to this mulberry tree 'be pulled up by the roots and be planted in the sea,' and it would obey you." *(Lk. 17:6)*

An endless amount is written and said about the necessity of having faith. However, when confronted with a serious problem, many people have great difficulty in exercising their faith. The main cause for this is the fact that human nature is fallible. When our faith is being tested, we are inclined to fall back on what we know, rather than to trust God to carry us through the unknown into the safety of His flock.

A penetrating study of God's holy Word, reveals countless examples of those people who put their steadfast trust in God. And for this they received their reward in Christ Jesus. God wonderfully met their needs according to the riches of His grace. If this were true about people, it was especially true in the life of His Son, Jesus Christ. The classic example of this is the arrest, death, resurrection and ascension of our Saviour. In what seemed to be the most impossible, appalling situation, His love for God was so deeply rooted that He could say with assurance, *"nevertheless, not as I will, but as You will"* (Matthew 26:39).

Trust God steadfastly. Find your strength through the Holy Spirit. Trust God to carry you through your problems and you will be rewarded when His perfect will is revealed to you.

> Faith is to believe what we don't see and the reward of such a faith is to see what we believe. (Augustine)

Counsellor and Finisher of my faith, I trust You to _____

_____

*W*atch over your faith

"Woe to you who are at ease in Zion, and trust in Mount Samaria."
(Amos 6:1)

hose who are too much at ease are usually woken up with a shock. History teems with many such examples. This is what led to the devastating fall of the once mighty Roman Empire. This kind of indulgent apathy has brought about the failure of business concerns. Families and marriages have been torn apart as a result of this kind of indifference. There can be no doubt in any mind that anything that is worth having is also worth nurturing. As soon as you take something of great value for granted, you are in danger of losing it.

And the Christian's faith is no exception. What in the whole world could be more precious than the church of Jesus Christ? Christ's concern for it was so great that He was willing to lay down His life for His people. The apostle of love writes that there is no greater love than this.

A great responsibility rests on you as a Christian never to take your faith for granted or to regard the church of Christ with little concern. More than anything else of great value, your faith needs to be cosseted, protected and offered in service to glorify Christ.

This requires an act of total commitment to the Master from you personally. He was willing to give His life for you. What value is to it for you to nurture your faith?

> It is not faith and works; it is not faith or works; it is faith only that works. (Anonymous)

Faithful Guide, keep me from being too much at ease with regard to my _____

_____

*W*hen doubt eats at your heart

"Now while Peter wondered within himself what this vision which he had seen meant ... " (Acts 10:17)

*Y*ou might live with trust in God and your fellowman for some time. Everything you attempt ends in success and you are sure that your future will be good, better than your past has ever been. But suddenly, for reasons that cannot be explained, your faith and trust start to wane. Things suddenly start going wrong and there is a dissonant note in your life. Then you suddenly start doubting God as well as your ability to handle matters successfully.

If you allow doubt to penetrate and control your mind, it is only a matter of time before you are overwhelmed by a feeling of incompetence. You start convincing yourself that you have no value and don't mean anything to anyone. The sooner you get out of the picture and are forgotten, the better.

The minute you become aware of it, you must handle destructive doubt which undermines your faith, scars your trust in God and destroys your confidence. Don't allow it to swell like a poisonous abscess in your inner being. It will undermine your mental and spiritual vision. Banish it from your life through positive and creative actions. Recall those things which you do feel confident about and concentrate on them. Then do something purposeful for someone who needs encouragement. It is amazing how you can get rid of your own doubt as well as strengthen the faith of another person. By doing this you won't fall prey to a sense of false security, but you'll strengthen your own faith every time.

> Speak faith. The world is a better place without your expressed ignorance and morbid doubt. (Ella Wheeler Wilcox)

When doubt eats at my heart, O Father, please give me _____

The core of a living faith

"He who does not love does not know God, for God is love." (1 Jn. 4:8)

Your faith can have many facets. There are times when it is an immeasurable source of inspiration; in times of weakness you have experienced its power in your spirit; when sorrow washed over you, you experienced the comfort that is only to be found through a living faith in God; in times of confusion it made you aware of a great calm. Your faith fits into your complex life in such a manner that every one of your needs is fulfilled. The result is that you use all your energy trying to do the perfect will of God.

Although it is true that God finds pleasure in lavishing His blessings upon your life, He can only do so if your heart is in harmony with Him and your whole life is filled with love for Him. Love is the key word which unlocks all Christian experience and it is also the lifeline of faith. It is impossible to know God unless you love Him. Because His whole being is love, He can only reveal Himself to those who are tuned in to His divine person even in a minute and imperfect way. Because God is love, you too must allow love to become part of your nature and being if you really want to get to know Him.

This may sound like an impractical ideal and foolish suggestion. But, Jesus has called you to such a way of life, and He will not mock you by calling you to an unattainable ideal. It is of course impossible to reach this through your own abilities, but because He promised to live in you and take possession of you, Christian love is an attainable ideal through faith which lives in your heart.

> Love is ownership. We own those whom we love. The universe belongs to God because He is love. (Henry Ward Beecher)

Lord Jesus, through Your Holy Spirit, I can _____

_____

ⓘn what do you put your faith?

"He did not waver at the promise of God through unbelief, but was strengthened in faith, giving glory to God." (Rom. 4:20)

Every person on the face of the earth believes in something or someone and that which you put your faith and trust in, determines the quality of your life. Some people believe in failure. Even before they make an attempt to do something new or creative, they have already formed an atmosphere of failure over the whole project through their attitude and words.

Then, when they do fail, they say with a feeling of false pride that that is exactly what they expected to happen. The misfortune they expect comes over them mainly because they believe in failure.

If you put your faith in God in a calm and purposeful manner, you appeal to His omnipotence. This will strengthen you beyond your wildest dreams. There is no part of your life or mind which cannot be revived by the Holy Spirit. You need only keep your mind focused on Him.

To have a realistic and practical faith in God, means that you will live in harmony with Him. This will result in the riches of His grace and love becoming yours. Your life will have meaning and purpose; He will lead you along constructive paths; fear will be removed from your life and peace of mind will fill your being. A practical faith in God is the greatest treasure you could ever own.

The most precious thing is within reach, available without price or money. You only need to stretch out the hand of faith and appropriate it by grace. (John Burroughs)

Precious Saviour, I put my faith in _____

_____

Faith is the answer

"And we know that all things work together for good to those who love God, to those who are called according to his purpose." (Rom. 8:28)

Undoubtedly there are days in your life when you find it hard to understand why certain things happen: a child dies in an accident; a good person is killed by lightning; a loved one is diagnosed with cancer; the business concern of an honourable man is declared insolvent. Inevitably the question comes to your mind, "Why?"

After Job's outburst because of all the misfortune that broke loose over his life, Sophar said to him, *"Can you search out the deep things of God? Can you find out the limits of the Almighty?"* (Job 11:7). This statement is still just as true today. Equally true is the fact that your faith in God needs to be just as steadfast as Job's. In spite of his suffering, in spite of his wife's foolish advice that he must curse God and die, he held on to the omnipotence and wisdom of God and to His unchanging goodness. This was how Job eventually found peace and lived in prosperity.

God loves you and only wants what is best for you. This was proven beyond all doubt by Jesus Christ on Golgotha. Just as Jesus was required to suffer in order to execute God's perfect will, it is necessary that sometimes, in certain situations, we have to endure suffering before the will of God becomes clear to us. If this is what you are presently experiencing, remember then that the living Christ is with you in your suffering. Trust Him to carry you through these difficult times. With Him you will be able to move through this temporary darkness into the bright light of His perfect will.

> God will not ask for medals, degrees or diplomas. He will ask for the scars of your faith. (Dwight L. Moody)

Almighty Father, I will not get upset, because _____

_____

Grow in faith

"Immediately the father of the child cried out and said with tears, 'Lord, I believe; help my unbelief.'" (Mk. 9:24)

Many dedicated Christians urge their fellowmen with the words, "Just believe!" They assure them that wonderful things will happen if they do that. But they don't tell them how such a faith can be obtained. The cry of the father quoted in our verse of Scripture resounds in innumerable hearts through the centuries, "I believe; help my unbelief." How can you and I become partakers of this faith?

As a modern-day follower of Jesus Christ, you believe in Him for the common things in life, things which would have happened anyway. However, you need a faith that will work when storm clouds gather ominously around you.

Start with the process of developing a mature and genuine faith. Through the grace of God it isn't very difficult and it is a very inspiring experience. Recall an incident in your life when something quite out of the ordinary happened. Look for something small to thank God for, an instance when you believed that God had answered your prayer. It is probably not something big or important, but when you recall the memory, it strengthens your faith in a wonderful way. Suddenly you are able to say, "God was really at work in my life."

Make a habit of remembering small revelations of answered prayers. Your faith will gradually grow to the extent where you acknowledge and appreciate bigger revelations from God. Don't go on yearning, asking God to give you greater faith. Use that which you already have and you will grow in faith and grace.

Faith ascends the steps built by love and looks through the window opened by hope. (Charles H. Spurgeon)

Loving Master, I want to grow in my faith so that _____

_____

*W*hen your faith grows dim

"And be renewed in the spirit of your mind, and put on the new man." (Eph. 4:23, 24)

*O*nce you start out on the spiritual path, there is no room for self-indulgence. It is true that the Word calls on us to find rest in the Lord, but even during periods of rest there needs to be a spiritual alertness.

If your faith has lost its trust, vitality and power, you ought to know what the cause is. It is in times like these that the Holy Spirit rushes to assist you. If you seriously ask Him, He will reveal your weaknesses and shortcomings. This revelation can be a challenging experience. He will reveal your inner self to you without withholding anything, even those sins you wanted to conceal in secrecy.

After a period of serious soul-searching by the Holy Spirit, which could sometimes be very painful, a new spirit – the Spirit of Jesus Christ – will start flowing through your life and your faith will be renewed. You cannot just take for granted that because this renewal has a spiritual dimension, it won't affect your everyday, practical life. When your spirit is in harmony with the Holy Spirit and your sense of values becomes balanced and real, your life will develop a constructive purposefulness and you will experience the peace which passes all understanding. In conjunction with all these blessings comes the assurance that you are a child of God. Then you live to His honour and glory only. Then your faith becomes fresh and vigorous.

The doubter turns the saying around and insists that faith, the size of a mountain, is required to move a mustard seed. (Webb B. Garrison)

Through the consciousness of your indwelling Holy Spirit, I possess the _____

Faith or feeling?

"Though He slay me, yet will I trust Him, even so, I will defend my own ways before Him." (Job 13:15)

The faith of many people depends exclusively on their emotions. They worship God when they "feel" like it; they pray when they "feel" they have to pray. Their faith is nothing but an addendum to their life, a quality which can be used if and when it suits them, or if circumstances allow it.

The problem with an "emotional faith" is that it is unstable and leaves you in the lurch during a crisis situation. The moment when you specifically need the support of a positive faith, there is nothing to back you up. An emotional faith is never able to handle a big crisis, while a positive faith can carry you even when your world falls apart. It enables you to cling to God and to draw strength from Him even when your spirit is drained. Such a faith can handle anything which might occur with confidence and can carry you through triumphantly.

Obtaining real faith is not a matter of luck. It is the product of numerous spiritual disciplines. A steadfast trust in your heavenly Father and in His love for you is the primary requirement. To know God through the living Christ is the ultimate spiritual experience. Such a knowledge is the result of an ever-growing prayer life, spending intimate moments with the Master. It is more than just hastily repeated words every now and again. It is to cultivate a consciousness of the presence of Christ in the midst of the gruelling routine of life. Union with Christ elevates our faith above a mere emotion into the sphere of practical experience.

> Faith is an act of commitment in which the will, the intellect and the emotions each has its rightful place. (William Inge)

Dear Guide, please grant me a faith which _____

_____

A faith that is self-testifying

"The works that I do in My Father's name, they bear witness of Me."
(Jn. 10:25)

The unique character of your Christianity arises out of your relationship with Jesus Christ. If you regard Him only as a historical figure who had a tremendous influence for good, but with whom you don't have a personal relationship, you are missing the core truth of the Christian gospel.

God came through Jesus to enter into a personal relationship with ordinary people. Until such time that this relationship is sealed, man has not yet experienced the joy of faith or got to know the Holy Spirit of God.

The difference between an orthodox faith and a vibrant faith in the living Christ, is the possession of His Holy Spirit. He promised to give His Spirit to all who love Him and accept Him. To be possessed by the Spirit of Christ is more than an emotional experience. In conjunction with that, joy, peace and all the other spiritual gifts are added to us through grace. To be a Spirit-filled Christian means that you experience a very real sense of the living presence of Christ, and that at all times and under all circumstances.

If you have disappointed Christ and feel very miserable about that, remember the words of Deuteronomy 33:27, *"The eternal God is your refuge, and underneath are the everlasting arms."* In moments of depression He is your light and inspiration. Then your religion is no longer a burden that has to be carried, but a force which gives inspiration and meaning to your life.

> Everything I see around me teaches me to trust my Creator with everything I can't see. (Ralph Waldo Emerson)

Father in Heaven, I rejoice in _____

_____

*W*hen unbelief gnaws at you

"O wretched man that I am! Who will deliver me from this body of death? I thank God – through Jesus Christ our Lord!" (Rom. 7:24)

It appears as if some of the Lord's children are permanently living on spiritual heights. It seems as if they never experience times of struggle and never even go through depression or doubt. And their fellow pilgrims envy them.

Even though your faith may fluctuate between the valley and the mountaintop and even though there may be times when you despair of your ability to lead a committed spiritual life, there are certain core truths of which you should never lose sight. Even though you might be tossed between the highest and the lowest poles, your salvation definitely does not depend on your emotions. Christ always remains the same (see Hebrews 13:8). It is impossible for you to sink so low that the love of Christ cannot reach you and that His arms are not under you. You have not been saved by your emotions, but through your faith in the atoning sacrifice of your Saviour.

To acknowledge and receive the love of God as a gift of grace; to plead in deep remorse for the forgiveness of sin; to allow His Holy Spirit into your life – these things bring unparalleled experiences into your life. Worries and affliction will still be part of it, but you can always share them with your Saviour.

Don't ever be ashamed, depressed or fearful when you experience times of spiritual recession. Through your fellowship with the living Christ you will eventually rise above them and you will even taste a more powerful experience of faith.

> Sanctification is the working of God's free grace; through this the whole person is being renewed into the image of God and enabled to die more and more to sin and live in faith and righteousness. (Westminster Catechism)

Thank You Lord that I can be sure of _____

_____

Victory through faith

"But we are not of those who draw back to perdition, but of those who believe to the saving of the soul." (Heb. 10:39)

There are many circumstances in life where a lack of faith can reduce you to a helpless, pathetic shadow of your former self. Think about the impact of death, financial failure, a family crisis, poor health and many other disasters which can befall man in this life. Unless you have a steadfast faith in the love and supporting grace of God, all your dreams will tumble down like a house of cards and your life will be destroyed by the storms which come across your path.

It cannot be denied that situations like these do occur. Perhaps you are presently going through just such a time. The fact that you are a Christian does not exempt you from tribulation. Nevertheless, your faith can and will help you to survive the storms and eventually come forth as an enriched victor on the other side.

Jesus, our Saviour, who was tested also, ensured us that He will be with us always (See Matthew 28:20). In conjunction with that you also have testimony that during His life on earth your Master also experienced every possible human experience that you are exposed to. Who will know better than He what impact the storm has on your life? Because of this it is obvious that nobody on earth will be able to assist and support you better than Jesus the Lord. He will enable you to handle the problems and tribulations triumphantly if you only trust Him unconditionally. With such a comforting assurance you can put your trust in Him and live life victoriously.

> There is no victory without conflict; no rainbow without clouds and a storm. (Aristotle)

I look to You in faith, because _____

_____

Maintain a balanced faith

"Some therefore cried one thing and some another, for the assembly was confused and most of them did not know why they had come together." (Acts 19:32)

In many ways the church of Jesus Christ today reflects the picture painted by Luke in the book of Acts. In recent years the church has been spoiled by politics. In this regard just consider the teachings of Marxism and "liberation theology". Various forms of worship exist and some are alarmingly intolerant towards other Christians who don't follow their specific pattern. Scandals have shaken the church, charges of heresy and hypocrisy have caused damage to the faith, division has brought a wedge between denominations.

The tragedy that resulted is that many people turned away from the church while Satan attacked and undermined it, not from the outside, but from inside.

Two things are urgently required to enable you to maintain a balanced approach to your faith. Firstly you must never judge God by the actions of people who imply that they are serving Him. All people are fallible and inconstant, but God is infallible and unchanging. Don't allow the behaviour of people to influence you, but fearlessly hold on to your faith in Jesus Christ. In the final analysis He will overcome evil.

Secondly you must never forget that God is love. We are commanded to love Him and our fellowmen as He loves us. Pray for those who upset and slander you. Through the power of Jesus Christ you must love them until they are back in the kingdom of God. That is your Christian duty and privilege.

He who loves, believes the impossible. (Elizabeth Barret Browning)

Lord Jesus, help me to hold on to _____

Faith in the valley of darkness

"Yea, though I walk through the valley of the shadow of death, I will fear no evil; For You are with me." (Ps.23:4)

*L*et us say it to one another again: Every pilgrim along life's journey has times of depression which sometimes border on despair. For a long while you may experience the joyful assurance of God's living presence and then, for no obvious reason, doubt stealthily enters your life; it overshadows your enthusiasm like an ominous cloud and you lose all interest in spiritual matters.

If this is what you are currently experiencing, your vision of God has dimmed. You need a new and fresh realisation of the love of Christ to expel the darkness. You need the Holy Spirit to keep you from being insensitive and to revive the joy of your fellowship with Him.

In the dark depths of doubt and depression you have to hold on tightly to your faith in an unchanging God. Regardless of how much your spiritual state may fluctuate, God's love for you is strong and unchanging. He has always loved you and even though you may feel far from Him at the moment, His love for you does not change. He has never left you. You can trust Him unconditionally, regardless of the spiritual state you may find yourself in.

One of the beneficial results of your walk in the dark depths of the spirit, is that you develop a greater appreciation for the sunlight of God's love and a deeper sympathy and understanding for the problems of others. God can use even your experience in the dark valley to serve your fellow pilgrims.

We have need to suffer in order to learn to have sympathy. (Elizabeth Landon)

Grant me a new and a fresh realisation of _____

_____

*W*hat is the real essence?

"For we through the Spirit eagerly wait for the hope of righteousness by faith." (Gal. 5:6)

*W*e live in a time of great contrasts. Never before has there been a deeper yearning for church unity and yet never before have there been so many churches and splinter groups who claim that their teachings are true beyond a shadow of doubt. In the midst of contrasting viewpoints of Bible-expositors and theologians, many humble Christians find it hard to maintain a balanced approach concerning their faith.

Christianity needs to be founded indissolubly on faith in God and the revelation of His person in Jesus Christ. Anything less creates a subspecies of Christians and is a denial of scriptural Christianity.

Faith in Jesus Christ, as the revelation of the eternal God, is more than a theological exercise. It is a real experience which occurs in the spirit and mind of a person when Christ becomes a living reality for that individual. It is essential to accept in childlike faith that the Spirit of Christ can fill our mind and emotions. When Christ lives in you, your spiritual vision is extended and you develop a deep understanding and love for those whom you differ from. It enables you to rise above clashing doctrines and contrasting expositions of Scripture.

According to the apostle Paul, faith in God and love for Christ are those things which are of essential value in the Christian's life. There is nothing greater than faith in God and allowing His love to be revealed through your life.

Faith separated from love is not faith, but merely science. In itself it is void of spiritual life. (Emanuel Swedenborg)

Lord Jesus, show me _____
_____

ℱaith overcomes fear

"Suddenly, when they had looked around, they saw no one anymore, but only Jesus with themselves." (Mk. 9:8)

𝒯here are extremely few, if any, people who have never known anxiety or fear. We fear so many things: we have fears concerning the future, the past, our finances, our health, our old age and death. In conjunction with these we can name numerous other issues which fill us with fear. No doubt you can compile your own personal list. The fact, remains, however, that insecurity with regard to the future is inclined to make you vulnerable. Then you become susceptible to feelings of anxiety and fear concerning yourself and those who are dependent on you.

It is therefore imperative that you should strengthen your faith in order to be able to handle the challenges of the future. For you to do that, you must build an intimate relationship with the living Christ through the Holy Spirit. He is the only one who can help you overcome the storms of life which can descend upon you so unexpectedly. The encouraging fact here is that He undertook to be with you in all circumstances and to help you to handle life with all its fear-inspiring demands.

Through prayer and meditation you can allow Jesus to become an essential and intimate part of your life. By maintaining a personal relationship with the Master, you will experience His guidance in all things. Through the strengthening and reinforcement of your faith in Him, all fear will be banned from your life.

> Fear knocks at the door. Faith answers the door. There is no one. (Anne Jameson)

Saviour and Friend, set me free from my fears _____

_____

A home for Christ

"[I pray] that Christ may dwell in your hearts through faith; that you, being rooted and grounded in love ... " (Eph. 3:17)

Your lifestyle reveals whether you are in harmony with life or not. If you are aggressive and always on the defensive, you will live a restless life and also experience bitterness and frustration. Guard against the misconception that life is in constant conflict with you.

In order to enjoy fulfilment and gratification it is important for you to be controlled by the highest wisdom. And this wisdom is not the result of education. If that were the case, few people would have had it. It becomes yours through your spirit.

While you seriously and incessantly, through prayer and meditation, search for a deeper understanding of God, you develop a wisdom which comes from your heavenly Father. This inspired wisdom saturates every part of your being. Then your values are no longer determined by human standards. Then you see people, situations and circumstances as God sees them.

Trying to observe life from God's all-wise viewpoint creates in you a new understanding of values and also a new lifestyle. When you are in harmony with God, all unacceptable aggression vanishes. You no longer so easily feel hurt or insulted, you experience the joy of cooperating with your fellowmen and of serving them with the wisdom given to you by the Holy Spirit.

> The wise person is also honest, pious and trustworthy, someone who walks the path of truth. The respect for Christ, which is the principle of wisdom, consists of total commitment to God. (Otto Zöckler)

Because You grant me wisdom, I am able to _____

_____

*L*et your faith live

"He who has the Son has life; he who does not have the Son of God does not have life." (1 Jn. 5:12)

There are many people, even those who are zealously involved in church activities, who will admit that their spiritual life has lost its momentum, that the spark has died, that they feel empty and have need of a revived faith. The great danger of this lies in the fact that these people could be permanently lost to Christianity.

Jesus came to the world so that we can have life in abundance (See John 10:10). As part of His Godly mission He died and rose again to destroy the fear of sin and death and to give you the promise of eternal life. And in order to make His promise an actual reality, the living Christ offers us the Holy Spirit. This is valid for all who believe in Him and accept Him as their Saviour.

If your faith has reached the low-water mark, or if you are anxious to prevent an arid desert from developing in your faith life, then now is the proper time to open up your life for Jesus Christ. It follows as a matter of course that you will have to submit your will and desires to the Master. In return for that, He will revive you. He will live within you and give you self-confidence, joy and peace. Through your faith and your intimate walk with Christ, you will live anew spiritually.

Your life is not a futile dream, but a solemn reality; it is yours and it is all you have before you enter eternity. (Thomas Carlyle)

Lord, I have great need of _____

_____

Bear testimony of your faith

"Preaching the kingdom of God and teaching the things which concern the Lord Jesus Christ with all confidence, no one forbidding him."
(Acts 28:31)

There are many followers of Jesus Christ who are afraid to speak out about their faith in the company of other people. Delegates at ecclesiastical meetings often keep quiet because they fear they will be ridiculed if they partake in the debate. Members of study groups will not participate in discussions because they are afraid their ignorance will show or because others might think they don't understand the matter under discussion. Yet others are reluctant to take part in ordinary conversations and confess their faith for fear of embarrassment or the possibility of being branded as fanatics.

These fears should not dominate your life. You can prepare yourself through prayer, Bible study and meditation. People cannot help but listen to the voice of someone who has authority.

In your Christian involvement it is extremely important for you to spend time with God in prayer and meditation. Submit your desire to be filled with the Holy Spirit to Him. Pray that He will enable you to develop a clear understanding of His Word as well as the ability to convey it to others in a way which they can understand. In your times of meditation listen to the Master and to the Holy Spirit. God's thoughts with regard to the path you should walk on will then become clear to you. Study His Word diligently. If God is working through you, you don't have to fear derision.

> Don't witness just to say something, but because you have something to say. (Richard Whately)

Lord, I lay my fear of talking in the company of others about You so that _____

_____

"*I* know for sure!"

"The Spirit Himself bears witness with our spirit that we are children of God." (Rom. 8:16)

It is one thing to know about God, but quite something else to know God Himself. The acceptance of lofty principles, interest in theology and enthusiasm for religious debate, linked to a serious desire to convert as many people possible to your personal view-point, are all insufficient substitutes for the consciousness of the presence of the living God in your mind and emotions.

The things which you may regard as important on your pilgrimage may be nothing but indicators pointing towards a more vibrant and realistic experience with God. Be careful not to fall into the trap of stopping at the road-signs to worship there as if they are God Himself. If your spiritual hunger is not stilled and your yearning for assurance about God remains unfulfilled or increases in intensity – thank God for that. You would never have experienced this spiritual hunger if you were dead spiritually.

You will have a living experience with God when you invite Him to come into your life and to take possession of you. This is much more than an act of courtesy: it is the unconditional commitment of yourself to God and then living only to reveal His Spirit wherever you may be.

If this sounds impractical and uninteresting to you, I wish to assure you that there are numerous people who will be able to testify that when they did just that, God became a reality to them and they were able to understand life for the first time.

> "Assuredly, I say to you, unless you are converted and become as little children, you will by no means enter the kingdom of heaven." (Jesus Christ in Matthew 18:3)

Saviour and Friend, please make it possible for me to _____

There is power in a strong faith

"All things are possible to him who believes." (Mk. 9:23)

Nothing is impossible when faith is stong. History is studded with events which were regarded as impossible at the time, but because someone refused to accept the situation, the impossible became possible. People are very quick to say that something which is hard to do, is impossible. It is the person who refuses to accept public opinion who breaks through all barriers and achieves success.

To have a faith which requires your total trust, a faith you are willing to make any sacrifice for, is to have a treasure of immeasurable value. It gives steadfast direction to your life. Then you are not troubled by questions such as, "What is the meaning of life?" or "Why was I born?" Your inner conviction will supply you with the answer if your faith is powerful.

A vital requirement is that your faith must be worthy of your highest ideal. The power of faith is dynamic. Faith with a wrong goal in mind diminishes its tremendous power and can cause immeasurable damage to you and those who are in contact with you. When you maintain a noble faith which inspires you, the world you live in will be enriched by it.

When your faith in God is a consuming conviction and His presence becomes the motivating influence in your life, you will look at life from a totally different perspective. You start noticing things which you can do rather than those which you cannot do. Then you live creatively and victoriously.

> Faith is the courage of the soul enabling it to go further than the eye can see. (William Newton Clarke)

Holy God, give me a faith so strong that _____

_____

$\mathscr{S}$trengthen others in their faith

"For I rejoiced greatly when brethren came and testified of the truth that is in you, just as you walk in the truth." (3 Jn. v 3)

$\mathscr{P}$etty jealousy is a soul-destroying weakness in the human character. It robs a life of everything good and noble. And how infinitely more destructive it is when revealed amongst people involved in the Master's work.

It is a sad fact that in and around the church there is more proof of petty jealousy, envy, bitterness and aversion than in other areas – and all this because of professional jealousy. The damage caused by this attitude is incalculable. It can so easily harm or even destroy the good work done by the church, simply because people fall prey to their personal feelings.

There are many and varying examples of this: obtaining high positions in church, the acceptance of a scheme which is the brain-child of someone else and the denial of someone else's achievements. The list is inexhaustible. The sad fact of the matter is that one of the main causes of jealousy is because of someone else's personal experience of the glory of Jesus Christ and an intimate walk with Him.

God calls each one of us to serve Him in our own personal way. Different people have divergent experiences with Christ and sometimes their manner of worship is radically different. However, it is of primary importance for the Christian faith that we encourage and support one another and rejoice in the other person's experience with the living Christ. If you put Him above personal feelings, only then do you really start to glorify God through your faith.

Moral indignation is jealousy wearing a halo. (H.G. Wells)

Lord, I have also fallen prey to petty jealousy _____

_____

ℐo you desire a faith that is alive?

"He is not the God of the dead, but the God of the living." (Mk. 12:27)

ℱew things in life are as deplorable or sad as a faith which is dead. There was a time when it tingled with life, abounding with joy and beauty. Perhaps it was marred by famine or smothered by worldly circumstances that became more important. A dead or dying faith teems with evasions, poor excuses and increasing bitterness.

Nevertheless, God has not changed. He is still the source of inspiration and all life. Therefore it must be accepted that you yourself are the cause of all spiritual backsliding, and not God. If you truly desire a powerful living faith, it is your responsibility to grow such a faith. God wants you to have a genuine, living faith of which He forms the centre. He has not withdrawn Himself from you, He still gives Himself to you. The problem is that possibly He has been replaced by something else in your life. God doesn't give His fullness to those who have pushed Him back to a secondary place in their lives.

If you long to have a living, vibrant faith, God must be placed in the centre of your life again so that He can control every aspect of your life from that centre. Hate needs to be replaced by love; friendliness must replace bitterness; power must take the place of weakness. Then your faith will become alive, creative and constructive.

> A little bit of faith will bring your soul into heaven; a big faith will bring heaven into your soul. (Dwight L. Moody)

Heavenly Father, my deepest desire is _____

_____

Forward in faith

"But we are not of those who draw back to perdition, but of those who believe to the saving of the soul." (Heb. 10:39)

Over the years many nations have faced disaster. In some cases they experienced humiliation when their enemies defeated them. However, history bears testimony to the fact that God worked miraculous deliverance for those who turned to Him in faith and put all their trust in God's love and grace.

In our generation too there are nations and people who are threatened by serious dangers. Sometimes these dangers seem insurmountable and the problems insoluble. We live in a time of breathtaking changes. In some instances people find it difficult and almost impossible to reconcile themselves with the effects of these changes. The danger is that, unless you have faith which can serve as an anchor to you, you could get lost in the wilderness of doubt, confusion, insecurity and frustration.

Regardless of what challenge or problem you have to struggle with, it is essential that you must handle it in the faith and strength that only Christ can give you. He overcame the worst the world could do to Him. He is always at your side to help you overcome the obstacles of life.

Put your trust in Him and enter the future with the living Christ. All fear will vanish from your life, because the perfect love of the Master will dispel all fear and protect you against the dangers of life.

> Faith is neither a feeling nor an insight; it is not a philosophy either. Faith is taking God at His word. (Arthur Evans)

Finisher of my faith, because I believe and trust You unconditionally

The test of faith

"Therefore do not be unwise, but understand what the will of the Lord is." (Eph. 5:17)

Unfortunately there are many people who are overcome by doubt when their faith is tested. They spend considerable time in prayer and meditation and they study the Word of God to find out what His will is. However, when His will becomes evident to them, they are hesitant to move forward according to His will. Then they go down on their knees again in prayer, thus missing the golden opportunity to serve the Lord in faith.

Prayer is always of cardinal importance in every matter. It is your communication with God and therefore also the foundation of your Christian lifestyle. Because this is the case, every action in your life should be supported and carried by prayer. However, prayer is never to be an escape-mechanism for disobeying God's commissions. James rightly said, *"For as the body without the spirit is dead, so faith without works is dead also"* (James 2:26).

When God answers your prayers, your faith should be strong enough to encourage you to obediently do the will of God. If you spend quality time in the presence of the Master and you open up your heart and mind to Him, He will speak to you through His Holy Spirit. This may be through someone else, or through circumstances which occur; or you may know instinctively what to do. Whatever the case may be, if you are sensitively tuned in to the voice of the Holy Spirit, God's will will be revealed to you. Therefore serve God and your fellowmen in faith.

I will go wherever You send me, O Lord, over mountains, valleys or the sea; I will say what You want, O Lord and be who You want me to be. (Mary Brown)

O, Holy Spirit, strengthen my faith so that I _____

_____

Faith and good deeds

"Therefore we conclude that a man is justified by faith apart from the deeds of the law." (Rom. 3:28)

Good works are the by-product of a Christian lifestyle. It is impossible to live with a consciousness of the presence of Christ and still do mean or evil deeds. As man becomes like the friends he has, so Jesus Christ becomes the mould according to which you cast your life.

Many dedicated Christian believers believe that by performing noble deeds they obtain a good standing and will eventually go to heaven because they do good deeds. We must remember, however, that many agnostics and even atheists are "good" people who enjoy fighting for the rights of those who are less privileged. For them life is also an experience of joy and happiness.

The difference between a Christian and a "good" person is that the latter is good because it is in his nature to be a good person. The Christian on the other hand, lives in a pulsating relationship with the living Christ and is good because the life of His Master is being reflected by him. The difference between natural goodness and a life inspired by Christ, is that the Christian adds a spiritual quality to life. This creates an attitude of inner peace and joy in a life in which God is glorified and His will performed. Therefore it is not restricted to time but has eternal value.

A life that is inspired by the Holy Spirit has a quality which rises above natural goodness and makes something of Jesus Christ visible in our lives.

It is easier to cross the Atlantic Ocean in a paper boat than to try and get to heaven by good works. (Charles H. Spurgeon)

Lord Jesus, I plead that _____

_____

ℳaintain your faith

"'Yet now be strong, Zerubbabel,' says the Lord; 'and be strong and work for I am with you,' says the Lord of hosts." (Hag. 2:4)

The great majority of people who have just become Christians do the Lord's work with great zeal. They are excited about their new life in Jesus Christ. They are keen to share their feelings with others and to get them involved as well.

However, the problem they experience is that not everyone shares their zeal and enthusiasm. Some are just not willing to give up their old, familiar pattern of life. Others again may have been involved in the work of the Lord for many years and just don't like it when, according to them, immaturity encroaches upon their lives. Then there are those too, whose enmity is reflected in their efforts to discourage Christ's disciples through ridicule and contempt.

Regardless of what happens, never give in to the temptation to stop your work and your witnessing for Christ. At all times ask for the guidance of the living Christ. When things go wrong or when you feel discouraged, lay your problems before Him in prayer. Ask Him to point out to you through the Holy Spirit if and where you have gone wrong. Never be fearful or too proud to ask and accept the advice of God's more mature children. If you have respect for their viewpoints, you can act on their advice.

Seek for help, advice and guidance, but under no circumstances allow discouragement to overtake you. If you honestly strive to serve the Lord, He will guide you.

> Christianity can be condensed into four words: Admit, Submit, Commit and Transmit. (Anonymous)

Saviour and Redeemer, encourage me to _____
_____ *like before.*

The glory of our faith

"That He would grant you, according to the riches of His glory, to be strengthened with might through His Spirit in the inner man, that Christ may dwell in your hearts through faith." (Eph. 3:16, 17)

In spite of bitter opposition, contempt and efforts to stop the witnessing about it, and in spite of the messages of false teachers, the Christian faith is still a glorious reality in the lives of innumerable people.

What is the secret of the survival and success of this faith? Good organisation played an important role in it; pious and brilliant scholars expounded the gospel for all who wish to study the Word of God; persecution strengthened the spirit of those who acknowledged the lordship of Christ. The survival of the church of Christ is one of the greatest miracles of all times. Yet the true glory of the faith is not vested in good organisation, in upright and pious scholars or in mutual help in times of persecution, but in the wonderful and glorious truth that the living Christ conquered time and space and is just as alive today as He was two thousand years ago. If all Christians allow this truth to have top priority in their lives, the church would have been a still greater spiritual force in the world of today.

The reality of the living Christ can only be revealed in society if He is taken up in the hearts of His modern-day disciples. When Christians become aware of the fact that He lives in their hearts, their faith comes alive and inspiring and the indwelling Christ becomes the glory of their faith.

Our faith is kept alive and growing by applying it in practice and not by speculating about it. (Joseph Addison)

Lord Jesus I worship and honour You because _____

_____

*F*aith heals depression

"But to those who fear My name the Sun of Righteousness shall arise with healing in His wings." (Mal. 4:2)

*D*epression, melancholy and pessimism are soul-destroying afflictions. Apart from the fact that it is a negative state of mind, it can also affect your physical and spiritual well-being. Your vision of the future is restricted and your general attitude towards life is influenced negatively. The causes are too many to number, but they include anxiety and fear, sickness and financial insecurity, loneliness and failure of human relations.

You may try to fight against this mental condition by seeking man-made solutions and medications. However, they will never be permanent or lasting in nature. Sooner or later the impact of these remedies will tarnish and the condition will emerge again – often in a more intense form than before.

The only sure and steadfast manner of treating emotional disruption is to turn to Christ and to open yourself up to His influence and love. Acknowledge Him as the Lord of your life and submit yourself to His faithful care.

This will require from you the expression of a steadfast faith. When Christ takes control of your life and shows you the direction which He intends for you, you will find that through your obedience to Him, you are filled with self-confidence and joy which only the living Christ can give to you through the working of the Holy Spirit.

> He who has lost his faith has nothing to live off and nothing to live for.
> (Publius Syrus)

Dear Saviour, I cling to You knowing that _____

_____

Faith is to know Christ

"I know whom I have believed and am persuaded that He is able to keep what I have committed to Him until that Day." (2 Tim. 1:12)

With these immortal words the apostle Paul reaffirms his faith in and allegiance to his Lord and Master, Jesus Christ. He could have said, "I know what I believe," and having said that, he would have said something worthwhile. He could have said, "I know why I believe," and his logic would have been correct and sound. There are many people who cannot make these two statements with absolute honesty. Paul was a person of intense convictions: when he persecuted the early Christians, he did so with fiery zeal. When he became a Christian, his spirit burned like a bright light with commitment. It revealed a zeal for his new-found Saviour that was immortal.

Paul did not rejoice in his faith or his convictions, but in the life and personality of His risen, living Master. "I know whom I have believed," makes his relationship intimately personal. It not only implies the acceptance of a special religious approach or formula, it implies a relationship which does not depend totally on us. Jesus calls us to Him and we reply positively or negatively to that call. And our relationship with the One whom we call our Saviour, depends on this decision.

To know Him in whom you believe, at least in a technical manner, is to make your spiritual life glorious and real. This not only brings the gifts of God into your daily life, but it also brings Christ Himself into your life.

> The jar with oil and the pitcher with grain remained full because the widow had a powerful faith. (Agathius Scholasticus)

Lord Jesus, knowing You as Saviour _____

The area of the mind

"How is it you do not understand?" (Mt. 16:11)

Whether you have progressed a long way on the path of life or whether you are only at its beginning, eventually you come to the place where you are faced with a big question mark. When you have reached that point, you can sink back in blissful ignorance, willing to admit that there are many things you don't know. On the other hand you could, when confronted by a question mark, look beyond the problem and try to find an answer to that which seems to be a mystery.

Life is full of question marks and even the most brilliant scholars encounter them. The area between the mind and the spirit has not yet been clearly defined. The basic truth is that man has both a mind and a spirit. Only a privileged few have succeeded, through their training and interest, to discover the depths of the human mind. They are all single-minded, serious people who managed to make progress into the domain of the spirit. They approach the question from another vantage point. And this also gives you a new experience with God which gives new meaning and purpose to your daily living.

Not all of us can be mentally bright and gifted, but we can all approach the area of the mind by the way of prayer and meditation. This will bring us to a fuller understanding of life because that is exactly what is derived from an increased knowledge of God through fellowship with Him.

The development of the mind is a kind of food for the soul. (Cicero)

Thank You, Lord my God, that through daily prayer I can _____

_____

_____

THE FOUNTAIN

OF RENEWAL

In the Christian life there is no such thing as a monastery to withdraw into hoping that God will meet and bless you there. You must live and grow daily. (Alan Redpath)

Holy God, and in Jesus Christ my heavenly Father:

I plead that You will keep me from spiritual stagnation; from the danger of remaining a toddler in faith; from the law of atrophy – that that which I don't use I'll lose! Thank You that from Your throne flows a fountain of salvation which enables me to grow on a daily basis in all the spiritual gifts mentioned in Galatians 5:22: love, joy, peace, patience, kindness, goodness, faithfulness, gentleness and self-control. Through the working of the Holy Spirit keep me from thinking that I have arrived spiritually and don't need to grow any more. Please make it to be my life-long desire and a daily process. Let me keep on growing and bearing fruit befitting to my conversion, just like a branch which is grafted in You, the vine. I pray this in the transcendent Name of the source of all things, Jesus Christ, my Saviour and Redeemer.

November

The secret of gradual growth

"But grow in the grace and knowledge of our Lord and Saviour Jesus Christ." (2 Pet. 3:18)

You probably get impatient with yourself sometimes regarding to your spiritual growth. It is possible that you have made little progress since you committed your life to Christ, and you feel dissatisfied with yourself because of that. You know from Scripture that you were called to live a life of growth and strength through Jesus Christ. In spite of much effort and this knowledge you feel that your spiritual life is in a groove and that you are making no progress whatsoever on the road which will take you to a deeper experience with Christ.

Perhaps the impact of your rebirth made such a tremendous impression on you that you expect every moment of your life to contain the same spiritual excitement and emotion. You are looking for the supernatural and because you don't find it, you feel that your spiritual life is inferior and continually regressing.

The secret of a successful spiritual life is to grow gradually. Regardless of how wonderful growth may be, healthy growing is always slow. The things which grow fast in nature, like the mushroom for instance, don't have the same sustaining strength as the oak which grows slowly. The acorn takes many years to develop into a shady oak. Don't confuse God's timing with your own. In the Lord's eyes a thousand years are like a fleeting thought.

In times of doubt and spiritual depression you need to steadfastly keep on growing gradually in the knowledge of God. Only by doing this will your faith rise above your feelings, causing you to continually grow closer to your heavenly Father.

> Grace is just the beginning of growth; and growth is the perfection of grace. (Jonathan Edwards)

Lord, I still want to _____

_____

*Y*our source of growth

"But you shall receive power when the Holy Spirit has come upon you." (Acts 1:8)

It is a sad fact that so many people who confess the Christian faith lack goals, vigour and spiritual growth. As a result they accuse the church of being dead or dying. It is an even sadder fact that Christians themselves speak about a "dead" church, while in actual fact they are essentially the church. This can only mean that they are dead themselves.

According to the promise of Jesus Christ and in fulfilling the prophecies of old, God gave us the grace to be vibrant and effective witnesses of the living Christ. And this happens in a world where there is a desperate need of love, grace, hope and mercy such as Jesus revealed in His earthly ministry. To those who are willing to submit themselves to the sovereignty of Christ, He gave the glorious opportunity of becoming instruments through whom the power of God can be made known to the whole world.

God makes this priceless gift available to you today so that you may grow spiritually to become a dynamic witness for Him. In exchange for that He requires your unconditional commitment to Him and that you will invite Him into your life so that His Spirit can take control and use you in the area where He needs you.

For you to add a new dimension and meaning to your Christian growth, it is important that you should accept this gift of God in all sincerity.

> In the same way that it is impossible to grow flowers without an atmosphere, or fruit without light or heat, it is equally impossible to grow spiritually without the Holy Spirit. (Henry Ward Beecher)

Holy Spirit, re-create me _____

_____

*R*ebirth and growth

"For if when we were enemies we were reconciled to God through the death of His Son, much more, having been reconciled, we shall be saved by His life." (Rom. 5:10)

*S*alvation is both immediate and progressively ongoing. There comes a time in your life when you realise that you need Christ. Initially you are only vaguely aware of your need and you will have no yearning for anything of a spiritual nature. However, when the challenge of Christ is set before you, you know instinctively that He can satisfy your deepest need.

There are many of the Lord's disciples who acknowledge His lordship in their lives, but they make no progress in their relationship with Him whatsoever. They keep on looking back to the day on which they were reborn and forget the fact that a glorious future with Christ awaits them. Christianity is a state of constant growth towards a deeper experience with God.

While it is true that surrendering to God is of vital importance, the fuller and richer meaning of that experience only becomes visible when you start living in the consciousness of His holy presence on a daily basis. This then becomes the motivational power of your life.

Rebirth means that you commit yourself to Jesus Christ as your personal Saviour and Redeemer. This fills you with inner peace. You will no longer be oppressed by sin and you will no longer be exhausted by trying to bear your own burdens. Now you experience a new life in Christ; you are redeemed from sin and have joy and peace. However, this can only be true if you grow into the image of your Saviour, Jesus Christ.

> On the road of faith we should not only be beginners, we must be persisters. (Ralph Waldo Emerson)

Holy Spirit, my spiritual growth _____

_____

Growing towards God

"You are of God, little children, and have overcome them, because He who is in you is greater than he who is in the world." (1 Jn. 4:4)

For many Christians God is irreconcilable with the world. They believe that in order to be a Christian you need to move around in a heavenly atmosphere and be as remotely secluded from the world as possible. Because they find it virtually impossible to live according to such a high standard, they drift from their high calling in Jesus Christ (See Philippians 3:14). Rather than living their lives in hypocrisy, they lower their standard of living.

We must never forget that Jesus Christ, who once travelled along the dusty roads of this world, was on the one hand the revelation of the eternal God and on the other hand a real person. To separate the living Christ from the ordinary man, is to do Him an injustice. Jesus Christ moved among common men, sharing in their fears, frustration, hopes, sorrows and sadness. He was one of them.

Through His life and teachings He showed them what they could become through His power and strength. He did not only invite them to follow Him, making Him their example. He was much more than an example. He is the power that enables you to grow and to live victoriously because He lives in you. You are in the world, sharing its joys and afflictions, but you are not of the world. You have the indwelling Spirit who keeps you from becoming part of the world.

> Don't be afraid of growing slowly, yet be extremely afraid of coming to a standstill. (Marcel Proust)

Holy Spirit, through Your power _____

_____

Spiritual growth

"For Godly sorrow produces repentance leading to salvation, not to be regretted." (2 Cor. 7:10)

Different people attach different meanings to the Passiontide. For some it is only a time slot on the church calendar which leaves them somewhat embarrassed because they know so little about its real meaning. For the dedicated Christian however it should be a time of honest soul-searching when we take a close look at our own lives and compare it with what Jesus Christ expects from us because He laid down His life for us.

One of the most difficult things in our pilgrimage is to be absolutely honest with ourselves; to realise that we are in the presence of the living God who knows us better than we know ourselves. Most of us try to find excuses for our disobedience and lack of spiritual growth. Deep down in our being however we know that we are disobedient to God.

Then we have the privilege of making an honest assessment of our lives by comparing it to the life of our Master under the guidance of the Holy Spirit. As your weaknesses and shortcomings are revealed to you, He grants you the opportunity to come to Him in honest repentance and confession in order to find the strength to overcome your weaknesses and to grow. This also gives you the assurance of His loving forgiveness appropriated for you on the cross.

Make use of these opportunities of meditation and introspection to increase your knowledge and grace and to strengthen your witnessing for Him. Make sure that you have regular Passiontides in your life when, through meditation, repentance and conversion you grow into that which Christ meant you to be.

> Repentance is to change your view of life; it is to look at life from God's point of view rather than your own. (Augustine)

Holy Spirit, work in me so that _____

_____

Small things

"For who has despised the day of small things?" (Zech. 4:10)

Do not despise anything which had a small beginning, because great and important things can develop from it. A child may have an ambition which may sound impractical and foolish, yet never mock or despise it. Many a group of chain stores originated from the unsightly corner café. Many a general manager started out as a simple office clerk. This world teems with big things which had a small and humble beginning.

Our spiritual life is no exception to this rule. When you first got to know the living Christ as your Saviour and Redeemer, your emotions probably varied between thanksgiving, ecstatic joy and the steadfast assurance that all things were possible to you because you knew God.

Then after a time the reaction set in. Some people call it backsliding in the faith. In reality it is an indication that when you were young in the faith you accepted the advantages of your relationship with Christ, without accepting the responsibility to grow spiritually as well. Sanctification is never immediate. It is an ongoing process of growing into the image of Jesus Christ. The more intimately you walk with Him, the more you realise the necessity of growing in faith.

Persevere on the path of faith. Never consider that you are a failure or that you are not getting anywhere. Always remember that you must continue growing and that the living Christ is with you during each stage of growth. He enables you to make a great success of your spiritual pilgrimage which had a small beginning – to His honour and glory.

Real growth begins when we accept our own weaknesses and then ask the Holy Spirit to do something about it. (Jean Vanier)

Lord, help me to grow to _____

_____

Christlikeness

"It has not yet been revealed what we shall be, but we know when He is revealed, we shall be like Him" (1 Jn. 3:2)

It should be the goal of every Christian to cast his life according to the mould of Jesus Christ. It will vary according to every person's nature and personality, but the desire will always be to grow into the likeness of the Master.

The unconditional acceptance of the lordship of Christ is the point of departure towards a new and satisfying way of life. In the knowledge that you now belong to Him, your love, as well as your mental and spiritual energy, should be aimed at becoming like Him. He becomes your role model and your goal.

Obviously it is impossible to perfect this pattern in your own strength. Trying to do this in your own strength will only lead to frustration and disappointment. With the acceptance of Christ as the Lord of your life, He becomes a living reality to you. If you ask Him in prayer, He will grant you His Holy Spirit. When you are united with Him, your faith comes alive and your whole life is lived in total obedience to Him.

This vitality in the faith and your obedience develop a Christlike character. The strange truth is that a person with such a character is usually not aware of his Christlikeness. There is no hypocrisy or false pride. A Christian is too busy loving and serving to have time to try and impress his fellowman. His Christlikeness is the by-product of his walk with the Master.

> Christian character is a by-product. It is manufactured in the factory of daily commitment. (Woodrow Wilson)

Master, I plead that Your Spirit _____

_____

Christ makes the difference

"Therefore, if anyone is in Christ he is a new creation; old things have passed away; behold all things have become new. Now all things are of God." (2 Cor. 5:17, 18)

If your life has deteriorated to a constant monotony and every day is but the prologue to the next, it is possible that some where along the line you have lost the spirit of anticipation. Perhaps you firmly believe that nothing will ever change and that your life will continue this way till the end.

It may seem impossible to change your circumstances. When a grey commonness and boring monotony seem to have settled on everything you do, it sounds foolish and even unkind to speak of change. How can a housewife change her routine? How can a businessman change his methods or how can a jobless person who is anxiously looking for a job maintain his self-respect when all his efforts seem to be doomed?

Regardless of what your circumstances may be, the living Christ has a message for you. He can change your attitude. Where monotony has smothered the spirit of expectancy, He lights the flame of ambition and vision again to prove to you what can be achieved when you allow His Spirit into your life.

When you acknowledge Him as the Lord of your life, the Master will take you and re-create you into that which He wants you to be. Your courage and enthusiasm will be renewed. Outwardly things may seem to be unchanged, but inwardly you will be aware of a new vision and fresh approach towards life. This experience of the presence of the living Christ in your life makes all things new for you. And you can obtain it nowhere else, except with Christ.

The greatest value of life is to live life in such a way that it has eternal value. (William James)

Master, please let Your Spirit inspire me _____

_____

Develop your inner life

"Abide in Me, and I in you. As the branch cannot bear fruit of itself, unless it abides in the vine, neither can you, unless you abide in Me." (Jn. 15:4)

Developing a vibrant spiritual life is imperative if you wish to grow in the knowledge of God. To know God is the highest experience and it is within your reach. Even though there is a difference in degree regarding such knowledge, there can be no doubt about the reality of its existence.

Unfortunately many people who maintain that they are spiritually well developed, suffer from shameful ignorance about the harsh realities of life as experienced by thousands of people. In their effort to touch the hand of God they lose contact with the world they live in. When this happens, their faith goes against the grain of those who don't know God, and their hyper-piety becomes a stumbling block to the world.

Jesus' life on earth reflected His holiness, but also true love and empathy. He was very practical in this regard. While His teachings were amazing, He also cared about people's physical needs. He went as far as saying that man cannot love God without loving your neighbour as well, and that true love cannot exist without service and the giving of "oneself".

Your spiritual growth must go hand in hand with a practical expression of inspired service. What value would your spirituality have for God or man if ordinary people are not touched by your service to God and man? Allow your inner growth to be reflected through creative service.

> It must be your joy to serve God. That is what our Master did. Will His servants then not follow the same road? (Horatius Bonar)

Lord, make it clear to everyone that I _____

*L*et Christ reform you

"He saw there was no man, and wondered. Therefore His own arm brought salvation for Him." (Is. 59:16)

*J*ust the mention of the word "justice" usually calls to the human mind images of courts and legislation where the lofty ideals of the law are being administered and debated. Justice however also applies to the everyday life. It means to be just and sincere in your actions.

In order for you to live a Christian life of love it is imperative that the qualities of righteousness and justice are evident in your negotiations. The basis of a Christian business concern is to be honest and fair towards your employees and clients so that the glory of Christ can be reflected through your life and actions.

It is not always easy to make this a reality in your life, and it requires growth in your spiritual and moral life. That which is fair to one person is unfair to the next. Righteousness in the eyes of one man could be regarded as hard-heartedness by the next. You must however discipline yourself to live in harmony with God, you must have an open mind and you must be sensitive to the prompting of the Holy Spirit. He will guide you in your dealings with other people.

Allow the Holy Spirit to influence and guide your mind, to determine your judgement and decisions. Then you will act according to His perfect will. Gradually you will develop to the point where righteousness becomes a corner-stone of your life.

Righteousness is truth in action. (Joseph Joubert)

Holy Judge, honesty and justice _____

_____

Inner beauty

"And let the beauty of the Lord our God be upon us, and establish the work of our hands for us." (Ps. 90:17)

People sometimes spend large amounts of money to make themselves beautiful. Some succeed while others don't. Unfortunately most people accentuate outward beauty. Yet others go farther and follow courses to develop their personality and social virtues. To be well-dressed and skilled in the social etiquette of high society, doesn't necessarily create a strong character or inner beauty. It is in man's character that the true beauty of a person's life has its basis. Man can be beautified with artful skill, but if his heart is self-centred and malicious, it will be a hard and unattractive beauty in the eyes of the beholder.

Others again may perhaps not be physically beautiful, but the quality of their inner life could be so beautiful that people don't notice their outward unattractiveness but only the inner beauty which they emanate.

Those who accentuate the importance of outward physical beauty and perfection, miss the important inner spirit and attitude of man. The inner life can only prosper and be reflected in the physical when there is perfect harmony between man and his Creator.

True beauty does not start at the cosmetics counter, but in that sacred place where you are intimate and alone with God. That is where you gather inner peace of mind and dignity which keeps you balanced at all times. Allow the beauty of your spirit to develop through your fellowship with God and then your whole life will emanate beauty.

> Piety is the foundation of all virtue. It is the golden chain which links up heaven and earth. (Edmund Burke)

Lord, I pray that my life will _____ your beauty

Make optimum use of God's gifts

"... and these things I want you to affirm constantly, that those who
believed in God should be careful to maintain good works" (Tit. 3:8)

It should be the desire of every disciple to strive towards an ever deeper experience of God's love as revealed through Jesus Christ. Regardless of how much you may love Him and even though you know that He loves you, you yearn for the relationship to keep on growing in depth.

You are aware of the fact that prayer, Scripture-reading, meditation and other spiritual disciplines all play an important role to enable you to grow in love. However, the practical application of these principles dare not be underestimated or ignored.

Many of Christ's disciples long for more, or a more powerful faith but they do not use the faith which they already have. Put your small faith to the test and you will find it becomes a working proposition in your everyday life.

The disciple who fully accepts his responsibility regarding faith, always desires a more meaningful prayer life. He may ask God to grant him this beautiful gift, but he already has it. The way to God has been opened by Jesus Christ, and it is the privilege of the disciple to regularly walk upon this path with a firm step. God has already given you the roadmap for prayer – all you have to do is to use and develop it.

Faith and prayer are wonderful gifts which God has given you to help you grow spiritually. You dare never allow them to become a burden which is executed sluggishly.

Prayer is like an electrical switch. It does not create the current, but creates the channel through which the current can flow. (Max Handel)

Father, help me to use my gifts _____

_____

*S*piritual growth is important

"For we do not wrestle against flesh and blood, but against spiritual hosts of wickedness in heavenly places." (Eph. 6:12)

The greatest forces in this world cannot be seen or analysed. People with restricted spiritual vision regard material things which can be seen, handled and judged to be of the utmost importance. They don't realise that the things which they see are the expression of thoughts. Love, hate, friendliness and bitterness, creativity or the desire to break down, all are expressions of a person's mind. That is why the basis of a balanced and constructive lifestyle is vested in the realisation that spiritual and mental powers are of much greater importance than material values.

The destructive forces of the world have their origin in the spirit of man, therefore it is in the area of the spirit that you need to equip yourself for a victorious life. It is in your spirit that you grow mature enough to forgive; that is where you calmly and peacefully develop a positive and constructive attitude towards life. That is the place where you wait upon the Lord to receive His strength and guidance.

It is only when you give time and energy to prayer in order to develop and nurture your spiritual reserves that you can dare to take on the negative and destructive powers which continually fight to obtain a foothold in your spirit.

Prayer is and always remains the deepest impulse of the human soul. (Thomas Carlyle)

Lord, let Your Holy Spirit inspire me _____

*S*piritual responsibilities

"Work out your own salvation with fear and trembling; for it is God who works in you both to will and to do for His good pleasure." (Phil. 2:12, 13)

*J*ust how serious are you about your spiritual responsibilities? As a committed Christian you have adopted a lifestyle which requires from you everything you could possibly give. In order to fully accept your responsibility you need to give your all to God and steadfastly place your faith and trust in Him. This commitment is not just an emotional experience, but a lifestyle which requires the practical application of your faith in life's everyday situations.

To be able to execute this requirement, you need the inspiration, wisdom and power of the indwelling Christ. It is impossible to live as "a redeemed human being" in your own strength. If, however, you allow Christ into your life, giving Him the freedom to reveal Himself through you, that which is impossible to you, does become possible through His power.

Your submission to Christ, so that He can work through you, requires total commitment and dedication. You are morally responsible for your actions, your behaviour and your attitudes. You are responsible for the amount of time you spend in prayer; your attitude towards other people; for the mercy that needs to be shown to your fellowman; for the thoughts which you harbour in your heart. In the final analysis you are responsible for what you are. Only if you abide in Christ and He in you, will you be able to realise this ideal.

> Only the one who can see the unseen, can do the impossible. (Frank Gaines)

Holy God, in Your wisdom _____

_____

Grow spiritually: help others

"Nevertheless God, who comforts the downcast, comforted us by the coming of Titus." (2 Cor. 7:6)

Paul was having a difficult time with the problems of the early church. Persecution and spiritual sabotage pressed heavily on his heart. Even though his faith remained strong, he felt down-hearted from time to time. He regarded the arrival of Titus as a form of encouragement from God to His servants in times of need. This is a testimony of Paul's dedicated discipleship.

God used Titus to ease Paul's burden and to encourage him. There are many disciples who are depressed and discouraged. Perhaps some of them work in dreary, dismal circumstances, they have lost their vision and their faith and so have become ineffective. Others again are involved in a hopeless struggle against strong persecution and consider giving up hope.

It may be that in your sphere of influence there are discouraged Christians who urgently need spiritual support. If you should happen to know such a disciple of the Lord but refuse to do something to restore his faith and hope again, you are disappointing God and denying your Christianity.

You may feel totally inadequate for the task, but through prayer and by opening your heart to the influence of the Holy Spirit, God will be able to use you constructively. It may involve offering of your friendship; perhaps listening to someone with a deep-seated grudge who is calling out for healing and forgiveness; or just praying with another person. God will bless you in this and make you a blessing. Thus you will grow a small step on the way to spiritual maturity.

> One of man's highest duties is the duty of encouragement. (William Barclay)

Father, please strengthen my faith to _____

ℛeal change

"And do not be conformed to this world, but be transformed by the renewing of your mind." (Rom. 12:2)

ℱamiliarity is one of the great dangers of our Christianity. You may have heard the gospel so many times already that it no longer has any impact on your spirit. Worship time doesn't succeed in lifting your spirit any more. Even though Christianity is part of your heritage and tradition, it no longer plays an active role in your daily life. You are classified as a Christian simply because you are not a pagan or an agnostic. The power, joy and gladness that Jesus Christ promised His followers, are just not part of your life.

Living Christianity implies an experience with the living Christ – an experience so meaningful that even the thoughts that flash through your mind are being changed. As you are being confronted with the realities of Christ's teachings, that love is stronger than hate, that forgiveness achieves much more than revenge and that God really guides those who are confused, a whole new meaning of what Christianity really is dawns on your spirit.

This new awareness of the Christian faith is not the product of a self-made illusion, but the direct result of the working of the Holy Spirit in your mind. If you open yourself up to the prompting of the Holy Spirit, you become aware that God is at work in your life. When He expresses Himself through your life, your Christianity becomes alive and meaningful and you change because Christ has changed your mind. This is glorious growth in the life of any Christian.

The indwelling of the Holy Spirit is this: to always keep God in sight and establish His temple in your life. (Walter Hilton)

Father, I praise and thank You _____

_____

Quality and quantity

"So you may walk in the way of goodness, and keep to the paths of righteousness. For the upright will dwell in the land." *(Prov. 2:20, 21)*

One of the superficial expressions that we have grown used to is that we need to choose between quality and quantity in our lives. The majority of people believe that you cannot enjoy both and thus you are faced with the choice: do you want the best or do you want the most?

As Jesus Christ so often did when He was confronted with the standards and teachings of His time, He refutes the theory that one cannot have both quality and quantity. Jesus said, *"I have come that they may have life and that they may have it more abundantly"* (John 10:10). If you acknowledge the lordship and sovereignty of Christ in your life, you become a new person. Rebirth occurs and you lay down your old life altogether. Selfishness is changed into a new, unselfish lifestyle which Christ offers you. In Jesus Christ your total existence becomes meaningful when you live according to the new values. Paul says, *"Therefore, if anyone is in Christ, he is a new creation; old things have passed away; behold, all things have become new"* (2 Corinthians 5:17).

This new life awaits you too and you need to grow towards it in your spiritual life. It is God's gift to you in Jesus Christ and all it requires from you is to give yourself unconditionally to Him. In exchange you will receive fullness of life far beyond your wildest dreams – a life of unparalleled quality and quantity because in reality you receive Jesus Himself.

Do you experience life as one big misery? Isn't it rather that your hands are too small and your vision too restricted? It is time for you to start growing into maturity. (Dag Hammerskjold)

Spirit of God, teach me to _____
_____ *in Christ.*

A life of fulfilment

"For now we live, if you stand fast in the Lord." (1 Thes. 3:8)

Knowing that your testimony for Jesus Christ is really effective is always a source of great joy. It may be something you said; a friendly or kind deed; your support in times of need; a sympathetic ear lent to someone who was in trouble. Regardless of what you have done, the fact that the Master used you to draw someone closer to Him, always leaves you with a feeling of humility, awe and fulfilment.

As during His earthly ministry, the living Christ is still inspiring people through His Holy Spirit to be His witnesses, to proclaim the gospel and win souls for God. This is the role God expects you to fulfil on your pilgrimage because you are the bearer of His holy Name.

True discipleship is never easy and you will have to overcome many barriers along the way, you will experience setbacks, you will taste disappointment and will even have to handle adversity. In spite of all that, you dare never give up hope, but persevere in your service as your Master did – even though He had to suffer and die for it.

Seek the Lord in prayer and open up your heart to the influence of the Holy Spirit so that Christ can become an essential part of your existence. As He leads you along His path and among His people, you will experience unparalleled fulfilment which can only be obtained when you grow in serving Jesus Christ.

Honest service according to our ability, even in the small things in life, is a sign of spiritual progress to the honour of God. (Wilfred Grenfell)

I want to serve You, O Lord, _____

Your responsibility

[I pray that] "the eyes of your understanding being enlightened; that you may know what is the hope of your calling, what are the riches of the glory of His inheritance in the saints." (Eph. 1:18)

It is true that salvation is God's free gift to all who want to accept it, but if you want to possess the total fulfilment and joy of your faith, you must concentrate on it with all your strength. It is a matter of course that people who are enthusiastic about their faith, derive much greater blessing from it than those who are lukewarm and happy-go-lucky about the truths of God.

It is our personal responsibility to develop optimal spiritual skill and effectiveness. It is useless to beg God to strengthen your prayer life if you are not willing to give more time to prayer. The desire to become more Christlike is praiseworthy, but unless you are willing to sacrifice time for meditation about the life, personality and character of the Master as revealed in Scripture, your desire will remain unfulfilled.

If you have accepted the Lord's free offer of salvation and have dedicated yourself to Him, you have committed yourself to the responsibility of growing closer to Jesus in every respect. This responsibility requires discipline, or you condemn yourself to spiritual immaturity. Such an unhappy situation is the consequence of a neglected quiet time with God.

Spiritual growth requires sustained nourishing through prayer and edifying Bible study. These two requirements must be met if you wish to remain true to your Lord and want to develop spiritually.

Spiritual maturity is not obtained through verbosity, but by constant submission to the will of God. (D.W. Lambert)

Lord, my spiritual life is _____

_____

The source of spiritual power

"For I know that this will turn out for my deliverance through your prayer and the supply of the Spirit of Christ." (Phil. 1:19)

Nobody can be totally independent as a Christian. If you had the privilege of a Christian background, you have an unpaid debt towards those who put you on the Christian road. If you are a new-born Christian, you will discover the value of spending time in the company of mature Christians. You will receive inspiration and encouragement from them.

Although the gospel of Jesus Christ is focused mainly on the individual, we don't find one person in the New Testament who is totally independent. The first disciples obtained their strength from their relationship with other disciples. Undoubtedly this is the answer to those who claim that they don't need the fellowship of the believers.

While fellowship is of the utmost importance, it must always be Christ-centred. There are too many Christian fellowship groups that function like religious debating societies where personal opinions are flung around while little time is given to a thorough study of God's Word and to prayer. While you are waiting upon the Lord in fellowship with other Christians, you can be encouraged and at the same time learn to know an intimacy with Christ which will strengthen and increase your faith.

The basic source of spiritual power is Jesus Christ who dwells in you. He promised to dwell in all who accepted Him as Redeemer and Saviour. For you to keep this wonderful experience fresh and alive, the New Testament maintains that it is imperative to live in fellowship with others who feel the same as you.

It is only when people start to worship that they start to grow. (Calvin Coolridge)

Thank You Lord, that my faith is strengthened _____

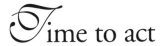ime to act

"He who has an ear let him hear what the Spirit says to the churches."
(Rev. 2:17)

In our day much is said and written about church members' unwillingness to attend church services. In church circles people are rightfully very upset about the fuss which is made about other faiths and sects, the threat of a drug culture and about Satanism.

Christians should give long and serious consideration to this situation. If we really want to be honest, we will find the cause for all this is that Christ is no longer at the centre of the church. In many congregations politics play a very important role; while we also find so many spouses are unfaithful in their marriages. How often we find that the social activities of the congregation we belong to are questionable. The various denominations are divided with regard to theology and doctrines while efforts to unite them are often sabotaged. In the meantime, the opposing forces are gaining ground at the expense of the church of Jesus Christ.

Whether you are an office bearer in your congregation or not, your highest duty is to strive to ensure that your congregation will be Christ-centred; that the members will acknowledge His sovereignty in all things and obediently follow His will. Thus you will do your part to exalt His glorious Name. You can only do this if you are sensitive to the voice of the Holy Spirit in your inner-being and react to it in obedience.

> The church of Christ is not an institution; it is a new life with Christ and in Christ, led by the Holy Spirit. (Sergius Bulgakov)

Holy Spirit, make me sensitive _____

$\mathscr{S}$piritual growth is essential

"I fed you with milk and not with solid food; for until now you were not able to receive it ... For where there are envy, strife and divisions among you, are you not carnal and behaving like mere men?" (1 Cor. 3:2, 3)

$\mathcal{M}$ any people believe in a God who is great and awesome, yet their outlook remains restricted: in faith they accept that He is love, but refuse to allow Him to bring that love into their lives. He promised His power to all who serve Him, but they remain weak and powerless; they maintain that they believe in God, but they don't experience His loving presence.

The tragedy is that these people live their lives on an ordinary human level and are therefore spiritually immature. They may be quite active in Christian work, but if things don't go their way, they refuse to cooperate. If they cannot be leaders, they refuse to be followers. In this, and in many other ways, they prove that they are still spiritually immature.

The Christian's way of life enriches the life of the disciples and extends their outlook. When you start becoming mature in the spiritual life, you develop a greater understanding of your fellow-man. If the love of Christ controls your life through His Spirit, all immature attitudes such as pettiness, jealousy and strife are wiped out because they are dissolved and removed through the love of Christ.

It is only when you have an intimate walk with the Master that you receive the grace to see these negative things for what they really are. Then you rise above this immaturity and live on the solid food which the Holy Spirit places at your disposal.

> Personality and individuality are engraved on the face of every person by God: It is something holy, it is for the resurrection, for eternal life. (Leon Bloy)

Lord, daily I want to _____

_____

Growth through understanding

"Beloved, let us love one another, for love is of God; and everyone who loves is born of God and knows God. He who does not love does not know God, for God is love." (1 Jn. 4:7, 8)

Many people don't find it easy to love at all. Perhaps they work with people who are a source of alarm to them; they may find the habits of others repulsive and their character traits disturbing. To live and work with such people makes the command of Christ to love seem impossible.

John, the apostle of love, writes about practical love. Perfect love is a slow process of growth in Christ. But it must have a starting point. When you are confronted with someone whom you find difficult to love, remember that this person has been created in the image of God. Regardless of how badly you may be repelled by this person, remember that beneath the exterior there are eternal values waiting to be released.

Do not judge people on their outward appearance. Rather see in them individuals whom God regards worthy of salvation. If you should change your attitude from dislike to understanding, you will experience a change in your own spiritual life. Then you will, by the grace of God and through the working of the Holy Spirit, develop a greater appreciation for those whom you previously found hard to love.

> Instead of making yourself unhappy, just allow your love to grow as God wants it to grow; look for goodness in others; express your love more freely, less selfishly and without expecting anything in return. Do not fear, you will receive your reward. (Henry Drummond)

Holy Spirit, teach me to love those _____

_____

ᒐnner strength

*"[I pray] that He would grant you, according to the riches of His glory,
to be strengthened with might through his Spirit in the inner man."
(Eph. 3:16)*

ᒐt is amazing to see how many people are neglecting their
spiritual life. They will go to unprecedented trouble to develop their body and increase their knowledge, yet totally ignore the
spirit. And this is where the great motivational power of a person's
life is to be found. If someone has a mean spirit, it simply means
that he has not yet had a real experience of the warmth and mercy
of God's love. He is not only missing the very greatest experience
of life, but is also losing a source of strength and inspiration which
is not equalled by anything on earth.

When you become conscious of God's indwelling presence,
you not only experience His strength, but you are made conscious
of the beauty and riches of life itself. It is impossible that Christ can
dwell in you, without His strength and beauty becoming part of
your life. To open up your life for the gracious influence of the
Holy Spirit is a life-changing experience with many blessings, but
the greatest blessing is the consciousness that Christ dwells in your
spirit and is present daily.

Such an experience changes your faith from the theoretical to
the practical, because the Christ who lives in you, wants to reveal
Himself through you to the world around you. If He is in control of
your life, your mind and emotions acquire a new sense of meaning
and your whole life is filled with His glory.

A true Christian can be described as someone whose life is controlled by
God whose presence is in him. (John Henry Newman)

Almighty God, through Your power _____

_____

To live anew

"[I will] put breath in you; and you shall live" (Ezek. 37:6)

If your faith has lost its energy, the time has come for you to take stock spiritually. It is not the will of your heavenly Father that your faith in Him should be a burden or a cross to you. Therefore, the cause of your spiritual deadness lies in yourself and not in Him.

Perhaps, in your zeal and enthusiasm to serve Him, you have set your mind more on getting things done, than on following the will of the Lord. The courage of your faith carried you for a time, but has now decreased alarmingly. Now you discover that though you were busy working for God, you have lost the consciousness of His Divine presence in your life. Something which is indispensable, has vanished visibly from your life.

There is but one way to revival. In order for you to taste the joy of an experience with God through Jesus Christ again, you must make your heart the home of His Holy Spirit. Through God's indwelling Spirit you will start living a victorious life in Jesus again. The greatest joy however, lies in the fact that your life is again reflecting the glory of Christ, even though it may be in a small measure. When this happens, your faith again becomes an inspiration and the motivational force in your life. It becomes the most important matter of your life, because Christ is a glorious reality.

> The Holy Spirit Himself, who is at work in God's children, is a consequence of God, which flows from Him and flows back to Him like the rays of the sun. (Athenagoras)

Holy Spirit, take control of my life so that _____

_____

A balanced inner life

"If any of you lacks wisdom, let him ask of God, who gives to all liberally and without reproach, and it will be given to him." (Jas. 1:5)

Our lives must be spiritual, but practical as well. So many people have the misconception that in order to live a truly spiritual life, you need to live in mystical seclusion where the realities of life are either ignored or forgotten. All your energy needs to be directed towards the development of the "spiritual life".

The teachings expressed by the Master along the dusty roads of Palestine, were intensely spiritual, yet essentially practical. It is extremely difficult to draw a line between that which He regarded as "spiritual" and "non-spiritual". For Him, everything – every thought and deed – was an expression of His relationship with His heavenly Father. Therefore a true Christian does not divide his life into compartments, because all of life must be an expression of the spiritual.

A faith which is so spiritualised that it dims the mind to the harsh realities of life, can definitely not be inspired by the Holy Spirit or by Jesus Christ. His Spirit sharpens the mind and makes it sensitive to discern the will of God. Paul Tournier wrote, "I wait upon God to renew my mind, to make me creative, instead of becoming the clanging cymbal that Paul speaks of." The spiritual expression of life touches the realities of every day and enables you to look, to a certain extent, at people's problems as God does. Thus the spiritual and the practical connect perfectly to make life complete.

> It is in the practical matters of life that people show their character. (Arthur Schopenhauer)

O Spirit, take possession of my life _____

*T*ruth leads to maturity

"But, speaking the truth in love, may grow up in all things into Him who is the head – Christ" (Eph. 4:15)

*S*ometimes life can become very complicated when the truth is forcefully expressed. Relationships can get tense and feelings are hurt. There are times when silence is kind and is required, but to steer clear of the truth only to prevent an unpleasant situation, often creates bigger problems.

The balm of the truth is love. If truth is expressed in a cruel manner, it can cause irreparable damage. It remains the truth, but leaves wounds which perhaps may never heal. Truth which is spoken in love doesn't lose any of its impact and benefits the one who speaks it and the one who listens to it.

Speaking the truth in love is an indication of spiritual maturity. To express truth without love reveals a lack of Christ's indwelling Spirit. An agnostic may be a person of truth because the truth is in good repute with honest people. But, to speak the truth because the living Christ reveals Himself through you, adds to it an extra quality which cannot be derived from any other source.

To speak the truth in the spirit and attitude of Jesus Christ, influences your approach towards your fellowmen and creates an attitude of love and understanding which liberates you from a judgmental attitude. Truth must never be used to oppress someone who is already burdened with guilt, but must offer forgiveness and healing. In conjunction with the truth, love will find expression through your life.

> While it is faith which makes all things possible, it is love which makes all things easy. (Evan H. Hopkins)

Holy God, may the quality of my life _____

_____

The power of the Holy Spirit

"I say then: Walk in the Spirit, and you shall not fulfil the lust of the flesh." (Gal. 5:16)

Nobody will ever deny that it is a difficult task to maintain the high standards of Christian living. Commitment and surrender to Jesus Christ, obedience to the will of God and strictly following the example and teachings of Christ, require a high level of dedication and self-discipline which is far above any human ability. The result is that there are many who want to become disciples, but let go of the challenge because they give in to the temptations and seductions of the world around them.

Jesus, our living Lord, is only too aware of the requirements of commitment to Him and His cause, and in order to encourage you along your pilgrimage, He warns us that we can do nothing without Him (see John 15:5). But, with God all things are possible, *"I can do all things through Christ who strengthens me"* (Philippians 4:13).

To enable you to accept the requirements and challenges of your commitment to Him, Jesus has made His Holy Spirit available to you. He grants you the ability to live as Jesus expects you to live and to overcome the temptations of the world around you.

If you should commit yourself to the Lord and allow His Holy Spirit in you to guide you, you will experience the power of the Holy Spirit more and more. Always remain sensitive to His influence and you will receive power of a quality as you have not known yet. This will enable you to live in obedience to the will of God.

> Obedience to God is the steadfast testimony of sincere and practical love for God. (Nathanael Emmons)

Lord, may the quality of my life _____

_____

Grow towards self-control

"A soft answer turns away wrath, but a harsh word stirs up anger."
(Prov. 15:1)

One of the distinctive characteristics of our Master's life on earth was His relationship with, and attitude towards people. He could be firm, yet tender; He could speak with authority without being cruel; He could encourage and reprimand. He could do all these things and yet there was never a show of swaggering or bitterness. Even in those rare moments of anger, He always acted in love.

Every word was perfectly chosen and expressed without a trace of bitterness. When one murderer on the cross gave vent to his feelings by blaspheming Jesus, He transformed that awful moment of horror and barbarity into a victory for love when He expressed His immortal words of sympathy, mercy and forgiveness.

We must remember this in our negotiations with other people, because bitter quarrels and unforgiveness are born from a loveless heart. It may well be that you have been provoked or hurt by a loveless remark. Perhaps you were accused falsely. If you react in a similar way, you will only fan the fire and drive a wedge between you and the opposing party causing a division which cannot be breached.

If you should feel that the criticism or treatment you receive is undeserved and unfair, or that you need to reprimand someone, follow the example of Jesus Christ and say what you want to say – but in love. Thus you will prevent someone from being hurt deeply and you will obtain victory in the Name of Christ.

> We must be anchored in self-discipline if we really want to be free.
> (Harold E. Kohn)

God, please enable me to _____

_____

The ripening Christian

"As you therefore have received Christ Jesus the Lord so walk in Him, rooted and built up in Him and established in the faith, as you have been taught, abounding in it with thanksgiving." (Col. 2:6, 7)

One of the weaknesses of modern Christianity is the great number of immature Christians. They maintain that they love Christ, and yet their love is weak and their witnessing ineffective. There was a time when they pledged their allegiance to Him, but since then they neglected to grow spiritually.

A dynamic Christian experience is an experience with the Holy God through the grace and love of the living Christ. The historical Jesus is included in this experience. It is only when the gospel story, as recorded in the Bible, is accepted that an understanding of and appreciation for God can be established. The historical Jesus is essential because He is the basis of everything the Christian believes about God.

You cannot meditate upon the historical Jesus for too long without becoming aware of the eternal and living Christ. A ripening Christian develops a consciousness about the presence of Christ in his life. This consciousness cultivates an intense desire to know Christ more intimately; a willingness to discipline the mind and feed it with lofty ideas and spiritual literature; a willingness to obey the will of the Master. As you ripen and mature as a Christian, you become more like your Master and you experience the fullness of your faith.

Maturity starts to grow when you experience a greater concern for others than for yourself. (John MacNaughton)

God of love, give me more love so that _____

_____

THE FOUNTAIN OF
SANCTIFICATION

All of us can reach the Christian door of sanctification, regardless the situation or circumstances of our life and regardless what our life-work is. (Francis de Salles)

"Holy is Your being, O God, more pure than the light of the sun!" Holy Father, by grace You call me, sinful man to a life of holiness.

Without Your abundant grace I would not even be able to start out on the path of sanctification.

But, through my Saviour, Jesus, Your Son, the possibilities of living a holy life are unlimited.

Holy Spirit, flow through me and cleanse me from all my sin. Capture my thoughts and submit them to Your will. Touch my words with Your Godly grace. May every deed I do be done in love and may I reflect the holiness of my Lord. I bring You all the honour and praise. You are the light of my life and the guide along my path. My heart is filled with love for You and I shout for joy to the glory of Your Name.

You are my Saviour O Lord, and the King of my heart!

December

A balanced spiritual life

"For you are a holy people to the Lord your God; the Lord your God has chosen you to be a people for Himself, a special treasure above all the peoples on the face of the earth." (Deut. 7:6)

Holiness has become a very unpopular word which doesn't appeal to many people. It seems to be something remote from everyday life. The ordinary person thinks to himself, "I am not a saint" and leaves the characteristic of holiness to the people with a religious inclination.

One of the roots of the word holiness is "well-lived". To really live a life of sanctification, is to live really well and fulfilled. This implies a well-balanced approach to every facet of life. Neither the spiritual nor the material life is neglected. All of life must be permeated with a spirit of appreciation and the knowledge that spiritual forces can function freely through every aspect of life.

Life is thrown off balance if the spiritual aspect is being neglected or ignored. Frustrations and disappointments start to reveal themselves. Personalities become distorted if the spiritual loses contact with the realities and facts of everyday life. Living without spiritual appreciation causes unapproachable personalities to develop, while losing sight of the facts of life creates unbalanced religious enthusiasts. Christian holiness is a balanced way of life. This stresses the importance of the human spirit, but does not neglect the pilgrimage through life with all its responsibilities.

> There is no simple definition for holiness. For me it means to get up every time I stumble and to do it with humility and joy. I like to think of it that way. (Helder Camara)

Holy Spirit, teach me the way to a balanced spiritual life so that

A life in fullness

"For God did not call us to uncleanness, but in holiness." (1 Thes. 4:7)

It is extremely sad that there are many people who think there is nothing as boring as living a "holy" life. Holiness has become synonymous with misery and the average person finds it appalling because he prefers a pleasant life.

The fact of the matter however is that "holiness" really means fullness of life – living well! God has called us to a full and fulfilling life. This implies that a truly spiritual life is balanced and level. It is not shocked by the revelation of any sin, regardless how vulgar and destructive it may be. It has a pleasant maturity which creates trust. Holiness should be the goal of all spiritually-minded people, because it is the foundation of a mature life.

The path to holiness is equally exciting and satisfying as the end-goal in itself, because you are travelling this road with God. This means there are times spent in His divine presence. You cannot experience such times without their having a tremendous impact on your life. You cannot spend time with Christ and still remain the same person. Something of the character and personality of the eternal Father and Son penetrate your spirit and you become totally holy.

Fortunate is the person whose feet are on the path of sanctification, because he already experiences a full and fulfilled life.

A holy life is not ascetic, sombre or lonely, but is a life controlled by Godly truth and faithful Christian service. It is to rise above the world while we are still living in it. (Tryon Edwards)

Holy Father, I sincerely desire that You _____

_____

True holiness

"For My thoughts are not your thoughts, nor are your ways My ways"
says the Lord." (Is. 55:8)

It is generally believed that living a holy life causes you to miss out on the sparkle and enthusiasm of life. Many people find it incomprehensible that a life of fullness, joy and completeness could be linked to holiness. Yet true holiness is the most dynamic, creative and meaningful force in the world.

To be holy implies that you live in right relationship with God. Nobody can know a relationship like that without a deep understanding of God: it causes you to enjoy life to the full and also gives you a greater understanding of people. True holiness consists of two important aspects. There is the burning desire to grow into Christlikeness and a willingness to be identified with people. Thus the image of Christ is reflected in the community where you live.

Holiness detests hypocrisy. It urges one to live through the power of the Holy Spirit and results in a balanced approach to life. Nobody who strives to obtain holiness will ever find life monotonous or uninteresting, because they are busy living according to God's standard.

The secret of a balanced and gratifying life is to live in such a way that it is easy for the Master to express Himself through you. This is the way of true sanctification, but it is also the road to a successful life according to God's standard.

> When people submit themselves to the Holy Spirit and live a holy life, they will learn more about God and Christ, salvation and immortality in one week, than they will learn in a whole life-time without the Holy Spirit. (John Brown)

Teach me, O Holy Spirit, the true meaning of holiness and enable me to _____

On the presence of God

"Therefore ... having boldness to enter the Holiest by the blood of Jesus, by a new and living way which He consecrated for us, through the veil." (Heb. 10:19, 20)

There are many people whose perception of God is clouded and vague. They visualise a fear-inspiring figure who rules over the affairs of the world, makes demands and hands out punishment. Even the thought that it is possible to come into the presence of God overwhelms them with a feeling of fear. The great tragedy is that these people rob themselves of the most glorious of all experiences in life – to be still and to know God.

The reason why Christ came to this world was to reveal God to man. Through the death of His Son, the God of love opened the way to the throne of grace for all who believe in Him. Now He is with the Father to intercede for us. Through His Spirit He is willing to live in your heart and guide you along the right path on a daily basis so that your everyday life can be to His glory.

If you desire to live a fulfilled life and to experience the joy of an intimately personal relationship with the living Christ, you only need to open up your heart and mind to Him. Surrender yourself unconditionally to His lordship and allow the Holy Spirit to control your life. By doing this you will experience the wonder of the fullness of life in Jesus Christ to the utmost. This is an important step on the road to sanctification.

> You must live a holy life in the manner that God expects from you. God doesn't expect you to be a Trappist monk or a hermit. He expects you to sanctify the world around you as well as your everyday life. (Vincent Palotti)

I open up my heart and mind to You, Lord, sanctify me that I

2 Peter 3:8-18 ~ 5 December

*W*hat is a mature Christian?

"But grow in the grace and knowledge of our Lord and Saviour Jesus Christ." (2 Pet. 3:18)

*S*piritual immaturity is a self-imposed cross which you carry. Many people call themselves Christians because they were born and bred in Christian homes or even because they are part of a Christian civilisation. Nevertheless, they have never fully surrendered to Jesus.

True Christianity starts with the acceptance of Jesus Christ as your Saviour and Redeemer. From that moment onwards you start with a new way of life. If you want this lifestyle to be meaningful, it requires a daily submission to the will of your Master.

If you confess your faith in Him, Christ accepts you as His disciple. He is true to all His promises, but the responsibility to develop a dynamic and living faith rests with you. You may have the desire to pray for a richer prayer life, but unless you are willing to spend more time in prayer it will remain only a desire. You may long to have a stronger faith, but you must utilise the faith which you already have.

A real, committed and ripening Christian never stops working at his growth towards identification with his role model, Jesus Christ. It may sound like a high ideal, but no Christian is fighting alone. Christ is always there to strengthen you in your weakness and frustration. The Christian life is an ongoing ripening process. If you stop working at it, your spiritual life will stagnate and eventually be non-existent.

In our era, the road of sanctification necessarily passes through the world of action. (Dag Hammerskjold)

Dear Lord, I humbly ask that during my periods of spiritual laziness You will activate me to _____

_____

Inspiration unto sanctification

"But there is a spirit in man, and the breath of the Almighty gives him understanding." (Job 32:8)

When our spiritual mind is restricted to religion, it can never reach its full potential. To think about the Holy Spirit only in terms of religious clichés restricts the greatness of God and lessens His impact on a person's life and experience.

Because He is eternal and omnipresent, the Holy Spirit is working today exactly as He did in the early days of the church. Every sphere of the human life which is enriching, ennobling and inspiring and which lifts man's thoughts to higher truths, is under the ministry of the Holy Spirit. Great works of art give expression to the Spirit's love of beauty. Music written by inspired composers echoes the harmony in the mind of God. Modern science exposes the hidden mysteries which suggest that there are even greater secrets still waiting to be discovered. Everything which is good in life is under the lordship and sphere of influence of the Holy Spirit.

Regardless what your life-work may be, if it can have the seal of God's approval, it can draw unlimited benefits from the ministry of the Holy Spirit. He can inspire you to greater achievements, give you ideas that will enrich your efforts, lead you on paths which you would never have discovered if you had leaned on your own understanding.

Allow the Spirit of God to be your guide and inspiration and react to the road which He opens up before you: the road to sanctification.

> Sanctification is not an optional extra to the process of creation, but rather the total goal thereof. (Donald Nicholl)

I thank You, Holy Spirit of God, for Your inspiration which _____ my life.

Don't miss out on the best

"But earnestly desire the best gifts." (1 Cor. 12:31)

It is a natural inclination of man to desire only the best which life has to offer. However, it is of the utmost importance to know what is best and not subconsciously accept that which is second best. It is disturbing that many people strive towards a goal because they believe it to be the best, while their aim should actually be higher.

Unfortunately this mistake is made because people have a distorted understanding of values. They regard financial riches to be of greater importance than an honourable character, they believe it is better to receive than to give, that the means justify the end and that only a fool will help someone else free of charge.

In order for you to know what is best for you, it is necessary for you to take stock of what you are and what you do. It takes courage to acknowledge your mistakes, to understand your weaknesses and to be committed to doing something positive about your goals in life.

Such courage requires standards against which it can be measured and the highest available standards are those given to man by God. They are the old crystallised values of love, honesty, unselfishness and purity. When you allow these God-given principles to govern your conscience, you will become aware of their challenge and impact upon your life, even though it may be very difficult to adhere to them. If, however, you carry on living according to these divine standards, God's best for you outshines by far all the plans you can make for yourself.

Faith has to do with the foundation, the ground on which we stand. Hope is to reach out in expectation of what is still to come. Love is to be there only and to act. (Emil Brunner)

Grant me wisdom, O divine Master, to _____

Let others see Christ in you

"And He said to them, 'Go into all the world and preach the gospel to every creature.'" (Mk. 16:15)

Why is it that so many people who call themselves Christians are hesitant to confess their faith in Jesus Christ before the world? Perhaps it is because of the ingrained pattern of society which believes that religion, like politics, is taboo in good company. Every other subject of conversation seems to be acceptable, even those of a dubious moral standard, while just the mention of your faith causes eyebrows to be raised.

It is understandable that people can be put off by those whose hyper-enthusiasm speaks of insensitivity. Nevertheless, in the world of today, there is an increasing need for Christians to identify themselves. This includes an unashamed confession of your faith in Jesus Christ. At the same time it is important that you should know when to speak and when to be quiet.

However, there is one way in which you can confess your faith without insulting or tiring other people, and that is to live like Jesus Christ by following His example. His whole life was a testimony of dedication to His task, sympathy, mercy and love for all people, regardless of their rank or circumstances. This is the very best way to be a witness for the gospel of Jesus Christ.

Ask the Holy Spirit to control your life to the extent that others will see Christ in everything you do and say. In this way you will give expression to the command of the Master.

> The world is much more willing to receive the gospel than what Christians are willing to give. (George W. Peters)

Help me, Lord Jesus, to live through the Holy Spirit in such a way that _____

To live for Christ

"For to me, to live is Christ." (Phil. 1:21)

Too many people live aimlessly. Days become months and months become years without their establishing for themselves what the goal of their life is. Often their objectives are shallow and unrealistic: they want to gather riches, pleasures and earthly possessions. In themselves these things cannot bring real satisfaction. In order to live joyfully and fulfilled, it is important to have a high goal in life, which Christ can approve of.

If you truly love Christ, you already have a high ideal and goal in your life. With that you also have the necessary strength and inspiration to give expression to that goal in your daily life. Your goal should be to spend every moment which God gives you in His grace, living steadfastly to His glory. There will not be room in your life for sporadic spiritual experiences. You will not be "spiritual" only if the mood strikes you. Your faith will remain constant, in spite of your fluctuating emotions.

Living for Christ means the commitment of your spirit, soul and body to Him; to walk along the road of sanctification in earnest; to accept Him as your only Redeemer and Saviour. If you live for Him, He will be alive for you and you will know the ecstasy of a life poured out before God as a thanks-offering and which is lived to His glory.

Never compare His perfection with your imperfection. Accept the gift of Himself in your life and allow Him to work through you. Then for you to live, is Christ!

Spirituality means "the Holy Spirit is at work"; it is an amazing act of the Holy Spirit in the human heart which renews him from the inside. (Leon Joseph Suenens)

Holy Jesus, live in me so that I _____

_____

Values that cannot be defiled

"Therefore, as the elect of God, holy and beloved, put on tender mercies, kindness, humility, meekness, longsuffering." (Col. 3:12)

In this highly competitive world we live in, there are many people who are striving for position. They strive towards higher and higher goals and cry out for attention and recognition. Becoming better than the next person has become a way of life for them. They search for an egocentric lifestyle which is willingly accepted.

Generally you will find that people who fit into this pattern do not have peace of mind and are not very happy. Deep inside their being they are fearful and insecure. They lack security. Take away their possessions, their position and their social status and there is little or nothing left for them in life.

Jesus established the foundation for a life of fulfilment and joy when He stressed man's complete love for God and commanded us to love our neighbour as we love ourselves – and as He loves us. That love was so great that it urged Christ to lay down His life for us. This love forms the basis of the good life and of peace. It creates a peaceful and full life under the lordship of God.

The living Christ is still there to help us through His Holy Spirit to adapt to this pattern of life. If you do this, His qualities will appear in your life. Your approach to other people will reveal just how unimportant and insignificant worldly achievements are when compared to the wonder of serving God and pursuing sanctification.

Sanctify yourself and the community you serve will be sanctified. (Francis of Assisi)

Jesus Christ, You are the Rock on whom I want to build because

To walk with Christ

"So it was, while they conversed and reasoned, that Jesus Himself drew near and went with them. But their eyes were restrained, so that they did not know Him." (Lk. 24:15, 16)

The first disciples were astounded by what happened. Their spiritual perception could not penetrate the darkness caused by the death of their Master. In their sorrow they also could not remember His promises. For the disciples the road to Emmaus was clouded with darkness and sorrow.

Jesus joined them on their journey, but initially they did not recognise Him. After requesting Him to stay over they recognised Him as the Master Whom they loved so much.

The Emmaus road is not unique in the Christian's experience. Many walked in His company for a long time without recognising Him. He lavished His blessings upon them and yet they did not react to His love. Perhaps they listened for many years as the gospel was preached by faithful ministers and yet they did not realise its full importance. They might even maintain that they experienced conversion but that the joy and reality of the faith eluded them.

Actually the wonderful truth is that the Master is walking with you on every step of the pilgrimage. Even when you treated Him as a stranger, He was your friend. When His blessings are recognised and appreciated, He keeps on giving and when you listen to His Word, He reveals Himself to you. Christ is walking with you now and is waiting to be recognised and accepted as your Master and Saviour.

It is useless to go somewhere to preach, unless you preach wherever you go. (Francis of Assisi)

Loving Master, thank You that You are not a stranger, but a _____

*C*rue spirituality (1)

"You are the light of the world. Let your light so shine before men, that they may see your good works and glorify your Father in heaven." (Mt. 5:14, 16)

*I*n many circles of society the word "spirituality" is not very popular. It conjures images of well-meaning people who are intensely religious, but don't succeed in handling the practical problems of everyday life.

True spirituality is the most beautiful and powerful force known to mankind. It is free from all deception and hyper-piety and is able to handle any situation that might occur. It is possible because it is not the result of storm and stress, but the expression of inner peace of mind which is the direct result of sustained fellowship with the Master.

The person who is truly spiritual is essentially practical. A truly spiritual employee will reveal his inner experience of spirituality through excellent and honest work and service. A mother who experiences spirituality in the true sense of the word, will reveal it through establishing a loving and well-organised family. Regardless of the role you have in life, you will fulfil it to the glory of God if you develop true spirituality.

The rich fruit of true spirituality is there for everyone to see. High-sounding words and religious clichés can never be a substitute for the spirituality which loves the living Christ so much that His glory is reflected by the lives of those who truly love Him. This is the essence of true spirituality: to love Christ with all your soul and mind and to allow His love to flow through you.

> The Holy Spirit is the living presence of God in your inner being. (Romano Guardini)

Loving Master, through Your Spirit, open up my life for Your love that _____

_____

True spirituality (2)

"Yet indeed I also count all things loss for the excellence of the knowledge of Christ Jesus my Lord." (Phil. 3:8)

There are people who don't succeed in reaching their full potential in life, because they feel inadequate to meet the challenges of life. This inadequacy can be caused by a feeling of insecurity or inferiority. Probably one of the most general causes is failure in the academic area. Success in this field is praiseworthy, but failure should not ruin your life. Tertiary education doesn't necessarily mean that you are better equipped to overcome the battles and hard knocks of life.

There is a consciousness which is superior to the intellect. We call it "spirituality". The spiritual life is supported by a sharp intellect, but does not depend on it. Those people who walk in the Spirit are in harmony with the heavenly Father and receive qualities and gifts from Him which help them to grow in grace and love. They live in peace with themselves, and under the guidance of the Holy Spirit of God they become balanced and mature personalities.

This wonderful lifestyle is available to all, educated and illiterate, who live on a spiritual basis and acknowledge the lordship and guidance of Christ, God and the Holy Spirit in their lives every day. The spiritual path of life becomes of the utmost importance to you when you consecrate your love and allegiance to Jesus your Saviour.

> It is much better to live a holy life than to talk about it. Lighthouses don't ring bells or fire cannons to draw attention – they just shine. (Dwight L. Moody)

Father, I feel inadequate so often that I _____

_____

The perfect way of life

"And do not be conformed to this world, but be transformed by the renewing of your mind." (Rom. 12:2)

How many people are there who yearn for peace of mind? In the rat race of this fast-moving modern society you see the unmistakable signs of tension, stress and anxiety. Afflicted people try to maintain the pace which becomes more hectic every day. It seems as though most people meekly accept that there is nothing they can do about the situation.

There is a proven method to handle stress and tension. But, as with all effective means, it requires the application of self-discipline. The answer is to seek the Lord while He is still to be found, to surrender yourself to Him and to allow Him – and not the modern way of life – to dictate the pattern of your life.

If this seems to you like an over-simplification of an intricate and difficult problem, you must not lose sight of the fact that the Holy Spirit is more than willing to help you. When He enters your life, He will take over and give to you an inner strength and peace of mind you never dreamt possible. And in conjunction with this, He gives you the ability and wisdom to handle any situation in life.

The living Christ is with you and is ready to come in and take control of your life for the better. Accept Him without delay and receive His power to live to the full, *"I have come that they may have life and that they may have it more abundantly"* (John 10:10).

> The peaceful quiet beauty of a sanctified life is, next to the power of the Holy Spirit of God, the most powerful influence in the world. (Blaise Pascal)

Holy Spirit of God, touch my life and give me _____
_____

*L*et wisdom control your life

"[I pray] that Christ may dwell in your hearts through faith; that you, being rooted and grounded in love ... " (Eph. 3:17)

*Y*our way of life reveals whether or not you are in harmony with life. If you are aggressive, you will be extremely restless and will experience bitterness, frustration and failure. Don't convince yourself that life is constantly at war with you. This line of thought is often an indication of your dissappointment and spiritual inability to reach your objective.

In order to experience fulfilment and satisfaction, it is important that your life should be controlled through Godly wisdom. This wisdom is not the result of education. You receive it through your spirit. While you constantly seek for a deeper understanding of God through prayer and Bible study, you develop a wisdom which can only be imparted by God.

This wisdom permeates your whole being. Your values are no longer determined by human standards, but you will see people, circumstances and situations as God sees them. Disciplining yourself to look at life from this Godly viewpoint, will give you a new sense of values and a changed lifestyle.

When you are in harmony with God you will lose all unpleasant aggression because you are no longer hurt so easily and also don't pity yourself any more. You will also experience the joy of co-operating with your fellowmen through the wisdom God gives you. This is an important step on the road to sanctification.

> Wisdom is the ability to use knowledge to successfully utilise the emergencies of life. People can gain knowledge, but wisdom is a direct gift from God. (Bob Jones)

Lord Jesus, because in Your grace You have given me wisdom, I can _____

The power of the Holy Spirit

"We have not so much as heard whether there is a Holy Spirit." (Acts 19:2)

If you are a follower of Jesus Christ, your witnessing must be effective. You are compelled to make a contribution to the church of Jesus Christ. Your worship must have purpose and meaning to you in your everyday life. These are matters which every Christian must consider regularly if he is serious about his commitment to his Saviour. If you are unsure about it, it is time that you should do some introspection about the quality of your pilgrimage in following Christ.

Unless you open up your life to the blessed working of the Holy Spirit and allow Him to take control, you will find your Christian zeal to be lacking. Your own personal efforts to live a committed Christian life are good up to a certain point. But, regardless of how zealous you may be, you will only be able to witness effectively and to the full if you are being enabled to do so through the Holy Spirit.

Those who try to serve Christ in their own strength will eventually find that their ministry lacks purpose and meaning and the well of their faith will run dry.

Always be sensitive to the Spirit and open up your heart and life to His influence. He will enable you to serve Jesus in the way that He meant you to. This is an important component of God's finishing school which we call sanctification.

> In order for you to know what holiness is, it is imperative that the Holy Spirit should teach you what sanctification is. (Donald Nicholl)

O, Holy Spirit, fill me with _____

_____

Inspired by Christ

"I have been crucified with Christ; it is no longer I who live, but Christ lives in me." (Gal. 2:20)

The central core fact of the Christian experience is the indwelling Christ. All Christian theology must be subordinate to this. Without this truth, Christianity becomes a code of conduct which is impossible to maintain. When the disciple realises that the end-goal of the Christian road is not reached through striving towards the impossible, but through faith in the living Christ, then his faith rises above theological debating and becomes a glorious reality.

When Christ really lives in you, He must be able to reveal Himself through you. It may seem to be religiously presumptuous and regarded as impractical, but it is the natural result of a life that is being inspired by Christ. If you have faith that Christ is living in you, you will do everything in your power to maintain this standard. Of course, there will be times when you disappoint Him and yourself. In moments of despondency you will feel like letting go of the spiritual life with its many demands. Remember then that you are the one feeling like that, not Christ. He is waiting for you to overcome your spirit of despair in order to become His instrument of blessing once again.

The experience of living in the consciousness of the living presence of Christ, becomes richer and more meaningful as the days go by. However, a start has to be made somewhere. Therefore, in spite of your feelings of inadequacy, start a new life in Christ today and live a rich and fulfilling life.

> A holy life is a voice that speaks; it speaks when the tongue is quiet. It is either a constant source of attraction or an eternal repulsiveness. (Robert Leighton)

In You, Lord, I experience _____

_____

True sanctification

"The night is far spent, the day is at hand. Therefore let us cast off the works of darkness, and let us put on the armour of light." (Rom. 13:12)

Real goodness has a strong appeal. Sham goodness is repulsive. This was the essential difference between the Master and the Scribes and Pharisees. Wherever Christ went, the throngs followed Him. The religious leaders of His time made the spiritual life hard.

The crowds who followed Him were excited when they saw in Him a holiness which they had never seen in any other person. They gladly wanted to understand it better and eventually possess it themselves. He initiated a desire for the living God in them. True spiritual light or holiness makes an overwhelming appeal to people.

The awfulness of sin and its terrible results can be stressed, the necessity for repentance can be held up. Yet, it is only when people see the beauty of the risen Saviour that they begin to understand something of His love for them. Only then are their hearts softened.

But how can holiness ever be understood and the light of Christ be noticed, other than in the lives of Christian disciples? This challenge is overwhelming and yet, because Christ promised to dwell in those who believe in Him, it is a glorious possibility.

The greatest challenge a disciple of Jesus Christ can present to the world, is not to give an exegesis on religious doctrine but to live a life that is conformed to Jesus Christ.

> Pentecost brought light, power and joy to the early church. It was not necessary to ask whether they had received the Holy Spirit. Fire is self-evident – as is power! (Samuel Chadwick)

Christ, let Your light shine through me, so that others _____

Spiritual renewal

"But you are a chosen generation, a royal priesthood, a holy nation, His own special people that you may proclaim the praises of Him who called you out of darkness." (1 Pet. 2:9)

The Bible tells us frankly that all have sinned and that we all fall short of the glory of God. Few people will argue about this. If however, you believe that God has forgiven your sins, it is a futile exercise to constantly remind yourself of those sins. If God has forgiven you, you must forgive yourself.

When God forgave your sins, He didn't leave a void in your life. Scripture says emphatically, *"Therefore, if anyone is in Christ he is a new creation; old things have passed away; behold, all things have become new. Now all things are of God"* (2 Corinthians 5:17, 18).

God made you new and the righteousness which He gave you, should have a positive meaning to you. When you have received forgiveness, forget about your sins because they are of no value to you. Allow the Spirit of the living Christ to take possession of your life and mind. Allow His goodness to take root and to grow in your character and personality.

This is a life which disciples often try to get away from. Often the cause for this is their unwillingness to commit themselves to Him unconditionally. A half-hearted commitment to Christ will always find excuses for self-fabricated feelings of unworthiness. If the Master has saved you and given you His Spirit, He also imparts a dynamic goodness to you which is a rich blessing to you and all those you come in touch with.

> What Christianity needs most in the midst of the forms of antagonistic unbelief, are holy lives. (Theodor Christlieb)

Lord Jesus, may I, through the power that You impart, live in such a manner that I _____

_____

Inner holiness

" They, without a word may be won [for Christ] by the conduct ... "
(1 Pet. 3:1)

Being a witness of the love and reality of God has an important role to play in the life of a Christian. Such witnessing should always occur under the guidance of the Holy Spirit. Without the ministry of the Holy Spirit witnessing about what God has done for you could become a form of self-glorification.

Regardless what form of witnessing God has called you to, it is imperative that you should obey Him. Your relationship with the Lord must result in a life which is holy and practical. Unfortunately the word "holy" has fallen into discredit amongst church people – to our great loss. It invokes the image of people who are religious, but without the love of Christ. True holiness means a well-lived life which is lived through the Spirit of God and which finds expression in practical ways.

A sanctified life is a form of life that is exempt from pettiness and is always keen to forgive and restore broken relationships. It harbours no grievances; is not guilty of character violation; is always keen to help those up who have fallen. Holiness in the true sense of the word is the most beautiful characteristic a person can have.

This lofty inner quality speaks more clearly than words. To strive to attain holiness without a speck of pride, is to glorify God and to reveal Him to those whom you rub shoulders with daily.

> Example is not the most important matter in influencing others – it is the only matter. (Albert Schweitzer)

O Master, help me in my striving to attain holiness to _____

$\mathscr{S}$et apart by God

"To all who are in Rome, beloved of God, called to be saints ... "
(Rom. 1:7)

$\mathscr{R}$ome is the symbol of the sinful world which lives in enmity with God. Paul is writing to the Romans and pointing out to them that they have been set apart for God; called to live holy lives. When you accept Christ as your Saviour and Redeemer, your greatest desire is to fully know Him and His ways. The fact that you experienced a real rebirth is only the point of departure on your spiritual pilgrimage. You still have a long way to travel before your life will start displaying the power and image of the living Saviour.

It may be that the idea of sanctification is not acceptable to the modern-day disciple, but that is because you associate it with people who have lost contact with the hard facts of life. Therefore many modern day disciples say, "Sanctification is not for me!" To live a sanctified life means to live separated, to be one of God's called ones. The reason God invites you to this high calling, is so that you should live to His honour and glory and that at least something of His holiness may flow through your life and be revealed in your life.

Aiming at such a high standard of living has a reward of its own and though you feel that you fall short of God's standards, He gives you the gift of perseverance, which enables you to walk along the path which Christ has prepared for you.

You may not regard yourself as a saint, but that is what the Master has called you to be and therefore you should never stop trying to be what God meant you to be.

> One can strive to attain holiness equally well in a factory and in a monastery. The one is just as sinful as the other. (Robert J. McCracken)

Heavenly Father, help me never to throw in the towel, thus _____

New life in Christ

"Examine yourselves as to whether you are in the faith. Test yourselves. Do you not know yourselves that Jesus Christ is in you?" (2 Cor. 13:5)

The great stabilising factor in the Christian experience is the fact that the living Christ is in us. It doesn't depend on how you feel and what you do, on your convictions or your emotions. The clearly outlined Christian doctrine is that Jesus Christ is in the mind and emotions of those who acknowledge His lordship, who love Him with all their might and are available to serve Him to the best of their ability.

The glorious truth that Christ lives in you, should cause a total revolution in your life. You will see other people in a new light, not as individuals whom you differ from, but as kindred spirits in the art of true living.

If the living Christ is in you, your whole concept of life is extended and you realise that the Godly truth in its rich fullness, is not comprehensible to the human mind. Your concept of truth may be correct, but others with another approach may also be correct. This understanding creates a broader vision and a spiritual depth and perception which can only be yours if you have the Spirit of Christ in you.

The indwelling Christ does not only give you a fresh approach to life, but also supplies you with the inner power which enables you to live victoriously. He grants those characteristics which are imperative for an inspired, goal-directed and satisfying quality of life. Because Christ lives in you, your whole life becomes a new, exciting and satisfying experience. This is God's finishing school to lead you to a sanctified life.

A saint is someone who makes goodness attractive. (Lawrence Housman)

I praise and thank You, Lord Jesus for _____

To live close to God

"I am Almighty God; walk before Me and be blameless." (Gen. 17:1)

Right through the world today perfection is stressed. In the arts, in science, in the business world, people are diligently striving towards perfect methods and machines – everything in the name of progress. In some instances people have developed such an obsession for perfectionism in material things that it has resulted in the decline and even extinction of spiritual and moral standards.

The beauty of God's creation is being marred through pollution and waste materials while man's convenience machines happily roll along. Deadly weapons are being produced and accumulated while one nation is trying to gain the upper hand over another. Personal moral standards are often relegated to second position beneath financial benefits and gain. Too often this is the price paid for progress.

There is only one lifestyle which is worthwhile and that is the life Christ offers us. Nothing apart from this can give us satisfaction and fulfilment in life because the life in Christ is permanent. Any other way of life is an inadequate substitute.

Regardless in which area you may be active, if you strive to attain perfection, make sure that God is your guide in this search of yours. Submit everything you do totally to Him, stay within His will in all your negotiations; maintain the standards set by Jesus Christ, and you will reach a standard of perfection that no worldly enterprise could ever offer you.

> There is no peace or tranquillity of mind to be bought over the counter. (Carey Williams)

Help me to strive towards _____
_____ *in my Christianity.*

The quality of your life

"We pray that our God would count you worthy of his calling, and fulfil all the good pleasure of His goodness and the work of faith with power." (2 Thes. 1:11)

It is a fact that the love of God is free and undeserved. Nothing you do or anticipate doing can earn it for you. God loves you because He is love and it is a truth you should be eternally grateful for.

Because God loves with such an amazing depth, you should be careful that you don't mistake His love for a kind of sympathy which allows you to go unpunished while living in sin. The moment you become aware that you are the subject of His godly love, you have responsibilities.

While God has lit a flame of love for Him in your heart, you need to do everything in your power to ensure that nothing you do would ever rob that flame of its glow. The only way you can do that is to allow your life to be ruled by the love of Jesus Christ. Your thoughts must be controlled by the Holy Spirit, your daily inspiration must flow from the quiet time you spend in God's presence every day.

God loves you with an undying love, just as He loves all people. As Christ's disciple it is your responsibility to transform His Godly love into a practical reality in the world where you live for Him. If you should fail in this, there is one less disciple doing His work here on earth.

People must stop blaming their environment for their problems and start learning to use their will that is their personal responsibility in the area of faith and morality. (Albert Schweitzer)

Lord my God, grant me a dynamic experience of Your love so that _____

May God's kingdom come

"For the kingdom of God is not in word but in power." (1 Cor. 4:20)

Many believing and committed Christians get involved in lengthy discussions and write books to prove that God exists. The majority of people are not impressed by this.

People feel instinctively that true spirituality is not complicated; that it is something which humble and uneducated people can understand. The inner consciousness of divine simplicity is confirmed by the incarnation of Christ: the God of heaven and earth came to the world as a tiny baby. When scholars and theologians asked Jesus what the greatest commandment in the law was, His reply could be understood by all, *"'You shall love the Lord your God with all your heart, with all your soul and with all your mind'. And 'You shall love your neighbour as yourself'"* (Matthew 22:37, 39).

It is not ingenious arguments that help people understand the kingdom of God, but it is the power of the living Christ as revealed through the lives of ordinary people. The kingdom of God is seen in the lives of people who once were slaves of sin but were set free by the grace of God and are now living Christlike lives; in people who once were failures and are now living victoriously. Every time when the living Christ is seen in a reborn personality, a facet of God's kingdom is seen. You don't have to be a brilliant student to be a reflection of Christ, but your life must be open to the generous influence of the Holy Spirit.

> There is no true holiness without humility. (Thomas Fuller)

Master, on this joyful day I once again open up my life to You so that _____

_____

The fruit of the Spirit

"But the fruit of the Spirit is love, joy, peace, longsuffering, kindness, goodness, faithfulness, gentleness, self-control." (Gal. 5:22)

Christian discipleship requires inevitable growth. There needs to be the constant desire to become more and more like the Master in my thoughts and actions. This demand might keep you from accepting the responsibility of discipleship, but for every serious follower of the living Christ, the challenge to become more and more conformed to Christ, is a matter of course which cannot be denied.

The fruit of the Spirit as set out here by Paul, are components of the mind of Christ. They have been called the nine main signs of God's presence, or aspects of the mind of Christ which can become the possession of every disciple who commits himself to make the attitude of Christ his own. To enable you to achieve this, the living Christ promised Himself to you. That which is impossible for you, becomes possible through Him.

Take one of the fruits quoted in our verse of Scripture and meditate on it for some time as the subject of your quiet time until it becomes an integral part of your nature. Repeat with concentration and intelligence the idea, "In Christ I am filled with love," until you feel how His love fills your life. Do the same with all the other gifts over a period of time. This may sound like a time-consuming process, but in matters that concern the spiritual life, growth can not be hastened. In this way you will develop a well-balanced spiritual life which you will live to His honour and glory.

> In this world durable things which need to last long, naturally grow slowly to reach maturity. (Vincent de Paul)

Mighty God, I desire to _____
_____ *in my life.*

*C*Attaining the unattainable

"Likewise the Spirit also helps in our weaknesses." (Rom. 8:26)

*W*hich of us have not experienced moments of intense discouragement along our spiritual pilgrimage? The goal of sanctification seems to be so high that it appears unattainable to us and you realise your own spiritual inadequacy. You start to wonder if the struggle is worth your while. Indeed you have seen the ideal of sanctification and you have felt it in your inner being, but you just don't have the ability to attain the seemingly unattainable. That which God expects from you and that which you could possibly attain, create in you a feeling of frustration and spiritual inefficiency. With Paul you are inclined to say, *"O wretched man that I am! Who will deliver me from this body of death?"* (Romans 7:24).

If God had left you in this insecure and unhappy condition, it would have been a sad situation. But God never implants a spiritual hunger in a person's spirit without satisfying it. This very hunger which upsets you so much is a gift of grace from God. It creates in you a desire for sanctification and the sense that God had meant sanctification for you as well, although you cannot attain it in your own strength. However, God is able to meet your every need.

He has called you to a way of life which is impossible for you to meet. Yet He promised His help to assist you in attaining those heights. He grants you the gift of the Holy Spirit and when you accept that gift you will definitely reach the heights He called you to.

> True holiness has love as its being, humility as its robe and doing good to others as its main task – and the honour of God as its final goal. (Nathanael Emmons)

Not in my strength Lord, but through Your strength _____

Surrounded by God's love

"And for their sakes I sanctify Myself, that they also may be sanctified by the truth." (Jn. 17:19)

As a matter of course there come those times when it feels to you as if your Christian pilgrimage is nothing but an uphill slog and a struggle. You may have an intense desire for sanctification, to walk daily in the presence of the Master, to have a meaningful prayer life, to work productively for the Master. These beautiful desires sometimes create tension. When your enthusiasm fades, your faith grows weak and you begin to wonder if it is worthwhile.

Perhaps you only looked at your spiritual life from your personal point of view and forgot to bring the Christ-factor into account. His involvement with your faith is more important than your own. In the first instance He is the one who called you. He Himself said, *"But you are a chosen generation ... His own special people ... "* (1 Peter 2:9). Therefore He has a living and loving interest in your discipleship. This divine calling does not depend on your changing emotions. He will tie you to your calling with the cords of love. When you become despondent or if your interest in spiritual growth starts to fade, remember then that the loving Christ never changes. You still belong to Him, He loves you and He is still your Master.

Christ's love for you is eternal and unfailing. It doesn't change according to your emotions. When you drift away from Him, He loves you just as much as when you are spiritually dynamic and conscious of His divine presence. Even though you should detach yourself from Him, you could never destroy His love for you.

> The will to persevere is often what makes the difference between failure and success. (David Sarnoff)

I thank You, O Guide, that my changing emotions need not _____

Divine piety

"But we all, with unveiled face, beholding in a mirror the glory of the Lord, are being transformed into the same image from glory to glory, just as by the Spirit of the Lord." (2 Cor. 3:18)

From time to time we all see the beauty of the Lord in one of His humble servants. This spiritual insight is given to us through grace and something is stirred within us which causes us to yearn secretly to become a better person, yes, even a saint.

Of course you don't express it in these words and you push the thought out of your mind, with the idea that you are no saint at all. Yet, as Christ's disciple you are called to be a saint.

A saint is not someone who lives secluded from the world or society and also not someone who is exempted from sin. A saint is a person who takes his position in his family, in the business world, in the workshop or factory and in the church, and then does his utmost to let the beauty of Christ flow through him. Even though he will still stumble and even fall along his pilgrimage, after every failure he will get up again, pledge his allegiance to his Lord afresh and keep on striving towards the final victory which has been assured for us through Jesus, the living Lord.

True sanctification is not attained through the amount of zeal which you add to your spiritual life, but by opening up your life to the influence of Jesus Christ and by allowing the Spirit to work through you.

> Every man has two life journeys to complete: there is the external journey with its various incidents and milestones; and there is the inner journey – a spiritual odyssey with a secret history of its own. (William R. Inge)

Lord Jesus, change me into a channel through which _____

*aturity*

"Till we all come to a perfect man, to the measure of the stature of the fullness of Christ." (Eph. 4:13)

Immaturity is one of the great shortcomings of human nature. On the one hand nature is taking its course and man moves through all the stages from youth to old age. On the other hand intellectual and spiritual maturity do not occur as a matter of course. The latter two qualities require your time and energy if you wish to develop them to the maximum potential imbedded in your personality.

In our efforts to reach maturity, it is necessary that we should have a standard against which we measure our progress. The apostle Paul maintains that this standard should be nothing less than the maturity of Christ. It almost sounds presumptuous to look at Christ and then strive to reach His stature, balance and maturity in your daily life. However, to aim at anything lower, is to accept a sub-standard Christianity. Christ is what He is and you must be encouraged and not discouraged, when you are challenged to be like Him.

When you realise what He is and what you are, you could possibly get pessimistic. You could easily decide that that is not the life for you. However, never forget His love for and His identifying with you. He is the inspiration to such a life and He gives you the strength to lead it if you would only confess your dependence on Him every moment of the day. Draw daily from the source of His strength which He puts at your disposal for this very reason.

> A saint is a saint not because he is "good" but because he is transparent for someone much bigger than himself. (Paul Tillich)

Through Your strength, Master and Saviour, I can _____

A Christian character

"But we know that when He is revealed, we shall be like Him, for we shall see Him as He is. " (1 Jn. 3:2)

It should be the goal of every Christian to build his life on the pattern of Christ's life. This pattern will vary according to our personalities, but the all-embracing desire should be to grow into conformity to Christ.

The acceptance of the lordship of Christ is the point of departure to a new and enriching way of life. Knowing that you now belong to Him, you should focus all your energy on Him. He becomes your pattern and your goal.

Of course, it is impossible to perfect this pattern of life by straining yourself, or to reach this goal through your efforts. Trying to do this in your own strength will only lead to frustration and disappointment. When you accept Christ as the Lord of your life, He becomes a reality to you. If you ask Him, He will give you His Holy Spirit. When you are united with Him, your faith starts to come alive and your whole life is submitted to Him in obedience.

From these dynamics and obedience, a Christlike character develops. The amazing truth is that the person who possesses a character like this is himself not aware of it. There is no false pride. People who are conformed to Christ are too busy loving their fellowmen. They don't have time to try and impress others. Their holiness is a by-product of their fellowship with their Master.

Grant me more holiness and a greater glow in my heart; grant me more comfort in sadness, more grief over my sin. (Adapted from Hallelujah 314:1)

Lord, at the end of the year my heart is so full, and I want to ____